HANDY WORDS
FOR THE BUSINESS SCENE
IN ENGLISH

ビジネス現場の英単語

Ｚ会編集部＋日本アイアール 編

Ｚ会

HANDY WORDS
FOR THE BUSINESS SCENE
IN ENGLISH

ビジネス現場の
英単語

定番単語＋日本式ビジネスフィールド

■はじめに

　ビジネスの現場で英語の読み書き・会話が必要とされているけれど，その実力が自分にはまだ十分に備わっていない――そんな不安を抱えている方が数多くいらっしゃることと思います。この本はそんな方々のために編まれました。

　本書には約 1,800 の英単語が収録されています。これらは，ビジネスライフを検証して必須の単語を厳選し，また TOEIC の出題傾向も加味したうえで決定されたものです。会社生活・取引先との交渉・プレゼンなどの用語から身の回り品まで，幅広くカバーされています。ビジネスパーソンの必修語が濃縮された一冊と言っていいでしょう。

　また，本書は多岐にわたるビジネスシーンを集約した 15 の章から構成されます。「会社の組織」「雇用」「会議」「営業」など，実際のビジネスのさまざまな場面を網羅的に扱っています。

　さらに，それぞれの章は 3 つの Section に区分されます。まず，Section 1 で，イラストを見ながら名詞を中心とした単語を覚えます。次に，Section 2 で，ビジネスに必須の単語とともに，ビジネスシーンで役に立つオリジナル用例に接します。切れば血の出るようなナマのビジネス英語を体感してください。さらに，Section 3 で，「履歴書」「雇用契約書」「アンケート」「クレームとそれに対応する E メール」などの文書や会話を読んで，実践力を身につけます。

　このような 3-Section 方式を採り入れることにより，本書はビジネス頻出単語を提示しただけの単語帳とは明らかに一線を画するものとなりました。

　もうひとつ，本書の特長としてリピート学習効果が挙げられるでしょう。各章の Section 2 の例文には Section 1 に掲載された単語が，また，Section 3 の文書には Section 1 及び Section 2 での掲載語が織り交ぜられています。したがって，順を追って学習していくと，自然とリピート学習ができるように工夫されているのです。

　毎日の生活の座右の書として，ぜひ本書をご活用ください。あなたのビジネスライフの新しい 1 ページが，ここから始まります。

2010 年 11 月　Z 会編集部，日本アイアール

■目　次

はじめに ……………………………………………………………… 3
目次 …………………………………………………………………… 4
本書の構成と使い方 ………………………………………………… 9

第1章　ビジネスパーソンの一日
Section 1　イラストで覚える！ ………………………………… 14
　　Schedule「スケジュール」
　　Commute「通勤」
　　Businessperson / man「ビジネスパーソン／男性」
　　Businessperson / woman「ビジネスパーソン／女性」
Section 2　例文で覚える！ ……………………………………… 18
Section 3　実際のスケジュールで確認！ ……………………… 30

第2章　会社と地域
Section 1　イラストで覚える！ ………………………………… 34
　　City「都市」
　　Desk「デスク」
　　Office「オフィス」
Section 2　例文で覚える！ ……………………………………… 38
Section 3　実際の会話で確認！ ………………………………… 50

第3章　オフィス機器
Section 1　イラストで覚える！ ………………………………… 54
　　Internet「インターネット」
　　Computer「コンピュータ」
　　Website「ウェブサイト」
　　Telephone「電話」
　　E-mail「電子メール」
　　Multifunction printer「複合機」

Section 2　例文で覚える！ ……………………………………… 58
Section 3　実際の会話で確認！ ………………………………… 70

第4章　会社の組織

Section 1　イラストで覚える！ ………………………………… 74
　Industry, Business「業界」
　Company, Firm, Business「会社，企業」
　Organization「組織」
　Company organization chart「組織図」
Section 2　例文で覚える！ ……………………………………… 78
Section 3　実際の文書で確認！ ………………………………… 90

第5章　雇用

Section 1　イラストで覚える！ ………………………………… 94
　Employment「雇用」
　Résumé「履歴書」
　Assessment「評価」
　Occupation「職業」
Section 2　例文で覚える！ ……………………………………… 98
Section 3　実際の文書で確認！ ………………………………… 110

第6章　勤務スタイル・福利厚生

Section 1　イラストで覚える！ ………………………………… 114
　Work「勤務」
　Terms of employment「雇用条件」
　Welfare program「福利厚生」
　Personnel change「人事異動」
　Retirement「退職」
Section 2　例文で覚える！ ……………………………………… 118
Section 3　実際の文書で確認！ ………………………………… 130

第7章 会議

Section 1　イラストで覚える！ …… 134
　Meeting「会議、打ち合わせ」
　Meeting[Conference] room「会議室」
　Presentation「プレゼンテーション」
　Chart, Graph「図表」
Section 2　例文で覚える！ …… 138
Section 3　実際のスクリプトで確認！ …… 150

第8章 企画・開発

Section 1　イラストで覚える！ …… 154
　Market research「市場調査」
　Survey「調査」
　Laboratory「研究室」
　Proposal「企画書」
Section 2　例文で覚える！ …… 158
Section 3　実際の文書で確認！ …… 170

第9章 製造

Section 1　イラストで覚える！ …… 174
　Production plant「生産工場」
　Product, Manufactures「製品」
　Out of order「故障して」
　Quality management「品質経営、品質管理」
Section 2　例文で覚える！ …… 178
Section 3　実際のウェブサイトで確認！ …… 190

第10章 宣伝・広報

Section 1　イラストで覚える！ …… 194
　Sales promotion「販売促進活動」
　Advertisement「広告、宣伝」
　Poster「ポスター」

Press[Media] conference「記者会見」
Section 2　例文で覚える！ ……………………………………… 198
Section 3　実際の文書で確認！ ………………………………… 210

第11章　営業

Section 1　イラストで覚える！ ………………………………… 214
　Sales representative[rep]「営業担当」
　Negotiation「交渉」
　Estimate, Quote「見積もり」
　Contract, Agreement「契約」
Section 2　例文で覚える！ ……………………………………… 218
Section 3　実際の文書で確認！ ………………………………… 230

第12章　販売

Section 1　イラストで覚える！ ………………………………… 234
　Sales floor「売り場」
　Complaint「苦情，クレーム」
　Payment「支払い」
　Inventory management「在庫管理」
Section 2　例文で覚える！ ……………………………………… 238
Section 3　実際のメールで確認！ ……………………………… 250

第13章　流通

Section 1　イラストで覚える！ ………………………………… 254
　Delivery service「配達サービス」
　Transportation「輸送」
　Distribution「流通」
　Trade「貿易」
Section 2　例文で覚える！ ……………………………………… 258
Section 3　実際のファックスで確認！ ………………………… 270

第14章　出張

Section 1　イラストで覚える！ ………………………… 274
- Business trip「出張」
- Airport「空港」
- ATM[Automatic Teller Machine]「ＡＴＭ」
- Currency exchange「両替」
- Airport timetable「空港の時刻表」
- Boarding pass「搭乗券」

Section 2　例文で覚える！ …………………………… 278
Section 3　実際の会話で確認！ ……………………… 290

第15章　ビジネスプラン・財務

Section 1　イラストで覚える！ ………………………… 294
- Business expansion strategy「事業拡大戦略」
- Corporate collapse「経営破たん」
- Marketing「マーケティング」
- Share, Stock「株」
- Financial statements「財務諸表」

Section 2　例文で覚える！ …………………………… 298
Section 3　実際の記事で確認！ ……………………… 310

INDEX ……………………………………………………… 313

■ 本書の構成と使い方

本書の構成

　本書は「ビジネスパーソンの一日」「会社と地域」「オフィス機器」「会社の組織」「雇用」「勤務スタイル・福利厚生」「会議」「企画・開発」「製造」「宣伝・広報」「営業」「販売」「流通」「出張」「ビジネスプラン・財務」の 15 の章に分けられています。
　各章には 3 つの Section があります。

各 Section の構成

Section 1　イラストで覚える！　　　ビジネスパーソンが頻繁に目にするもの〔こと〕を英語でどう言うのかをイラストとともに確認し，覚えることができます。

Section 2　例文で覚える！　　　各場面で多用される単語を，リアルな用例とともに覚えることができます。

Section 3　実際の文書〔会話，ウェブサイトなど〕で確認！　　　Section 1 と Section 2 で覚えた単語を実際の文書などで確認することができます。

各Sectionの使い方

Section 1 　イラストで覚える！

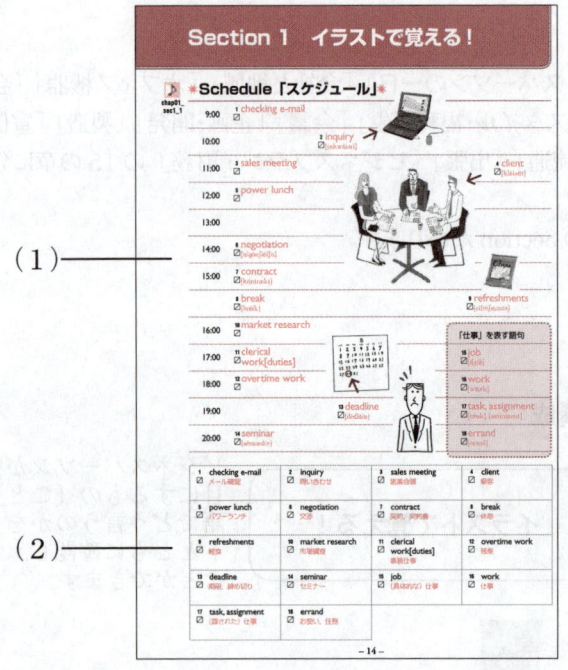

（1）イラスト
　ビジネスパーソンが頻繁に目にするビジネスの場面のイラストです。まず，イラストを見て，英語で何と言うのかを確認しましょう。

（2）単語リスト
　そのページに載っている単語のリストです。このリストで英語と意味を覚えましょう。このとき，音声ファイルを聞いて発音も一緒に覚えましょう。

赤シートを活用しよう！

・イラストに赤シートをのせ，該当する英語がわかるか確認します。英語が覚えられた単語はチェックボックス☐に印をつけましょう。
・単語リストに赤シートをのせ，意味がわかるか確認します。意味が覚えられた単語はチェックボックス☐に印をつけましょう。

音声

　各ページの左上にある♪が音声ファイルの番号です。音声を聞いて，単語を繰り返し発音して覚えましょう。

Section 2　例文で覚える！

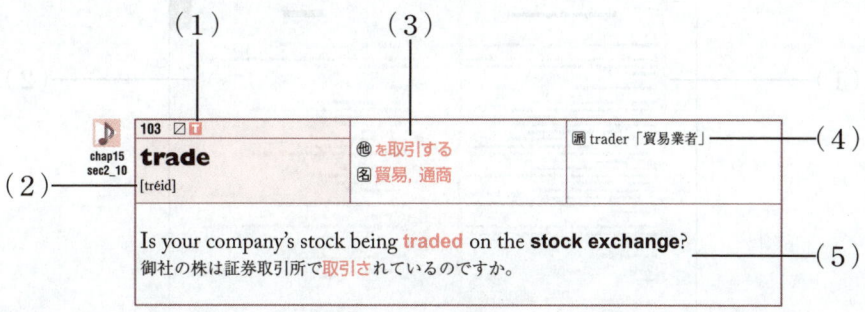

(1) **T** マーク
　20万語以上から成る TOEIC® Test のコーパスをコンピュータで分析し，出現頻度が 10 以上の見出し語にこのマークがついています。

(2) 見出し語と発音記号

(3) 訳語
　ビジネスシーンでよく使われる訳語を精選して掲載しています。

(4) 参考語
　類で類義語，関で関連語，派で派生語，反で反意語を掲載しています。

(5) 用例と用例訳
　ビジネスシーンで役に立つ実践的な用例を掲載しています。この用例で単語の使い方を身につけましょう。赤字は見出し語，黒い太字は同じ章の Section 1 に出てきた単語を示しています。

赤シートを活用しよう！

　赤シートをのせ，意味がわかるか確認します。意味が覚えられた単語はチェックボックス☑に印をつけましょう。

音声

　各ページの左上にある♪が音声ファイルの番号です。単語と例文を繰り返し聞き，また実際に発音することで，単語とその使い方を覚えましょう。

Section 3　実際の文書〔会話，ウェブサイトなど〕で確認！

（1）——— 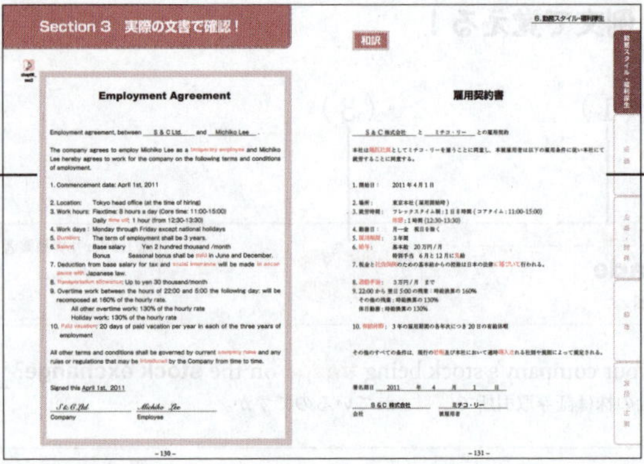 ———（2）

✳Review Words✳

☑ temporary employee ➡ Sec.1-23	☑ time off ➡ Sec.1-30	☑ duration ➡ Sec.1-24
☑ salary ➡ Sec.1-2	☑ pay ➡ Sec.2-74	☑ social insurance ➡ Sec.1-4
☑ in accordance with ➡ Sec.2-77	☑ transportation allowance ➡ Sec.1-50	☑ paid vacation ➡ Sec.1-31
☑ company rule ➡ Sec.1-5	☑ introduce ➡ Sec.2-93	

（3）———（Review Words）

（1）文書，会話など

ビジネスシーンで使われる文書や会話などが掲載されています。赤字は同じ章の Section 1 または Section 2 に出てきた単語です。実際の文書や会話に触れ，既出の単語の確認をするとともに，ビジネス英語の感覚を養いましょう。

（2）日本語訳

英語の赤字部分の訳は赤字になっています。

（3）Review Words

英語で赤字になっている単語の掲載箇所を示しています。その単語がまだ十分に覚えられていないと感じたら，➡の後の掲載箇所に戻って確認しましょう。覚えられたらチェックボックス☑に印をつけましょう。

赤シートを活用しよう！

- 日本語訳に赤シートをのせ，英語の赤字部分に対応する訳がわかるか確認します。
- 英文に赤シートをのせ日本語訳と対照し，日本語訳の赤字部分に対応する英単語がわかるか確認します。

音声

英文のページの左上にある♪が音声ファイルの番号です。音声を聞いて，実際のビジネス文書やビジネス会話に慣れるようにしましょう。

第1章
ビジネスパーソンの一日

英語で何と言うでしょうか？

☞答えはP.16

Section 1 イラストで覚える！

✳ Schedule「スケジュール」✳

9:00	1 checking e-mail
10:00	2 inquiry [inkwáiəri]
11:00	3 sales meeting
12:00	5 power lunch
13:00	
14:00	6 negotiation [nigòuʃiéiʃn]
15:00	7 contract [kɑ́ntrækt]
	8 break [bréik]
16:00	10 market research
17:00	11 clerical work[duties]
18:00	12 overtime work
19:00	13 deadline [dédlàin]
20:00	14 seminar [sémənɑ̀:r]

4 client [kláiənt]

9 refreshments [rifréʃmənts]

「仕事」を表す語句

15 job [dʒɑ́b]

16 work [wə́:rk]

17 task, assignment [tǽsk], [əsáinmənt]

18 errand [érənd]

---

1 checking e-mail メール確認	2 inquiry 問い合わせ	3 sales meeting 営業会議	4 client 顧客
5 power lunch パワーランチ	6 negotiation 交渉	7 contract 契約、契約書	8 break 休憩
9 refreshments 軽食	10 market research 市場調査	11 clerical work[duties] 事務仕事	12 overtime work 残業
13 deadline 期限、締め切り	14 seminar セミナー	15 job (具体的な) 仕事	16 work 仕事
17 task, assignment (課された) 仕事	18 errand お使い、任務		

1. ビジネスパーソンの一日

✳ Commute 「通勤」 ✳

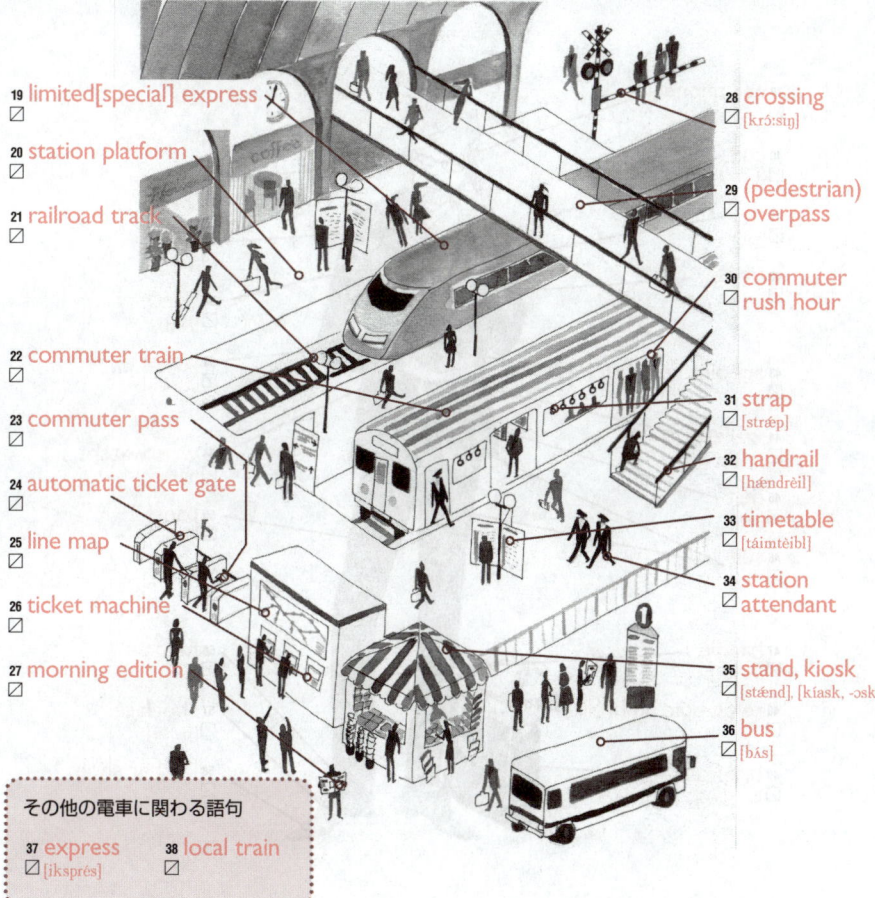

19 limited[special] express
20 station platform
21 railroad track
22 commuter train
23 commuter pass
24 automatic ticket gate
25 line map
26 ticket machine
27 morning edition
28 crossing [króːsiŋ]
29 (pedestrian) overpass
30 commuter rush hour
31 strap [strǽp]
32 handrail [hǽndrèil]
33 timetable [táimtèibl]
34 station attendant
35 stand, kiosk [stǽnd], [kíask, -ɔsk]
36 bus [bʌ́s]

その他の電車に関わる語句

37 express [iksprés]
38 local train

19	limited[special] express 特急	20	station platform プラットホーム	21	railroad track 線路	22	commuter train 通勤列車
23	commuter pass 定期券	24	automatic ticket gate 自動改札	25	line map 路線図	26	ticket machine 券売機
27	morning edition 朝刊	28	crossing 踏切	29	(pedestrian) overpass 歩道橋	30	commuter rush hour 通勤ラッシュ
31	strap つり革	32	handrail 手すり	33	timetable 時刻表	34	station attendant 駅員
35	stand, kiosk (駅の) 売店	36	bus バス	37	express 急行	38	local train 各駅停車

✴ Businessperson / man 「ビジネスパーソン／男性」

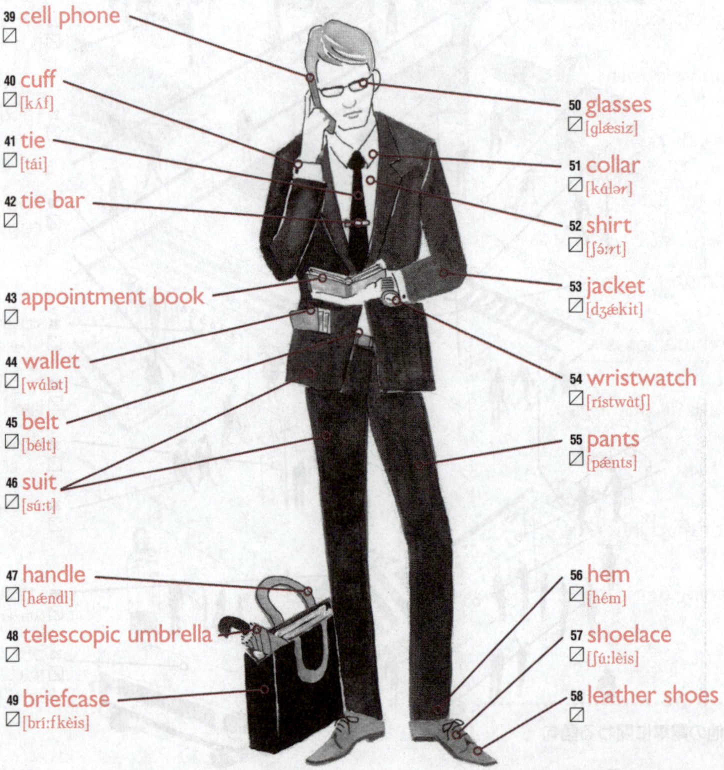

- 39 cell phone
- 40 cuff [kʌ́f]
- 41 tie [tái]
- 42 tie bar
- 43 appointment book
- 44 wallet [wálət]
- 45 belt [bélt]
- 46 suit [súːt]
- 47 handle [hǽndl]
- 48 telescopic umbrella
- 49 briefcase [bríːfkèis]
- 50 glasses [glǽsiz]
- 51 collar [kálər]
- 52 shirt [ʃə́ːrt]
- 53 jacket [dʒǽkit]
- 54 wristwatch [rístwàtʃ]
- 55 pants [pǽnts]
- 56 hem [hém]
- 57 shoelace [ʃúːlèis]
- 58 leather shoes

39	cell phone 携帯電話	40	cuff 袖口	41	tie ネクタイ	42	tie bar ネクタイピン
43	appointment book スケジュール帳	44	wallet 札入れ	45	belt ベルト	46	suit スーツ
47	handle 取っ手	48	telescopic umbrella 折りたたみ傘	49	briefcase ブリーフケース	50	glasses めがね
51	collar 襟	52	shirt ワイシャツ	53	jacket ジャケット	54	wristwatch 腕時計
55	pants ズボン	56	hem すそ	57	shoelace 靴ひも	58	leather shoes 革靴

1. ビジネスパーソンの一日

✱ Businessperson/woman「ビジネスパーソン／女性」✱

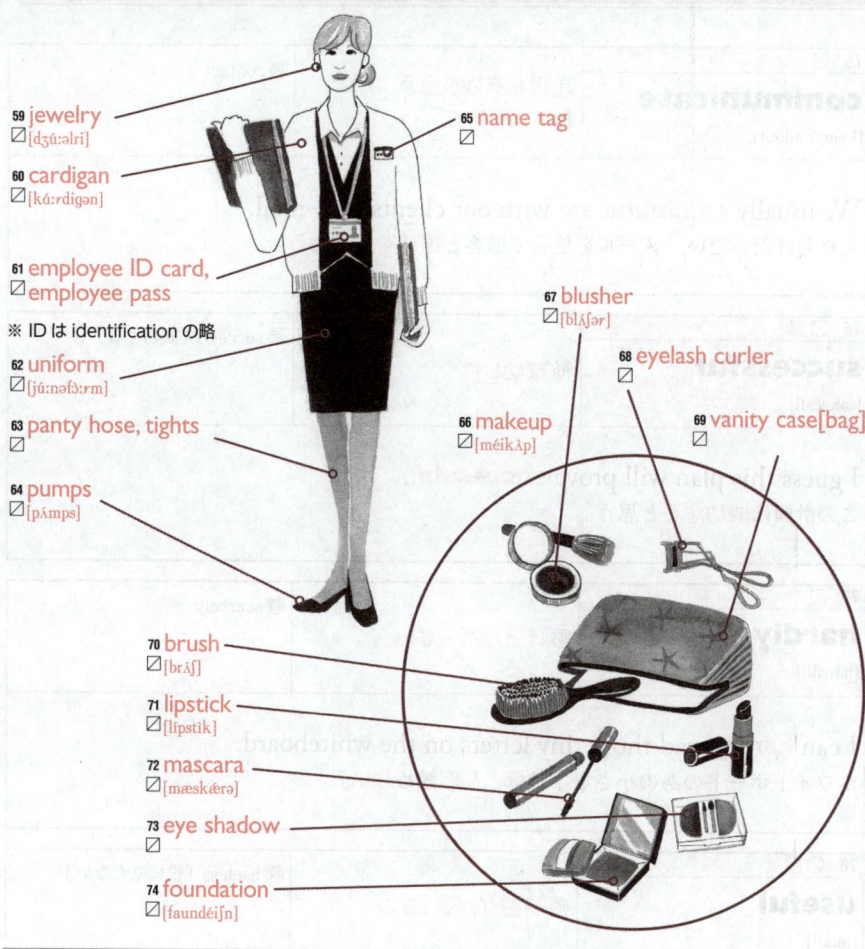

59 jewelry [dʒúːəlri]
60 cardigan [káːrdigən]
61 employee ID card, employee pass
　※ ID は identification の略
62 uniform [júːnəfɔːrm]
63 panty hose, tights
64 pumps [pʌmps]
65 name tag
66 makeup [méikʌp]
67 blusher [blʌ́ʃər]
68 eyelash curler
69 vanity case[bag]
70 brush [brʌʃ]
71 lipstick [lípstik]
72 mascara [mæskǽrə]
73 eye shadow
74 foundation [faundéiʃn]

59	jewelry	アクセサリー	60	cardigan	カーディガン	61	employee ID card, employee pass	社員証	62	uniform	制服
63	panty hose, tights	パンスト	64	pumps	パンプス	65	name tag	名札	66	makeup	化粧品
67	blusher	ほお紅	68	eyelash curler	ビューラー	69	vanity case[bag]	化粧ポーチ	70	brush	ブラシ
71	lipstick	口紅	72	mascara	マスカラ	73	eye shadow	アイシャドウ	74	foundation	ファンデーション

Section 2　例文で覚える！

chap01
sec2_01

75 ☐		
communicate [kəmjúːnikèit]	自 連絡を取り合う 他 を知らせる	類 contact

We usually **communicate** with our clients by e-mail.
私たちはだいたい、メールを使って顧客と連絡を取り合う。

76 ☐ T		
successful [səksésfl]	形 成功した	派 succeed「成功する」

I guess this plan will prove **successful**.
この計画は成功すると思う。

77 ☐		
hardly [háːrdli]	副 ほとんど〜ない	類 scarcely

I can **hardly** read those tiny letters on the whiteboard.
ホワイトボードのあの小さな字はほとんど読めない。

78 ☐ T		
useful [júːsfl]	形 有益な, 役に立つ	反 useless「役に立たない」

The information we gathered is **useful** for creating a new market.
我々の集めたその情報は新しい市場を生み出すために有益だ。

79 ☐		
challenging [tʃǽlindʒiŋ]	形 やりがいのある, 刺激的な	派 challenge「手ごたえ, やりがい」

The project was a **challenging** job for him.
そのプロジェクトは彼にとってやりがいのある仕事だった。

1. ビジネスパーソンの一日

chap01
sec2_02

80
explain [ikspléin]
他 を説明する
関 describe「の特徴などを述べる」

Our boss **explained** to us our problems with the project.
上司は私たちにそのプロジェクトの問題を説明した。

81
spare [spéər]
他 を与える, 取っておく
形 予備の

I would be grateful if you could **spare** a few minutes.
2, 3分お時間を割いていただけるとありがたいのですが。

82
share [ʃéər]
他 ①を分かち合う, 話す
②を分ける, 共有する

Mr. Sasaki will **share** some perspectives on strategic market planning.
佐々木氏は戦略市場計画の展望について話す予定です。

83
plan [plǽn]
他 ①[plan to do で]…する予定である
②を計画する
関 make plans「計画を立てる」

What are you **planning** to do this weekend?
今週末は何をするご予定ですか。

84
aware [əwéər]
形 ～に気がついている, ～を知っている
派 awareness「気づいていること, 自覚」

Were you **aware** that the meeting time had been changed?
会議の時間が変わったことに気づいていましたか。

― 19 ―

chap01 sec2_03

85 regularly
[régjələrli]

副 ①定期的に, 時間通りに
②規則正しく

類 periodically

Checking e-mail regularly is a must.
定期的にメールを確認することが必要だ。

86 tight
[táit]

形 ①(予定などが) ぎっしり詰まった
②堅い, きつい

I hope she can meet this tight schedule.
彼女がこのぎっしり詰まったスケジュールを守れるといいのですが。

87 sign
[sáin]

他〈書類・手紙など〉に署名する
名 標識, 看板

関 signature「署名」

The client signed a new contract with us.
その顧客は当社との新規契約書に署名した。

88 participate
[pɑːrtísəpèit]

自 参加する

類 take part

We all have to participate in the training seminar this afternoon.
我々は全員, 今日の午後研修セミナーに参加しなければならない。

89 attend
[əténd]

他〈会など〉に出席する

反 miss「を欠席する」
派 attendance「出席」

I can't attend the sales meeting this afternoon.
私は今日の午後の営業会議に出席できません。

— 20 —

90 submit [səbmít]
- 他 を提出する
- 類 hand in

I'm supposed to **submit** this **work** tomorrow morning.
明日の朝，この仕事を提出することになっているんです。

91 allow [əláu]
- 他 ①[allow + 名 + to do で] 〜が…するのを可能にする
- ②を許す
- 派 allowance「手当，経費」

The new idea **allows** us to save time and money.
その新しいアイデアは時間とお金を省くことを可能にする。

92 linger [líŋgər]
- 自 手間取る
- 他 〈時間〉を無駄に過ごす

We **lingered** over lunch and got back to work late.
ランチで時間を食ってしまい，会社に戻るのが遅くなった。

93 employ [implɔ́i]
- 他 を雇う
- 反 fire「を解雇する」

I'm **employed** here as an accountant.
私はここで会計士として雇われている。

94 meet [míːt]
- 他 ①〈必要・要求〉を満たす，〈期待〉に応える
- ②〈人〉に会う
- 関 meet the expectations「期待に応える」

I'm afraid we may not be able to **meet** the **deadline**.
申し訳ございませんが，締め切りに間に合わないかもしれません。

chap01
sec2_05

| 95 □ T **actually** [ǽktʃuəli] | 副 実は, 本当のところは | 類 to tell the truth |

Actually, we have to put off the plan.
実はですね, 計画を延期しなければなりません。

| 96 □ T **expect** [ikspékt] | 他 ①[expect +名+ to *do*]で]〜が…するだろうと思う ②を期待する | 派 expectation「期待」 |

When is the project **expected** to start?
そのプロジェクトはいつ始まる見込みでしょうか？

| 97 □ **accompany** [əkʌ́mpəni] | 他 と一緒に行く, 同行する | 派 accompanying「付随的な」 |

His wife **accompanied** him on his business trip to China.
中国への出張に彼の妻が彼に同行した。

| 98 □ T **complete** [kəmplíːt] | 他 を仕上げる, 終了する | 類 end |

This **task** should be **completed** by the end of the week.
この仕事は今週末までに終わらせる必要があります。

| 99 □ T **agree** [əgríː] | 自 同意する | 反 disagree「意見が合わない」 |

I'm afraid I don't **agree** with you.
残念ですが, あなたの意見に同意できません。

1. ビジネスパーソンの一日

100 ☑ T
serve
[sə́ːrv]
他 ①〈客〉に応対する
②〈飲食物〉を出す
派 service「サービス」

A new branch will be opened to **serve** clients in Beijing.
北京の顧客に応対するために，新しい支店が開かれる。

101 ☑
respond to
他 に答える
類 reply to

I'm **responding to** your e-mail **inquiry** about our new items.
弊社の新商品についてのメールでのお問い合わせにお答えいたします。

102 ☑ T
decide
[disáid]
他 を決意する
類 make up *one's* mind

He **decided** to attend the career development seminar.
彼はそのキャリア開発セミナーに参加することに決めた。

103 ☑ T
full-time
[fúltáim]
形 全時間勤務の, 常勤の
関 part-time「パートタイムの」

He has five years of **full-time clerical work** experience at a law firm.
彼は法律事務所で5年間の常勤の事務の経験がある。

104 ☑ T
consider
[kənsídər]
自他 (を) よく考える
派 consideration「熟考」

I'll **consider** your proposal and contact you by the end of the week.
あなたの申し出をよく考えて，今週末までにご連絡差し上げます。

— 23 —

chap01
sec2_07

105 dream
[dríːm]

名 夢
自 夢を見る

派 dreamless「夢のない」

My **dream** is having my own business someday.
私の夢は，いつか自分の会社を持つことだ。

106 overnight
[óuvərnàit]

形 夜通しの，夜間の
副 一晩中，夜通し

関 overnight courier「夜間便」

I took the **overnight** express from Tokyo to Hakata.
私は東京から博多までの夜行の急行に乗った。

107 hangover
[hǽŋòuvər]

名 二日酔い

It was hard to stand all the way on the train with my **hangover**.
二日酔いで，電車でずっと立っているのがつらかった。

108 cross
[króːs]

他 を横切る，渡る

派 crossing「交差点」

Many people are **crossing** the **overpass** to change trains.
たくさんの人々が，電車の乗り換えのために歩道橋を渡っている。

109 fulfill
[fulfíl]

他 ①〈要求など〉を満たす
　②〈義務など〉を実行する

類 fill

I am sure this product will **fulfill** the customers' demand.
この製品は顧客の要望をきっと満たすだろう。

chap01
sec2_08

| 110 ☐ **subscribe to** | 他 を購読する | 関 subscriber「定期購読者」 |

I **subscribe to** three business magazines to read while commuting.
私は通勤時間に読むために，3つの経済誌を購読している。

| 111 ☐ **approach** [əpróutʃ] | 他 自 (に)近づく，接近する | 派 approaching「間近な」 |

The train got crowded as it **approached** Tokyo.
東京に近づくにつれ，電車は込んできた。

| 112 ☐ **drop by** | 他 にちょっと立ち寄る | 関 call at「に立ち寄る」 |

Every morning, I **drop by** the **stand** to buy coffee.
毎朝，私はコーヒーを買うのにその売店に立ち寄ります。

| 113 ☐ T **affect** [əfékt] | 他 に影響する | 関 influence「に（間接的に）影響を与える」 |

The heavy snow severely **affected** highway traffic.
その大雪は道路交通に大変影響した。

| 114 ☐ **pull up** | 自 (車などが)止まる，(運転手が)車を止める 他 〈車など〉を止める | 類 stop |

A **bus pulled up** in front of my office building.
バスが私のオフィスビルの前に止まった。

chap01 sec2_09

115 commute
[kəmjúːt]

自 通勤する, 通学する
他 を取り替える

派 commuter「通勤〔学〕者」

I used to **commute** from Yokohama to Shinjuku by train.
以前, 私は横浜から新宿へ電車で通勤していた。

116 get on

他 に乗る

反 get off「から降りる」

The woman **got on** the **commuter train** in a hurry to get a seat.
その女性は, 座席を取るために急いで通勤電車に乗った。

117 check
[tʃék]

他 を調べる, 確認する

関 checkup「健康診断」

He **checked** the **timetable** and the fare on the Internet.
彼はインターネットで時刻表と料金を調べた。

118 remote
[rimóut]

形 遠い, 都会から離れた

関 remote control「リモコン」

It takes him three hours to commute from the **remote** town.
彼は都会から離れた町から3時間かけて通勤する。

119 bound for

〜行きの

The train is **bound for** Osaka.
その電車は大阪行きだ。

— 26 —

1. ビジネスパーソンの一日

120 avoid [əvɔ́id]
他 を避ける
類 escape

I take trains in order to **avoid** traffic jams.
交通渋滞**を避ける**ために，私は電車を使う。

121 grip [gríp]
他 をしっかりつかむ
名 取っ手, グリップ
関 grasp「をつかむ」

Gripping the **handrail**, he climbed up the stairs.
彼は手すり**にしっかりつかまって**階段を上った。

122 wear [wéər]
他 を着ている, 身に着けている
関 put on「を身に着ける」

This company's employees don't have to **wear** suits on Fridays.
この会社の従業員は金曜日はスーツ**を着**なくてよい。

123 slip into
他 〈衣類〉をさっと着る
関 slip「滑って転ぶ」

He **slipped into** his **jacket**.
彼はジャケット**をさっと着た**。

124 straighten [stréitn]
他 を真っすぐにする
派 straight「真っすぐな」

He **straightened** his **tie** before appearing in public.
彼は公共の場に出る前に，ネクタイ**を真っすぐにした**。

― 27 ―

chap01 sec2_11

| 125 **tie** [tái] | 他 ①〈ひもなど〉を結ぶ
②(ひもなどで)を結び付ける | 関 tie-up「提携」 |

He **tied** his **shoelaces** tightly so that they wouldn't come loose.
彼は靴ひもがほどけないよう，きつく結んだ．

| 126 **glance** [glǽns] | 自 ちらっと見る | 類 glimpse |

The man **glanced** at his **wristwatch** and left his office at once.
その男性は腕時計をちらっと見ると，すぐに会社を出た．

| 127 **be stuffed with** | 〜でいっぱいである | 関 stuff「を詰め込む」 |

Mr. Mori's **wallet was stuffed with** 10,000-yen bills.
森氏の財布は1万円札でいっぱいだった．

| 128 **button** [bʌ́tn] | 他〈衣服など〉のボタンを掛ける
名 ボタン | 反 unbutton「のボタンを外す」 |

Button your **shirt** fully before meeting the clients.
顧客と会う前に，ワイシャツのすべてのボタンを留めなさい．

| 129 **shoulder** [ʃóuldər] | 他 を肩で担ぐ，背負う
名 肩 | 関 shoulder bag「ショルダーバッグ」 |

He **shouldered** his **briefcase** and left for his office.
彼はブリーフケースを肩に掛け，会社に向かった．

1. ビジネスパーソンの一日

chap01
sec2_12

130 ☐		
a pair of	1対の，1組の	

You will get **a** free **pair of pants** with your purchase of $100 or more.
100ドル以上お買い上げの方には，ズボン1着を無料で差し上げます。

131 ☐ T		
remove [rimúːv]	他 ①を取り除く ②〈衣類など〉を脱ぐ，外す	類 take off

This product safely **removes lipstick**, oil and other tough stains without discoloring the surface.
この製品は，口紅や油やその他のしつこい染みを，表面を変色させることなく安全に取り除きます。

132 ☐		
swipe [swáip]	他〈磁気カード〉を読み取り機に通す	関 swipe card「磁気カード」

Workers must **swipe** their **employee ID card** at the entrance.
職員は入り口で社員証を読み取り機に通さなければならない。

133 ☐		
fold up	他 を折り畳む	関 folder「フォルダ」

The woman **folded up** her sunshade in front of the building.
その女性は建物の前で日傘を折り畳んだ。

134 ☐		
apply [əplái]	他 ①〈化粧品など〉を塗る ②を適用する	派 application「適用，申し込み」

She **applied** liquid **foundation** over her entire face.
彼女は顔全体にリキッドファンデーションを塗った。

Section 3　実際のスケジュールで確認！

chap01_sec3

Sunday	Monday	Tuesday	Wednesday	Thursday	Friday	Saturday
			1 9:00 a.m. Meeting with new **clients** at Star Café	**2**	**3**	**4**
5	**6** 12:00 p.m. **Power lunch** with Ms. Roberts	**7**	**8** 3:00 p.m. **Contract** meeting at Top Notch Service	**9**	**10** Shipment to the US headquarters (Product #332)	**11**
12	**13**	**14** ✓	**15**	**16** 5:00 p.m. **Negotiation** with Mr. Norton at Trade Room	**17**	**18**
19	**20** 4:00 p.m. **Sales meeting** at Room 122	**21**	**22**	**23**	**24** 8:00 p.m. **Attend** a business **seminar** at Tokyo Gakuin	**25**
26	**27**	**28** The **deadline** of report for #2 plan C	**29**	**30** 3:00 p.m. **Participate** in the monthly meeting at Room 144		

NOTE
- ✓ **Commuter pass** runs out on 14th!
- ✓ Also get a round-trip ticket for the **express** train for 16th.

– 30 –

1. ビジネスパーソンの一日

和訳

日	月	火	水	木	金	土
			1 午前9時 スターカフェにて新規顧客と打ち合わせ	2	3	4
5	6 12時 ロバーツさんとパワーランチ	7	8 午後3時 トップノッチサービスにて契約会議	9	10 アメリカ本社へ発送 （商品番号332）	11
12	13	14 ✓	15	16 午後5時 トレードルームでノートン氏と交渉	17	18
19	20 午後4時 122室にて営業会議	21	22	23	24 午後8時 ビジネスセミナーに出席 東京学院にて	25
26	27	28 プランCナンバー2の報告書の締め切り	29	30 午後3時 月例会議に出席 144室にて		

メモ
- ✓ 定期が14日に切れる！
- ✓ 16日の急行列車の往復切符も買う。

✴Review Words✴

☐ client → Sec.1-4	☐ power lunch → Sec.1-5	☐ contract → Sec.1-7
☐ negotiation → Sec.1-6	☐ sales meeting → Sec.1-3	☐ attend → Sec.2-89
☐ seminar → Sec.1-14	☐ deadline → Sec.1-13	☐ participate → Sec.2-88
☐ commuter pass → Sec.1-23	☐ express → Sec.1-37	

第2章
会社と地域

それぞれ英語で何と言うでしょうか？

☞ 答えは P.35

Section 1　イラストで覚える！

✳City「都市」

1. train station
2. highway [háiwèi]
3. shop, store [ʃáp], [stɔ́:r]
4. intersection [ìntərsékʃn]
5. parking, parking lot
6. apartment house
7. vehicle [ví:ikl]
8. road sign
9. traffic [trǽfik]
10. pedestrian [pədéstriən]
11. motorbike, motorcycle [móutərbàik], [móutərsàikl]
12. suburb [sʌ́bə:rb]
13. expressway [ikspréswèi]
14. billboard, signboard [bílbɔ̀:rd], [sáinbɔ̀:rd]
15. skyscraper [skáiskrèipər]
16. avenue [ǽvənjù:]
17. downtown area
18. commercial district
19. office building
20. complex [kámpleks]

1 train station 電車の駅	2 highway 幹線道路	3 shop, store 店	4 intersection 交差点
5 parking, parking lot 駐車場	6 apartment house マンション	7 vehicle 乗り物	8 road sign 道路標識
9 traffic 交通	10 pedestrian 歩行者	11 motorbike, motorcycle バイク	12 suburb 郊外
13 expressway 高速道路	14 billboard, signboard 看板	15 skyscraper 摩天楼	16 avenue 大通り
17 downtown area 繁華街	18 commercial district 商業地区	19 office building オフィスビル	20 complex 複合施設

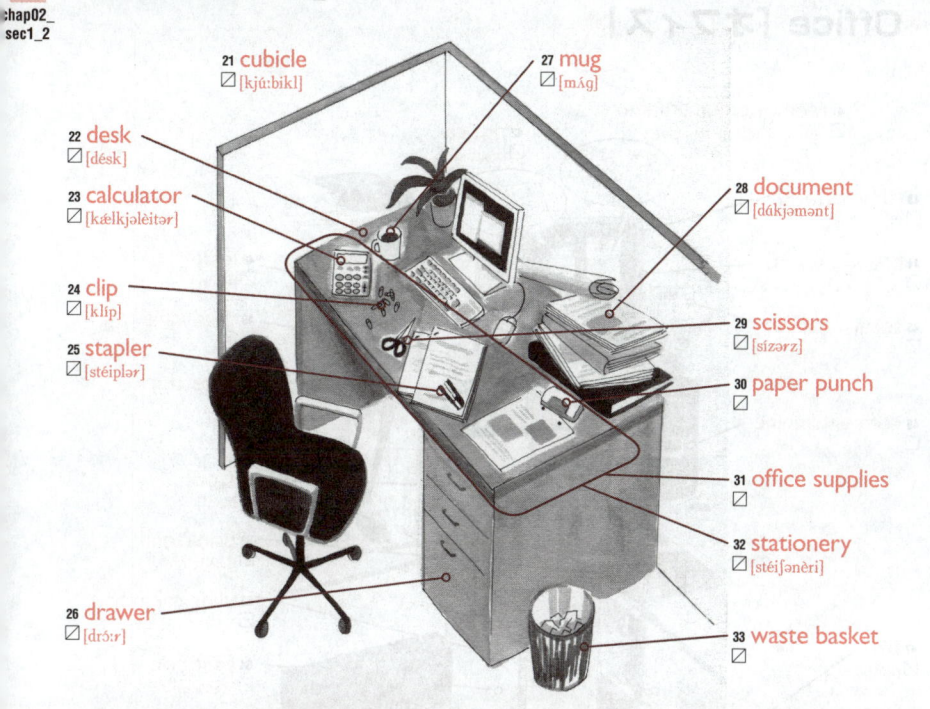

✱Desk 「デスク」✱

- 21 cubicle [kjú:bikl]
- 22 desk [désk]
- 23 calculator [kælkjəlèitər]
- 24 clip [klíp]
- 25 stapler [stéiplər]
- 26 drawer [dró:r]
- 27 mug [mʌ́g]
- 28 document [dákjəmənt]
- 29 scissors [sízərz]
- 30 paper punch
- 31 office supplies
- 32 stationery [stéiʃənèri]
- 33 waste basket

その他の文房具を表す語句

- 34 finger stall
- 35 glue [glú:]
- 36 rubber band
- 37 ruler [rú:lər]
- 38 shredder [ʃrédər]
- 39 staples [stéiplz]
- 40 correction tape

21	cubicle 小さい部屋	22	desk 机	23	calculator 電卓	24	clip クリップ
25	stapler ホチキス	26	drawer 引き出し	27	mug マグカップ	28	document 資料
29	scissors はさみ	30	paper punch 穴あけパンチ	31	office supplies 事務用品	32	stationery 文房具
33	waste basket くずかご	34	finger stall 指サック	35	glue のり	36	rubber band 輪ゴム
37	ruler 定規	38	shredder シュレッダー	39	staples 針（ホチキスの）	40	correction tape 修正テープ

✴ Office 「オフィス」 ✴

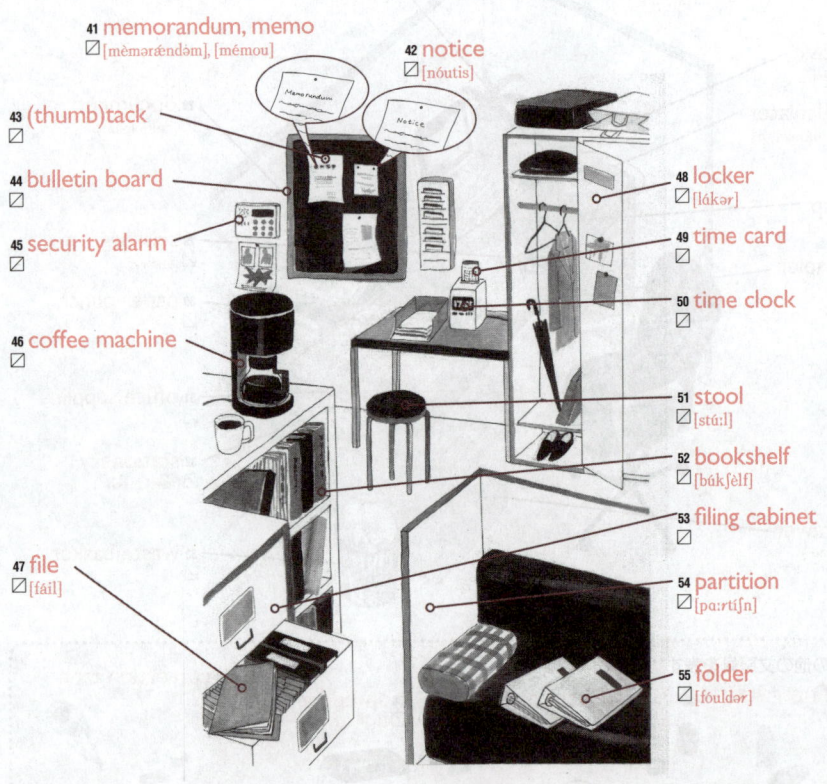

- 41 **memorandum, memo** [mèmərǽndəm], [mémou]
- 42 **notice** [nóutis]
- 43 **(thumb)tack**
- 44 **bulletin board**
- 45 **security alarm**
- 46 **coffee machine**
- 47 **file** [fáil]
- 48 **locker** [lákər]
- 49 **time card**
- 50 **time clock**
- 51 **stool** [stú:l]
- 52 **bookshelf** [búkʃèlf]
- 53 **filing cabinet**
- 54 **partition** [pɑ:rtíʃn]
- 55 **folder** [fóuldər]

41 memorandum, memo お知らせ	42 notice 掲示, 告知	43 (thumb)tack 画びょう	44 bulletin board 掲示板
45 security alarm 警報機	46 coffee machine コーヒーメーカー	47 file ファイル	48 locker ロッカー
49 time card タイムカード	50 time clock タイムレコーダー	51 stool 腰掛け	52 bookshelf 本棚
53 filing cabinet ファイルキャビネット	54 partition 間仕切り	55 folder フォルダー	

2. 会社と地域

- 64 emergency exit
- 56 conference room
- 65 ladder [lǽdər]
- 57 hallway [hɔ́ːlwèi]
- 66 supply room
- 67 storage [stɔ́ːridʒ]
- 68 office [ɔ́ːfis]
- 69 laboratory [lǽbərətɔ̀ːri]
- 70 elevator [éləvèitər]
- 58 stairs [stéərz]
- 71 side door
- 59 floor [flɔ́ːr]
- 60 visitor [vízitər]
- 61 visitor pass
- 73 cafeteria [kæ̀fətíəriə]
- 62 receptionist [risépʃənist]
- 72 lobby [lɑ́bi]
- 74 front door
- 63 reception desk
- 75 main entrance

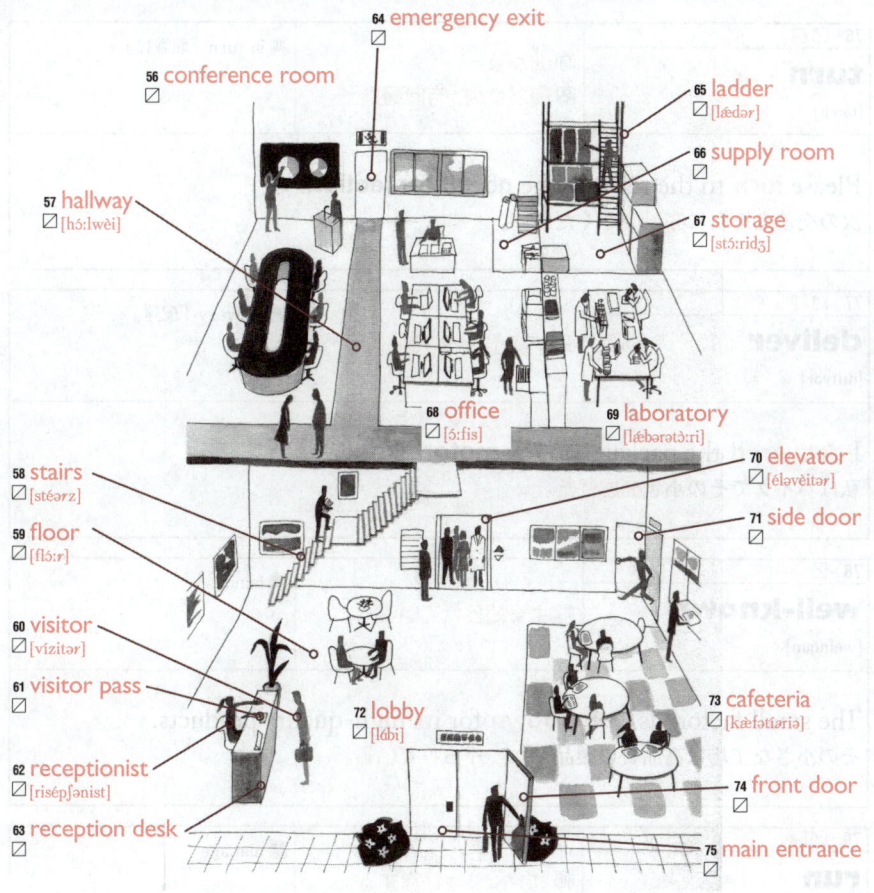

56	conference room 会議室	57	hallway ろうか	58	stairs 階段	59	floor 床
60	visitor 来客	61	visitor pass 入館許可証	62	receptionist 受付係	63	reception desk 受付
64	emergency exit 非常口	65	ladder はしご	66	supply room 備品室	67	storage 倉庫
68	office オフィス	69	laboratory 研究室	70	elevator エレベーター	71	side door 通用口
72	lobby ロビー	73	cafeteria 社員食堂	74	front door 正面ドア	75	main entrance 正面玄関

ビジネスパーソンの一日

会社と地域

オフィス機器

会社の組織

雇用

Section 2　例文で覚える！

---

76 **turn** [tə́ːrn]
- 自 曲がる
- 名 曲がり角, 方向転換
- 関 in turn「順番に」

Please **turn** to the right at the next **intersection**.
次の交差点を右に曲がってください。

---

77 **deliver** [dilívər]
- 他 を届ける, 配達する
- 派 delivery「配達」

I **delivered** the package on my **motorbike**.
私はバイクでその小包を届けた。

---

78 **well-known** [wélnóun]
- 形 よく知られている
- 類 famous

The small factory is **well-known** for its high-quality products.
その小さな工場は高品質の製品でよく知られている。

---

79 **run** [rʌ́n]
- 他〈店など〉を経営する
- 類 manage

My brother **runs** a small **shop** in Miami.
私の兄はマイアミで小さな店を経営している。

---

80 **advertise** [ǽdvərtàiz]
- 他 を宣伝する
- 自 広告を出す
- 派 advertising「広告」

The new product has been **advertised** on a **billboard** at the station.
その新製品は駅の看板で宣伝されている。

2. 会社と地域

81 park [páːrk]
- 他 を駐車する
- 名 公園
- 派 parking「駐車」

Not a few **vehicles** are **parked** near the station.
かなりの数の車が駅のそばに駐車されている。

82 be stuck in
- (渋滞など)にはまる

We **were stuck in** traffic near Times Square.
タイムズスクエアの近くで渋滞にはまった。

83 locate [lóukeit, –́–]
- 他〈建物など〉を置く，設ける
- 派 location「所在地」

The **office building** is **located** in the middle of the city.
そのオフィスビルは市の中心に位置して〔置かれて〕いる。

84 worldwide [wə́ːrldwáid]
- 形 世界中の
- 副 世界中に
- 関 nationwide「全国的な」

The bankruptcy of that company had an impact on the **worldwide** fashion industry.
その企業の倒産は世界中のファッション業界に衝撃を与えた。

85 base [béis]
- 他 の本拠を置く
- 名 基礎
- 関 basic「基本的な」

That company has been **based** in this town since 2000.
その企業は2000年からこの町に本拠を置いている。

— 39 —

| 86 | rental [réntl] | 名 レンタル, 賃貸し
形 レンタルの, 賃貸しの | 関 rental car「レンタカー」 |

Our company offers a wide array of apartment **rentals** in Chicago.
弊社はシカゴの賃貸マンションを幅広く提供致します。

| 87 | move out | 自 引っ越す | |

I plan to **move out** to a safer **suburb**.
もっと安全な郊外へ引っ越す予定です。

| 88 | lease [líːs] | 名 賃貸借契約
他 を賃貸しする | |

The **lease** on this building is renewed every two years.
本建物の賃貸借契約は2年ごとに更新される。

| 89 | rent [rént] | 他 を賃借りする
自 賃貸しされる | |

The young manager is going to **rent** a small room from his college friend.
その若い経営者は大学時代の友人から小さな部屋を賃借りする予定だ。

| 90 | tower over | 他 の上に高くそびえる | 類 rise |

Modern **skyscrapers tower over** the streets of Tokyo.
東京の通りには近代的な摩天楼が高くそびえている。

2. 会社と地域

91 ☐ T
access
[ǽkses]
　名 アクセス, 接近方法
　派 accessible「行きやすい」

Our office has good **access** to a **train station**.
私たちのオフィスは電車の駅への**アクセス**がよい。

92 ☐
under construction　工事中で

The **highway** will be **under construction** till next month.
その幹線道路は来月まで**工事中**だ。

93 ☐ T
build
[bíld]
　他 を建設する, 建てる
　派 builder「建設業者」

They are planning to **build** a new cinema **complex** in the downtown area.
彼らは繁華街に新しいシネコン〔複合映画館〕**を建設する**予定だ。

94 ☐ T
sum
[sʌ́m]
　名 総額, 合計
　他 を合計する

She worked out the **sum** on her **calculator**.
彼女は**総額**を電卓ではじき出した。

95 ☐ T
order
[ɔ́ːrdər]
　他 を注文する
　名 注文
　関 place an order「発注する」

The **office supplies** we **ordered** yesterday have already arrived.
昨日**注文した**事務用品はすでに届いています。

― 41 ―

96 lock
[lák] 他 に鍵を掛ける　　反 unlock「の鍵を開ける」

Workers should **lock** their **drawers** when they are away from their desk.
職員は机から離れる際に，引き出しに鍵を掛けるべきだ。

97 occupy
[ákjəpài] 他〈部屋など〉を使用する　　関 vacant「空いている」

The **cubicle** is **occupied** when the red light is on.
赤ランプがついているときは，その小部屋は使用中だ。

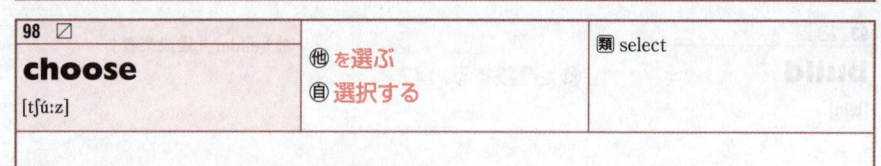

98 choose
[tʃúːz] 他 を選ぶ／自 選択する　　類 select

You can **choose** whatever **stationery** you want.
欲しい文房具を何でも選ぶことができますよ。

99 clear
[klíər] 他 を片付ける／形 はっきりした　　類 clean

We have to **clear** these documents off the **desk** immediately.
私たちは早急に，机の上からこれらの文書を片付けなければならない。

100 fasten
[fǽsn] 他 をしっかり固定する　　反 unfasten「を外す」

Fasten the top edges with a **clip**.
その上端をクリップで留めてください。

— 42 —

2. 会社と地域

101 discover
[diskʌ́vər]
他 を発見する
類 find

I **discovered** some spelling errors in his English report.
私は彼が書いた英語の報告書にいくつかの綴りの間違い**を発見**した。

102 realize
[ríː(ː)əlàiz]
他 〈希望・目的など〉を実現する
類 achieve

They have to come up with a new way to **realize** their goal.
彼らは目標**を実現する**ための新しい方法を考え出さなければならない。

103 borrow
[bɔ́ːrou, bɑ́r-]
他 〈物・金〉を(無料で)借りる
反 lend「を貸す」

Can I **borrow** something to write with?
何か書くもの**を貸**してもらえますか？

104 concentrate
[kɑ́nsntrèit]
自 専念する, 集中する
関 focus「焦点を合わせる」

It's so noisy outside that we can't **concentrate** on the job.
外があまりに騒がしいので, 私たちは仕事に**集中**できない。

105 pile
[páil]
他 を積み上げる
名 積み重ね
関 piles [a pile] of「たくさんの, 多量の」

The **documents** for the meeting are **piled** on her desk.
その会議の資料は彼女の机の上に**積ん**である。

| 106 | **belong to** | 他 ①のものである
②に所属している，の一員である | |

Does that jacket **belong to** Lisa or Jenny?
あのジャケットはリサ**の**ですか，それともジェニー**の**ですか？

| 107 | **clip** [klíp] | 他〈記事・絵など〉を切り抜く
名（はさみで）切ること | 派 clipping「切り抜き」 |

I **clip** articles from the economic newspaper every day.
私は毎日，経済紙から記事**を切り抜く**。

| 108 | **litter** [lítər] | 他 に散らかる
名 ごみ，くず | 関 No Littering.「ごみ捨て禁止」 |

His desk was **littered** with papers.
彼の机は書類が**散らか**っていた。

| 109 | **throw away** | 他 ①を投げ捨てる
②〈金など〉を浪費する | 関 dump「をごみとして投棄する」 |

When you **throw** something **away**, please use the **waste basket**.
何か**を捨てる**ときには，そのごみ箱をご利用ください。

| 110 | **measure** [méʒər] | 他 の寸法を測る | 派 measurement「測量，測定」 |

I **measured** the paper with a **ruler**.
私は定規でその紙**の大きさを測った**。

2. 会社と地域

111 in-house [ínháus]
形 社内の
副 社内で

Now they're editing the August edition of their **in-house** newsletter.
彼らは今，社内報の8月号を編集している。

112 pour [pɔ́ːr]
他 ①を注ぐ，つぐ
②〈金・物資〉をつぎ込む

She **poured** coffee into her **mug**.
彼女はマグカップにコーヒーを注いだ。

113 exit [éɡzit, éksit]
名 退出
他 〈場所〉から退場する
反 entrance「入り口」

I inserted my **time card** into the time clock and made a hasty **exit** from the office.
私はタイムカードをタイムレコーダーに挿し，事務所から急いで退出した。

114 contain [kəntéin]
他 〈情報など〉を含んでいる
派 container「容器，コンテナ」

This **folder contains** important information about the product.
このフォルダには，その製品の重要な情報が入っている。

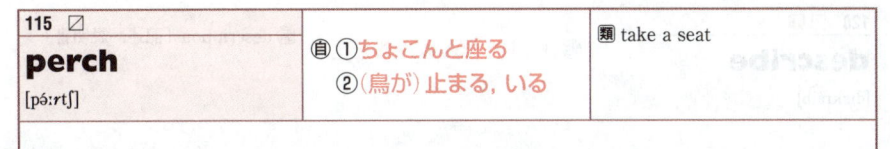

115 perch [pɔ́ːrtʃ]
自 ①ちょこんと座る
②〈鳥が〉止まる，いる
類 take a seat

He **perched** on a **stool** and ordered a drink.
彼は腰掛けに座り，飲み物を注文した。

116	**punch** [pʌ́ntʃ]	他〈タイムカードなど〉を押す	

I forgot to **punch** the **time clock** this morning.
私は今朝タイムレコーダーを押すのを忘れた。

117	**distribute** [distríbju:t]	他 ①を配布する ②を散布する, ばらまく	派 distribution「配給, 分布」

He asked me who had **distributed** the **memo** about the meeting.
彼は誰が会議についてのお知らせを配ったかを私に聞いた。

118	**separate** [sépərèit]	他 を分ける, 分離する	派 separately「別々に, 個々に」

These booths should be **separated** from each other by **partitions**.
これらのブースは間仕切りでお互いに切り離した方がいい。

119	**brew** [brú:]	他〈コーヒーなど〉を入れる	

This **coffee machine brews** 4 to 10 cups of coffee at a time.
このコーヒーメーカーは一度に4〜10杯のコーヒーを作る。

120	**describe** [diskráib]	他 を記述する, の特徴を述べる	派 description「記述, 説明書」

This **notice describes** the time, place and purposes of the meeting.
この掲示には会議の日時と場所と目的が記されている。

2. 会社と地域

121 post [póust]
- 他〈掲示など〉を貼る
- 名 柱
- 派 posting「任命，配属」

The schedule is **posted** on the **bulletin board**.
スケジュールは掲示板に貼られている。

122 stack [stǽk]
- 他 を積む
- 名 積み重ね
- 類 pile

Would you **stack** these books on the **bookshelf**?
これらの本を本棚に積んでもらえますか？

123 activate [ǽktəvèit]
- 他 を作動させる，活性化させる

Press this button to **activate** the **security alarm**.
警報機を作動させるにはこのボタンを押しなさい。

124 open [óupn]
- 形 営業中の
- 他 を開ける
- 反 closed「閉店した」

The **cafeteria** is **open** from 10:00 a.m. to 4:00 p.m. Monday through Friday.
カフェテリアは月曜日から金曜日の，午前10時から午後4時まで営業している。

125 various [véəriəs]
- 形 さまざまな
- 派 variety「多様性」

The **storage** in our office has **various** kinds of foreign documents.
当社の収蔵庫にはさまざまな種類の外国文書がある。

| 126 | extra [ékstrə] | 形 余分の,追加の | 類 additional |

Find some **extra** notebooks in the **supply room**.
追加のノートを何冊か備品室で見つけてきて。

| 127 | out of service | 使用中止で | 関 out of order「故障中で」 |

Almost all of the **elevators** are **out of service** now.
ほとんどのエレベーターが今,使用中止です。

| 128 | renovate [rénəvèit] | 他〈古い建物など〉を修復する | 類 repair |

This old building needs **renovating** as soon as possible.
この古いビルはできるだけ早く修復する必要がある。

| 129 | establish [istǽbliʃ] | 他①を設立する ②を確立する | 派 establishment「設立,確立」 |

Our team **established** a **laboratory** last year.
私たちのチームは昨年,研究室を設立した。

| 130 | improper [imprápər] | 形①不当な ②不適当な,ふさわしくない | 反 proper「適切な」 |

The penalty for **improper parking** in this area is thirty dollars.
この地区での不当な駐車に対する罰金は30ドルだ。

2. 会社と地域

131 **greet** [gríːt]
他 〈人〉を迎える, にあいさつする
派 greeting「あいさつ」

They **greeted** the **visitors** at the entrance.
彼らは入り口で訪問客**を迎えた**。

132 **obtain** [əbtéin]
他 を手に入れる

Please **obtain** your **visitor pass** at the reception desk.
受付で入館許可証**を手に入れ**てください。

133 **polish** [páliʃ]
他 ①を磨く
②〈技術〉に磨きをかける

The cleaning crew is **polishing** the **floor**.
清掃員たちが床**を磨いて**いる。

134 **ascend** [əsénd]
他 〈階段など〉を上る
反 descend「〈階段など〉を下る」

He **ascended** the **ladder** slowly.
彼はゆっくりとはしご**を上った**。

135 **emergency** [imə́ːrdʒənsi]
名 非常事態
派 emergent「緊急の」

You should take the **stairs** in case of **emergency**.
非常の場合には階段を使った方がいい。

Section 3　実際の会話で確認！

chap02_sec3_1

1

- M: I've heard you're going to relocate.
- W: Yes, we're **moving out** in October. Our **lease** expires that month, and the owner of this building says he wants to **renovate** it. So we've decided to move.
- M: What's your new **office** like?
- W: Well, it's in a rather new **office building** and **occupies** an entire **floor**. We'll have a spacious **conference room** and also a **cafeteria**, though a small one.
- M: Where is the building **located**?
- W: It's in the **downtown area**. It's within walking distance from two **train stations** and very close to an **expressway** ramp, which allows easy **access** for our clients.
- M: Will I be able to **park** my car in front of the building?
- W: No, you won't have to do that. We'll have some **parking** spaces for **visitors**, so you'll just have to tell our **receptionist** when you use one.
- M: That's great. I'm looking forward to visiting your new office.

chap02_sec3_2

2

- W: Koji, could you put this heap of **documents** away? They've been **piled** up here for weeks, and I need to **clear** the **desk** at once.
- M: But where should I put them? The **bookshelves** and **filing cabinets** are full, so we have nowhere to put them. If I could **throw** them **away** or put them in a **shredder** …
- W: No, you can't do that. They are important. We have to store them somewhere. What about the **supply room**?
- M: It's on the third floor! And it's always **locked**.
- W: The general affairs department has the key. And you can borrow a cart there.
- M: Oh, now I remember! A **notice** was **posted** on the **bulletin board**, saying the **elevator** will be **out of service** for maintenance this afternoon. It's already past noon.
- W: It looks like you'll have to use the **stairs**.
- M: Do you really mean that? You work me too hard.
- W: You can't **choose** your boss. Okay, I'll help you. Now let's get started.

— 50 —

和訳

1

- **M**：会社が移転すると伺いましたが。
- **W**：ええ，10月にここを出ます。賃貸契約がその月に切れるんですが，このビルのオーナーがビルをリフォームしたいと言うんですね。それで引っ越すことに決めたんです。
- **M**：新しいオフィスはどんな感じですか。
- **W**：そうですね，わりと新しいオフィスビルの中にあって，ワンフロア丸ごと占めています。広い会議室と，小さいですがカフェテリアもあります。
- **M**：場所はどこなんですか。
- **W**：繁華街です。電車の駅2つから歩ける距離で，高速道路の出入り口もすぐ近くなので，クライアントの方々のアクセスには便利です。
- **M**：ビルの前に車を駐車できるでしょうか。
- **W**：いえ，それには及びません。来客用の駐車スペースがあるので，利用されるとき受付の者に言っていただければ結構です。
- **M**：それはいいですね。新しいオフィスにおじゃまするのが楽しみです。

2

- **W**：コウジ，この書類の山をしまってくれない？ 何週間もここに積んであるんだけど，すぐに机の上を片づける必要があるのよ。
- **M**：だけどどこにしまえばいいんですか。本棚とファイルキャビネットはいっぱいだし，しまう場所なんてありませんよ。捨てるかシュレッダーにかけるかしていいのなら…。
- **W**：それはだめ。重要書類だから。どこかに保管しなくちゃ。備品室はどうかしらね。
- **M**：備品室は3階ですよ！ それにいつも鍵がかかっています。
- **W**：鍵は総務部にあるわ。台車も借りられるし。
- **M**：ああ，思い出したんですけど，エレベーターがメンテナンスで今日の午後使用中止になるって掲示が掲示板に張ってありました。もう昼過ぎですよ。
- **W**：階段を使うしかなさそうね。
- **M**：本気で言ってますか？人使いが荒すぎますよ。
- **W**：上司は選べないのよ。わかった，手伝うからすぐに始めましょう。

☀ Review Words ☀

☐ move out ➡ Sec.2-87	☐ lease ➡ Sec.2-88	☐ renovate ➡ Sec.2-128
☐ office ➡ Sec.1-68	☐ office building ➡ Sec.1-19	☐ occupy ➡ Sec.2-97
☐ floor ➡ Sec.1-59	☐ conference room ➡ Sec.1-56	☐ cafeteria ➡ Sec.1-73
☐ locate ➡ Sec.2-83	☐ downtown area ➡ Sec.1-17	☐ train station ➡ Sec.1-1
☐ expressway ➡ Sec.1-13	☐ access ➡ Sec.2-91	☐ park ➡ Sec.2-81
☐ parking ➡ Sec.1-5	☐ visitor ➡ Sec.1-60	☐ receptionist ➡ Sec.1-62
☐ document ➡ Sec.1-28	☐ pile ➡ Sec.2-105	☐ clear ➡ Sec.2-99
☐ desk ➡ Sec.1-22	☐ bookshelf ➡ Sec.1-52	☐ filing cabinet ➡ Sec.1-53
☐ throw away ➡ Sec.2-109	☐ shredder ➡ Sec.1-38	☐ supply room ➡ Sec.1-66
☐ lock ➡ Sec.2-96	☐ notice ➡ Sec.1-42	☐ post ➡ Sec.2-121
☐ bulletin board ➡ Sec.1-44	☐ elevator ➡ Sec.1-70	☐ out of service ➡ Sec.2-127
☐ stairs ➡ Sec.1-58	☐ choose ➡ Sec.2-98	

第3章
オフィス機器

英語で何と言うでしょうか？

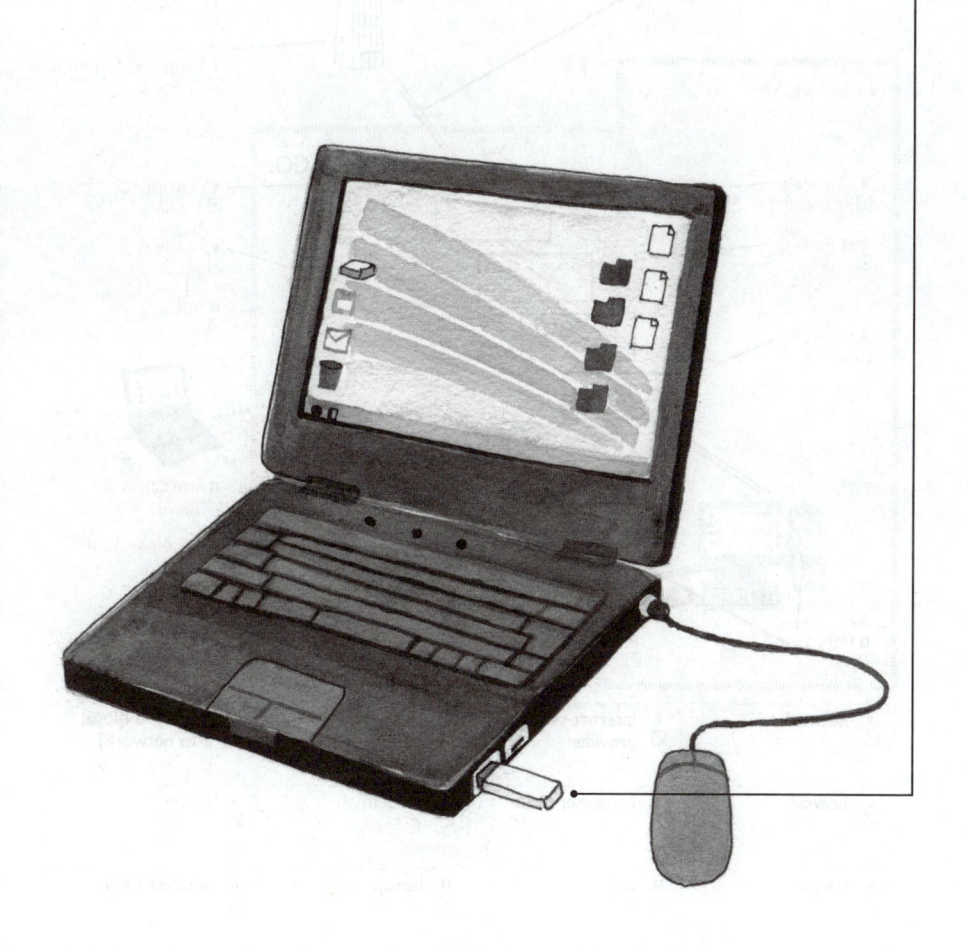

☞ 答えは P.55

Section 1 イラストで覚える！

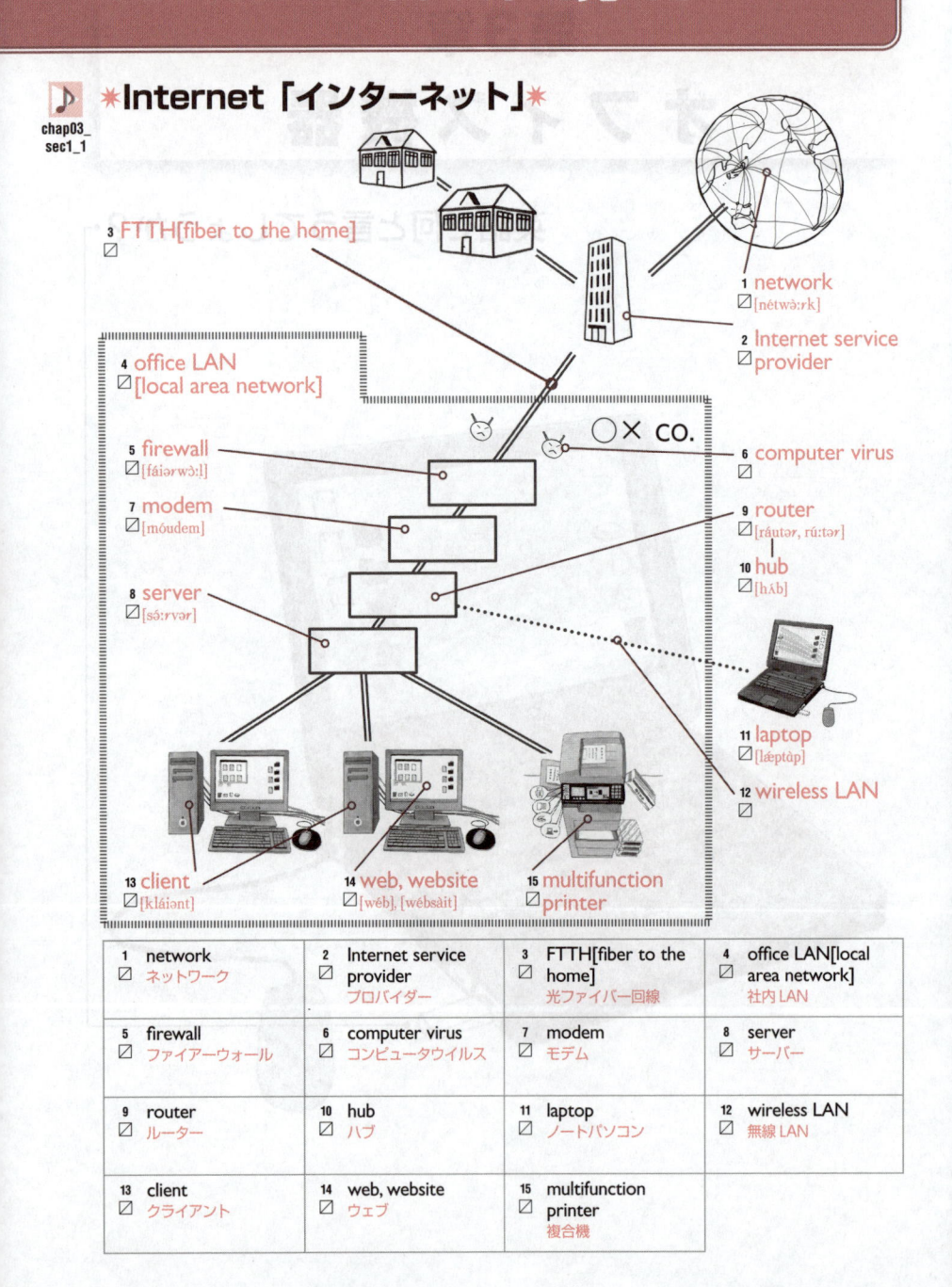

✲Internet「インターネット」✲

- 1 network [nétwə:rk]
- 2 Internet service provider
- 3 FTTH [fiber to the home]
- 4 office LAN [local area network]
- 5 firewall [fáiərwɔ:l]
- 6 computer virus
- 7 modem [móudem]
- 8 server [sə́:rvər]
- 9 router [ráutər, rú:tər]
- 10 hub [hʌ́b]
- 11 laptop [lǽptɑp]
- 12 wireless LAN
- 13 client [kláiənt]
- 14 web, website [wéb], [wébsàit]
- 15 multifunction printer

1 network ネットワーク	2 Internet service provider プロバイダー	3 FTTH [fiber to the home] 光ファイバー回線	4 office LAN [local area network] 社内LAN
5 firewall ファイアーウォール	6 computer virus コンピュータウイルス	7 modem モデム	8 server サーバー
9 router ルーター	10 hub ハブ	11 laptop ノートパソコン	12 wireless LAN 無線LAN
13 client クライアント	14 web, website ウェブ	15 multifunction printer 複合機	

3. オフィス機器

✳ Computer 「コンピュータ」 ✳

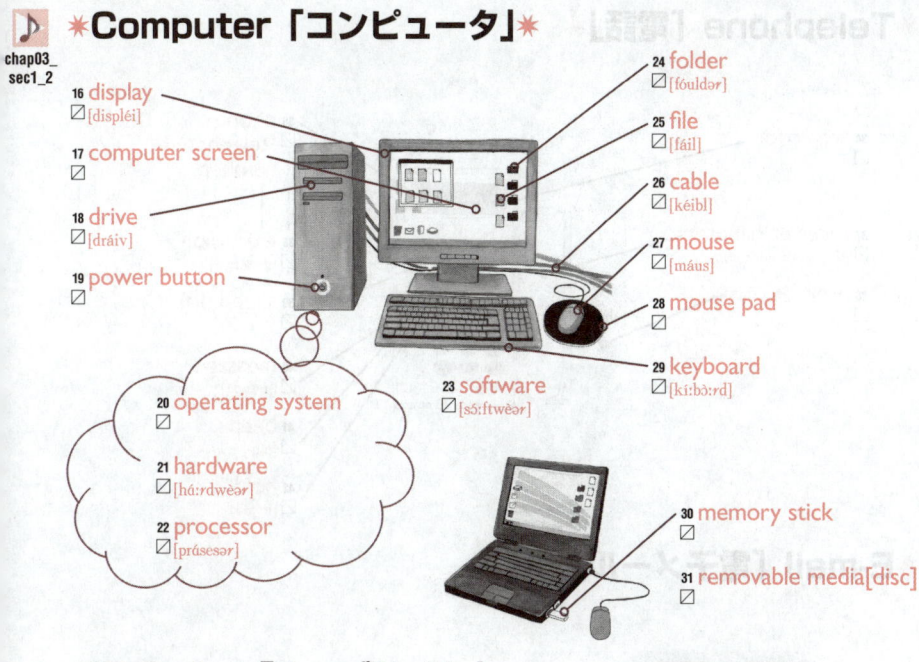

- 16 display [displéi]
- 17 computer screen
- 18 drive [dráiv]
- 19 power button
- 20 operating system
- 21 hardware [hɑ́ːrdwèər]
- 22 processor [prάsesər]
- 23 software [sɔ́ːftwèər]
- 24 folder [fóuldər]
- 25 file [fáil]
- 26 cable [kéibl]
- 27 mouse [máus]
- 28 mouse pad
- 29 keyboard [kíːbɔ̀ːrd]
- 30 memory stick
- 31 removable media[disc]

✳ Website 「ウェブサイト」 ✳

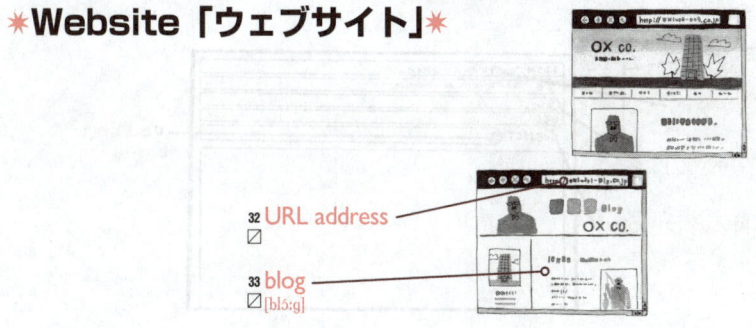

- 32 URL address
- 33 blog [blɔ́ːg]

16 display ディスプレイ	17 computer screen 画面	18 drive 駆動装置, ドライブ	19 power button 電源ボタン
20 operating system 基本ソフト, OS	21 hardware ハードウェア	22 processor 処理装置	23 software ソフトウェア
24 folder フォルダー	25 file ファイル	26 cable ケーブル	27 mouse マウス
28 mouse pad マウスパッド	29 keyboard キーボード	30 memory stick メモリースティック	31 removable media[disc] リムーバブルメディア
32 URL address URL アドレス	33 blog ブログ		

— 55 —

♪ *Telephone 「電話」*

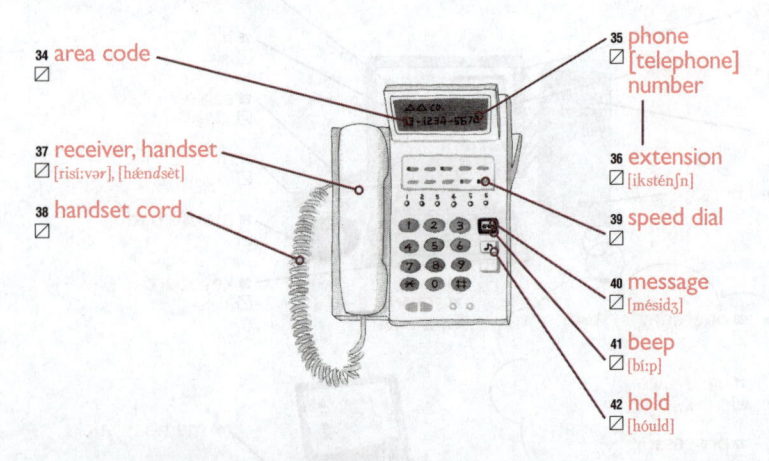

- 34 area code
- 37 receiver, handset [rɪsíːvər], [hǽndsèt]
- 38 handset cord
- 35 phone [telephone] number
- 36 extension [ɪksténʃn]
- 39 speed dial
- 40 message [mésɪdʒ]
- 41 beep [bíːp]
- 42 hold [hóʊld]

E-mail 「電子メール」

- 43 header [hédər]
- 44 e-mail address
- 45 CC [carbon copy]
- 46 BCC [blind carbon copy]
- 47 subject [sʌ́bdʒekt]

FROM: Yamada Ichiro <ichiro_y@sandc.co.jp>
TO: Susan White <susan_w@intero.co.jp>
CC:
BCC:
SUBJECT:

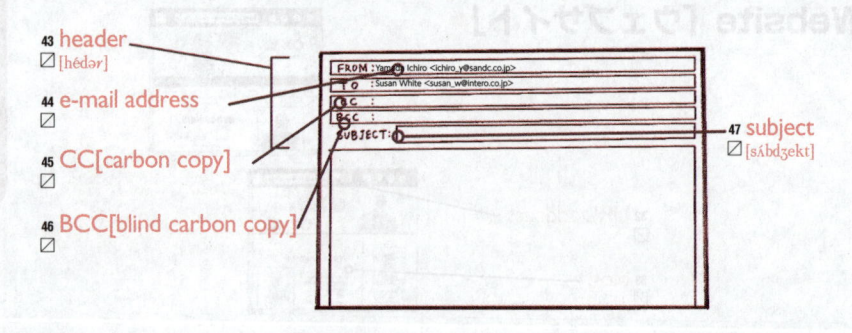

34	area code 市外局番	35	phone[telephone] number 電話番号	36	extension 内線	37	receiver, handset 受話器
38	handset cord 電話コード	39	speed dial 短縮ダイヤル	40	message 伝言	41	beep ビーッという音
42	hold 保留	43	header ヘッダー	44	e-mail address 電子メールアドレス	45	CC[carbon copy] CC
46	BCC[blind carbon copy] BCC	47	subject 件名				

— 56 —

3. オフィス機器

✳Multifunction printer 「複合機」

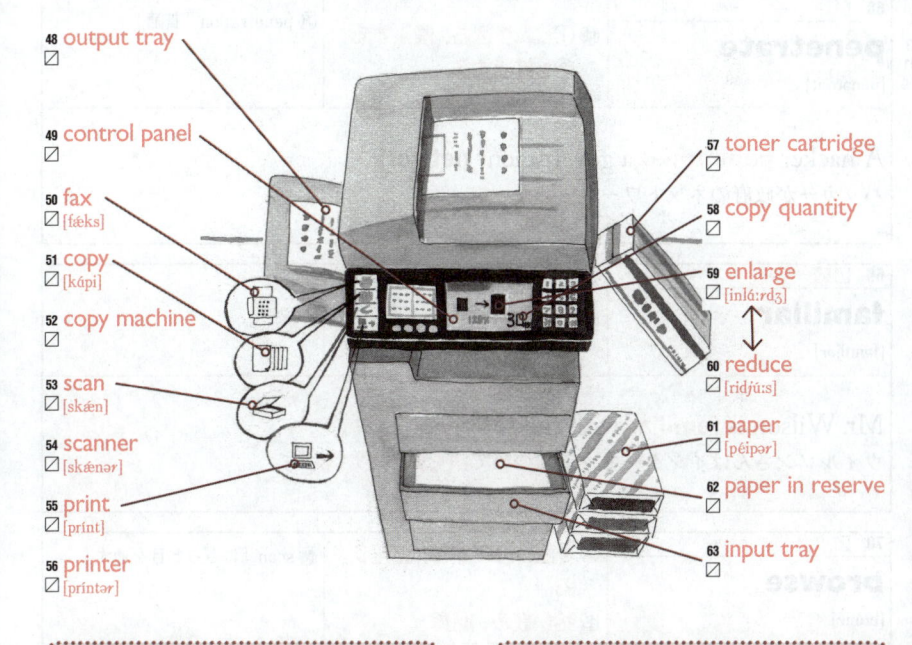

48 output tray
49 control panel
50 fax [fæks]
51 copy [kápi]
52 copy machine
53 scan [skǽn]
54 scanner [skǽnər]
55 print [prínt]
56 printer [príntər]
57 toner cartridge
58 copy quantity
59 enlarge [inlάːrdʒ]
60 reduce [ridjúːs]
61 paper [péipər]
62 paper in reserve
63 input tray

コピーの種類
64 black & white copy
65 two-sided printing

トラブル
66 out of paper
67 paper jam

48 output tray 排紙トレイ	49 control panel 操作パネル	50 fax ファックス	51 copy コピー，複写
52 copy machine コピー機	53 scan スキャン	54 scanner スキャナー	55 print 印刷
56 printer プリンター	57 toner cartridge トナーカートリッジ	58 copy quantity コピー枚数	59 enlarge 拡大する
60 reduce 縮小する	61 paper 紙	62 paper in reserve 補給紙	63 input tray 給紙トレイ
64 black & white copy 白黒コピー	65 two-sided printing 両面印刷	66 out of paper 紙がなくなって，紙切れ	67 paper jam 紙詰まり

Section 2　例文で覚える！

68　penetrate
[pénətrèit]

他 ①に入り込む，侵入する
　　②を貫通する

派 penetration「貫通」

A hacker **penetrated** a government **network**.
ハッカーが政府のネットワークに侵入した。

69　familiar
[fəmíljər]

形（物事を）よく知っている

Mr. Wilson is **familiar** with the Internet.
ウィルソンさんはインターネットについてよく知っている。

70　browse
[bráuz]

他 を拾い読みする，閲覧する
名 拾い読み，閲覧

関 scan「にざっと目を通す」

Just click here to **browse** our products.
当社の製品を閲覧するにはここをクリックしてください。

71　confuse
[kənfjúːz]

他 ①を混乱させる
　　②を混同する

派 confusion「混乱」

All of our team members are **confused** by the new system.
我々のチームのメンバーは全員，その新しいシステムに困惑している。

72　restrict
[ristríkt]

他 を制限する，限定する

Entrance to this laboratory is **restricted**.
この研究室への立ち入りは制限されている。

3. オフィス機器

73 infect [inflékt]
他 を感染させる
派 infection「感染」

My PC was **infected** with a **computer virus**.
私のPCはコンピュータウィルスに感染した。

74 design [dizáin]
他 をデザインする, 設計する
派 designer「デザイナー, 設計者」

She **designed** the **website** for the company.
彼女はその会社のウェブサイトをデザインした。

75 construct [kənstrʌ́kt]
他 を構築する
派 construction「建築」

We need to **construct** a high-speed **wireless LAN**.
私たちは高速の無線LANを構築する必要がある。

76 update [ʌ́pdèit, ⏑ ⏑́]
他 〈データなど〉を更新する
関 revise「を改訂する, 修正する」

He usually **updates** his **blog** every other day.
彼はたいてい1日おきにブログを更新する。

77 dispose of
他 を処分する
類 do away with

We **disposed of** the old batteries according to the rule.
我々は規則に従って古いバッテリーを処分した。

— 59 —

78 turn off

他 を消す

反 turn on「をつける」

He went out of the room without **turning off** his **laptop**.
彼はノートパソコンをオフにしないで部屋を出た。

79 attach
[ətǽtʃ]

他 を添付する

派 attachment「添付」

Please refer to the **attached** **file** for more information.
詳しい情報については，添付ファイルを参照してください。

80 link
[líŋk]

名 リンク
他 をリンクする

If you click on the **link**, you can go to that website.
リンクをクリックすると，そのウェブサイトに行くことができる。

81 up-to-date

形 最新の

反 old-fashioned「旧式の，流行遅れの」

Our office is equipped with **up-to-date** computers.
当社のオフィスには最新のパソコンが装備されている。

82 fix
[fíks]

他 ①を修理する
　②を固定する

類 repair

I sent my computer to a repair factory to **fix** the DVD **drive**.
私はDVDドライブを修理するためにコンピュータを修理工場に送った。

— 60 —

3．オフィス機器

83 ☑ 🇹
connect
[kənékt]

他 を接続する，つなげる

派 connection「連結，接続」

Connect the **cables** to the proper ports of your computer.
コンピュータの適切なポートにケーブルを接続してください。

---

84 ☑
revamp
[rìːvǽmp]

他 を改良する

類 improve

We have **revamped** our website.
ウェブサイトを一新しました。

---

85 ☑
click
[klík]

他 をクリックする

Please **click** the left **mouse** button.
マウスの左ボタンをクリックしてください。

---

86 ☑
insert
[insə́ːrt]

他 を挿入する，差し込む

派 insertion「挿入，新聞折り込み広告」

I **inserted** the **memory stick** in the computer to check the contents.
私は内容を確認するために，メモリースティックをパソコンに差し込んだ。

---

87 ☑ 🇹
enter
[éntər]

他 を入力する

He **entered** the **URL address** and browsed the site.
彼はURLアドレスを入力して，そのサイトを閲覧した。

88 install
[instɔ́:l]

他 ①〈ソフトウエア〉をインストールする
②を設置する，取り付ける

反 uninstall「をアンインストールする」

You shouldn't **install** unnecessary **software**.
不要なソフトウエアは**インストール**しないように。

89 touch-type
[tʌ́tʃtàip]

自 キーを見ないでタイプを打つ

She can **touch-type** quickly and correctly.
彼女は（キーボードを）速く正確に**キーを見ないで打つ**ことができる。

90 delete
[dilí:t]

他 〈データなど〉を削除する

類 erase

I **deleted** an important file by mistake.
誤って重要なファイル**を削除**してしまった。

91 upgrade
[ʌ̀pgréid] 動, [ʌ́pgrèid] 名

他 〈ソフトウエアやハードウエア〉をアップグレードする
名 アップグレード

We plan to **upgrade** our computers next month.
私たちは来月コンピュータ**をアップグレード**するつもりだ。

92 customize
[kʌ́stəmàiz]

他 ①〈コンピュータ〉を自分の好みに合うように設定を変える
②を注文に応じて作る

派 customer「顧客」

I advise you to **customize** your computer when you have time.
時間があるときに，コンピュータ**をカスタマイズする**ことをお勧めします。

3. オフィス機器

93 compatible [kəmpǽtəbl]
形 互換性のある
反 incompatible「気が合わない，互換性のない」

Is that printer **compatible** with this **operating system**?
そのプリンタはこの OS と互換性がありますか。

94 hesitate [hézitèit]
自 ためらう
派 hesitation「ちゅうちょ，ためらい」

Do not **hesitate** to contact me if you want to attend the party.
パーティーに参加したければためらわずに連絡してください。

95 bother [báðər]
他 の邪魔をする，を悩ます
類 interrupt

Sorry to **bother** you, but you got a phone call from Ms. Sato.
お邪魔してすみませんが，佐藤さまからお電話です。

96 receive [risíːv]
他 を受ける，受け取る
派 reception「歓迎(会)，受付」

We have **received** your e-mail of July 7 requesting the catalog.
7月7日付けの，カタログ請求のメールを受け取りました。

97 as soon as possible
できるだけ早く

Please reply **as soon as possible**, no later than tomorrow.
できるだけ早く，明日中には返事をください。

98 hold on
⾃ 電話を切らないでおく

Please **hold on**, I still have something to tell you.
電話を切らないでください，まだお伝えすることがあります。

99 leave
[líːv]
他 を残す

May I **leave** a **message** for Ms. White?
ホワイトさんに伝言をお願いできますか（残したいのですが）。

100 above
[əbʌ́v]
副 上に，前述の

反 below「下の方に」

Please contact us at the **e-mail address above**.
前述のメールアドレスまで連絡してください。

101 have a bad connection
電波の接続が悪い

We seem to **have a bad connection**, so I will call you back.
電波の接続が悪いようなので，電話をかけ直します。

102 accommodate
[əkɑ́mədèit]
他 ①〈要求など〉に応じる
②〈人〉を宿泊させる，収容できる

類 adapt

We are not able to **accommodate** your sudden request.
あなたの急な要求に応じることはできない。

3. オフィス機器

103 return
[ritə́ːrn]
他〈受けた電話〉を返す
名応答
類 answer

I **returned** her call soon after checking my call register.
着信履歴を見てすぐに，私は彼女に折り返し電話した。

104 urgent
[ə́ːrdʒənt]
形 急を要する
派 urgently「緊急に」

Excuse me, but I have an **urgent** message for you.
すみませんが，あなたに緊急の伝言があります。

105 out of the office
外出して
関 go out「外出する」

He is **out of the office** for lunch now.
彼は今，昼食のために外出中です。

106 retrieve
[ritríːv]
他〈データなど〉を検索する，呼び出す

I use an e-mail system that **retrieves** new messages every five minutes.
5分おきに新しいメッセージを取り込むメールシステムを使っている。

107 I wonder if
① …していただけますでしょうか
② …してもよろしいですか
関 Could you …?「…していただけますか」

I wonder if you could call back later.
後でかけ直していただけないでしょうか。

108 answering machine

名 留守番電話 類 answer phone

He recorded a message after the **beep** on the **answering machine**.
彼は留守番電話のピーという音の後にメッセージを録音した。

109 in use

使用中で

The telephone is **in use** right now.
この電話は現在使用中です。

110 write down

他 を書き留める 類 jot down

I **wrote down** his **phone number** in my diary.
私は彼の電話番号を手帳に書き留めた。

111 inquire
[inkwáiər]

自 尋ねる, 問う 類 ask

Thank you for **inquiring** about our exhibition.
私どもの展示会についてお問い合わせいただき，ありがとうございます。

112 wrong
[rɔ́ːŋ]

形 間違った 類 incorrect

I think you have the **wrong** number.
番号を間違えていますよ。

3. オフィス機器

113 further
[fə́:rðər]
- 形 さらに進んだ
- 副 さらに進んで
- 関 additional「追加の」

Would you give us **further** information on the market?
その市場について**さらに詳しい**情報を教えていただけますか？

114 spell
[spél]
- 他 〈語〉を綴る
- 関 spell out「を詳細に説明する」

How do you **spell** your name?
お名前はどのように**綴る**のですか？

115 verify
[vérəfài]
- 他 が正しいかどうか確かめる
- 類 confirm

Please **verify** your e-mail address and password.
お客さまのメールアドレスとパスワード**が正しいかどうか確認**してください。

116 I'm afraid
- （残念ながら）～でないかと思う
- 関 I'm sorry to say「残念ながら～」

I'm afraid she's gone home.
残念ながら，彼女は家に帰った**ようです**。

117 below
[bilóu]
- 副 下に，下記の
- 反 above「上に，前述の」

Answer each of the questions **below** and send us the form.
下記の質問に答えて，申し込み用紙を送ってください。

| 118 ☐ T **contact** [kɑ́ntækt] | 他 に連絡する
名 (人との)連絡, 交際 | 類 reach |

To **contact** me, give me a call at 03-1234-5678, **extension** 715.
私と連絡を取るには, 03-1234-5678, 内線 715 にお電話ください。

| 119 ☐ T **detail** [díːteil, ditéil] | 名 細部, 詳細な記述
他 を詳しく述べる | 関 in detail「詳細に, 詳しく」 |

See the attachment for more **details**.
さらに詳しいことは, 添付ファイルを見てください。

| 120 ☐ **proper** [prɑ́pər] | 形 適した, 正しい | 派 properly「適切に, きちんと」 |

All the staff members should be trained on the **proper** use of the copier.
スタッフ全員がコピー機の適切な使い方について訓練を受けるべきだ。

| 121 ☐ T **save** [séiv] | 他 を節約する | 反 consume「を消費する」 |

Two-sided printing helps **save** paper in the office.
両面印刷をすると社内の紙の節約になる。

| 122 ☐ T **function** [fʌ́ŋkʃn] | 自 (機械などが)機能する | 派 functional「機能上の」 |

This **scanner** doesn't **function** properly.
このスキャナーは正常に機能しません。

3. オフィス機器

123
forward
[fɔ́:rwərd]

他 ①を転送する
②を送る

Please **forward** this message along with the **copy** of the contract to your boss.
契約書のコピーとともにこのメッセージを あなたの上司に転送してください。

124
feed
[fí:d]

他 を補給する

関 feed off「を情報源として利用する」

We need to **feed** some **paper** into the copy machine.
コピー機に紙を補充しないといけない。

125
print out

他 〈データ〉を打ち出す, 印刷する

My boss asked me to **print out** some files.
上司は私にファイルをプリントアウトするよう頼んだ。

126
plug in

他 のプラグをコンセントにつなぐ

類 connect

That **printer** is not **plugged in**.
そのプリンターはコンセントにつながれていない。

127
replace
[ripléis]

他 を取り替える

関 replace A with B「AをBと取り替える」

Please **replace** the **toner cartridge** with a new one.
トナーカートリッジを新しいものに取り替えてください。

- 69 -

Section 3　実際の会話で確認！

1

W: Good morning, this is Orange Computing. How can I help you?
M: Hello, this is Ishigami Takashi from S&G. I'd like to speak to Julian Roberts in the technical department.
W: Sorry, he's out of the office, and I'm afraid he won't be back today. Would you like to leave a message?
M: No, I need to contact him as soon as possible. Actually, our office network seems to be infected with a computer virus. Our server's down, and strange sentences keep appearing on our computer screens. It was Julian who designed our network, so he's more familiar with it than anyone else in our office. We need his help right now. This is urgent.
W: Oh, I see.
M: I wonder if I could have his cell phone number or e-mail address.
W: I'll check. Could you hold on a second?
M: Sure. Thanks.
W: Here's his cell phone number. Could you write it down?
M: Yes. Go ahead, please.

2

M: Hello, this is Verox Customer Service. May I help you?
W: Yes, we're having trouble with our copy machine.
M: What's the problem?
W: Since this morning, we've been having a paper jam every time we try to copy something. Each time we have to pull out jammed paper from the output tray, which is really troublesome.
M: Did you make sure the input tray is in a proper position?
W: Of course I did. There is nothing wrong with the machine as far as I can see.
M: Do you happen to use poor quality paper?
W: No, we use only high quality paper. Besides, we replaced the toner cartridge last week.
M: Did you find anything else about the copier?
W: Well, it also functions as a printer and a fax, and in both cases it prints anything out just fine. No paper jamming occurs.
M: Okay, we'll send our technician to fix it. Could you tell me your company name and telephone number?

3. オフィス機器

和訳

1

W：おはようございます，オレンジ・コンピューティングです。ご用件を承ります。
M：S&G 社のイシガミ・タカシと申します。技術部のジュリアン・ロバーツさんをお願いしたいのですが。

W：あいにく外出中で，今日は戻らないと思います。伝言を残されますか。

M：いいえ，できるだけ早く彼と連絡を取る必要があるんです。実は，うちの会社のネットワークがコンピュータウイルスに感染したようなんです。サーバーがダウンして，コンピュータの画面に妙な文がずっと出ています。ネットワークを設計したのはジュリアンなので，うちの会社の誰よりも彼がネットワークのことをよく知っているんです。すぐに彼の助けが必要で，急を要します。
W：なるほど，わかりました。
M：彼の携帯の電話番号かメールアドレスを教えていただけないかと思うんですが。
W：調べますので，切らずに少々お待ちいただけますか。
M：はい。すみません。
W：彼の携帯番号です。書き留めていただけますか。
M：はい。お願いします。

2

M：はい，ベロックス・カスタマーサービスでございます。どういったご用件でしょうか。
W：コピー機の調子が悪いんです。
M：どういった具合ですか。
W：今朝から，何かコピーしようとするたびに紙詰まりするんです。そのたびに排紙トレーから詰まった紙を引っ張り出さなければならないので，とても困っています。
M：給紙トレーが正しい位置にあるのは確認されましたか。
W：もちろんです。私が見る限りコピー機におかしいところはありません。
M：もしかして質の悪い紙をお使いではありませんか。
W：いいえ，上質の紙しか使っていません。それに，トナーカートリッジも先週取り替えました。
M：コピー機についてほかに気がついたことはありますか。
W：ええと，プリンターとファックスとしても機能するんですが，どちらの場合も問題なく何でも印刷します。紙詰まりは起きません。
M：わかりました，サービスマンを修理に向かわせます。会社名と電話番号を教えていただけますか。

✳Review Words✳

☐ out of the office ➡ Sec.2-105	☐ I'm afraid ➡ Sec.2-116	☐ leave ➡ Sec.2-99
☐ message ➡ Sec.1-40	☐ contact ➡ Sec.2-118	☐ as soon as possible ➡ Sec.2-97
☐ network ➡ Sec.1-1	☐ infect ➡ Sec.2-73	☐ computer virus ➡ Sec.1-6
☐ server ➡ Sec.1-8	☐ computer screen ➡ Sec.1-17	☐ design ➡ Sec.2-74
☐ familiar ➡ Sec.2-69	☐ urgent ➡ Sec.2-104	☐ I wonder if ➡ Sec.2-107
☐ phone number ➡ Sec.1-35	☐ e-mail address ➡ Sec.1-44	☐ hold on ➡ Sec.2-98
☐ write down ➡ Sec.2-110	☐ copy machine ➡ Sec.1-52	☐ paper jam ➡ Sec.1-67
☐ paper ➡ Sec.1-61	☐ output tray ➡ Sec.1-48	☐ input tray ➡ Sec.1-63
☐ proper ➡ Sec.2-120	☐ wrong ➡ Sec.2-112	☐ replace ➡ Sec.2-127
☐ toner cartridge ➡ Sec.1-57	☐ function ➡ Sec.2-122	☐ printer ➡ Sec.1-56
☐ fax ➡ Sec.1-50	☐ print out ➡ Sec.2-125	☐ fix ➡ Sec.2-82

第4章
会社の組織

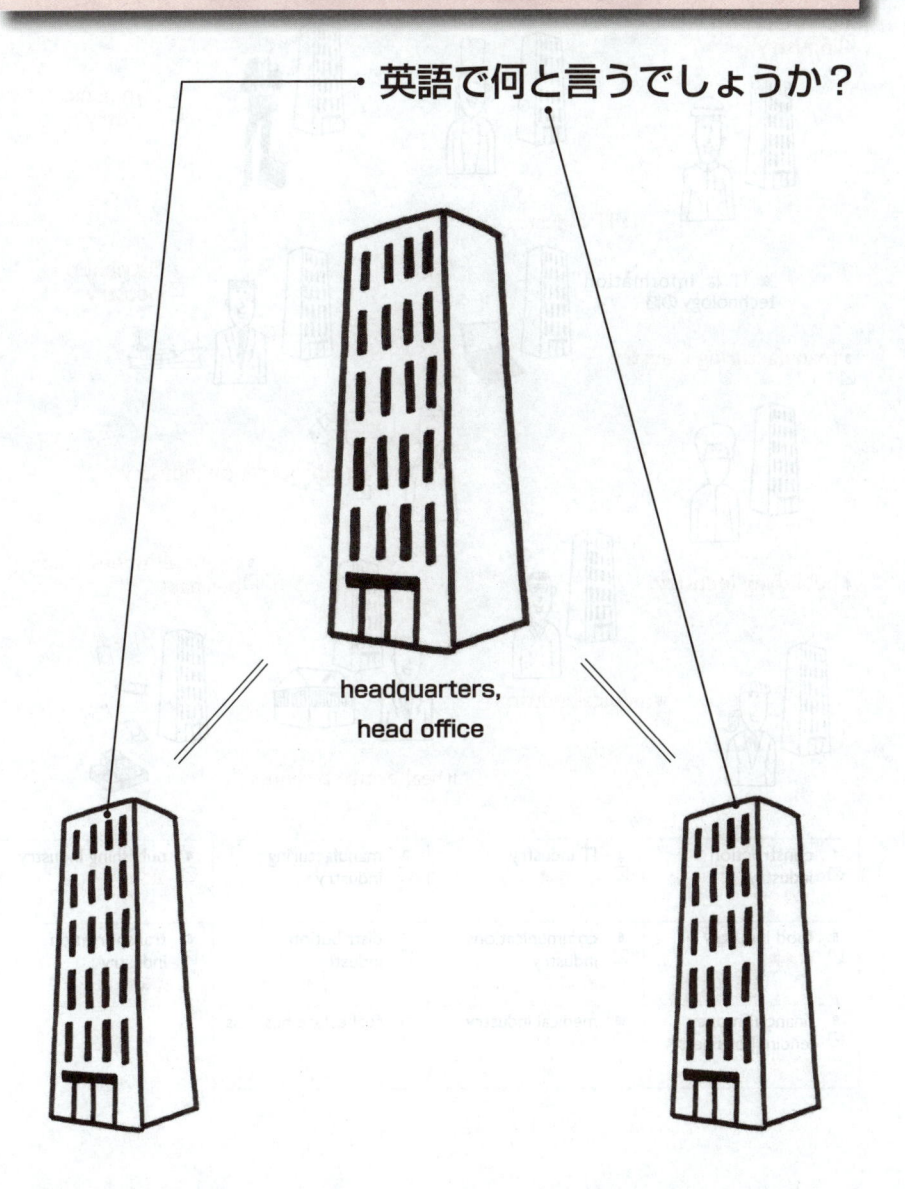

英語で何と言うでしょうか？

headquarters,
head office

☞ 答えは P.76

Section 1 イラストで覚える！

✽Industry, Business「業界」✽

1 construction industry
2 IT industry
  ※ IT は information technology の略
3 manufacturing industry
4 publishing industry
5 food industry
6 communications industry
7 distribution industry
8 transportation industry
9 financial[money lending] business
10 medical industry
11 real estate business

1 construction industry 建設業界	2 IT industry ＩＴ産業	3 manufacturing industry 製造業	4 publishing industry 出版業
5 food industry 飲食業	6 communications industry 通信業界	7 distribution industry 物流（流通）産業	8 transportation industry 運輸業
9 financial[money lending] business 金融業	10 medical industry 医療業界	11 real estate business 不動産業	

4. 会社の組織

✳ Company, Firm, Business 「会社, 企業」 ✳

12 (joint-)stock company

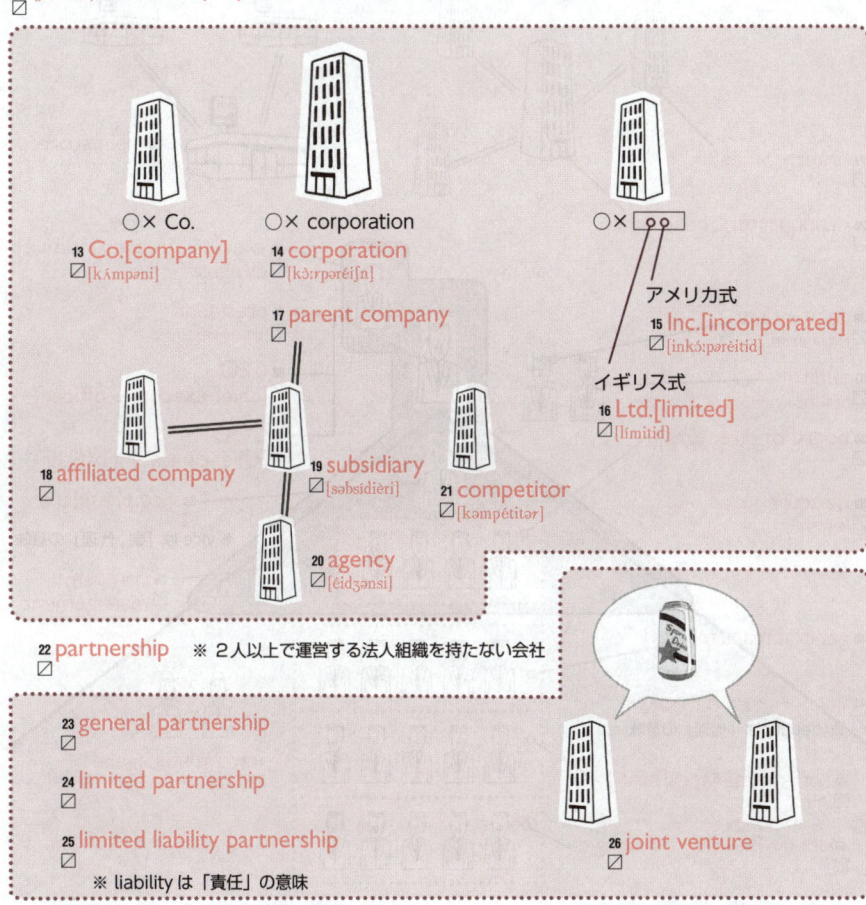

13 Co.[company]
[kʌ́mpəni]

14 corporation
[kɔ̀ːrpəréiʃn]

アメリカ式
15 Inc.[incorporated]
[inkɔ́ːpəreitid]

イギリス式
16 Ltd.[limited]
[límitid]

17 parent company

18 affiliated company

19 subsidiary
[səbsídièri]

20 agency
[éidʒənsi]

21 competitor
[kəmpétitər]

○× Co.
○× corporation
○×

22 partnership ※ 2人以上で運営する法人組織を持たない会社

23 general partnership

24 limited partnership

25 limited liability partnership

26 joint venture

※ liability は「責任」の意味

12	(joint-)stock company 株式会社	13	Co.[company] 会社	14	corporation （大きな）会社	15	Inc.[incorporated] 法人組織
16	Ltd.[limited] 法人組織の	17	parent company 親会社	18	affiliated company 関連会社, 系列会社	19	subsidiary 子会社
20	agency 代理店	21	competitor 競合他社	22	partnership 共同出資	23	general partnership 合名会社
24	limited partnership 合資会社	25	limited liability partnership 合同会社	26	joint venture 合弁事業		

Organization 「組織」

- 27 branch office
- 28 headquarters, head office
- 29 main store
- 30 executive[representative] director
- 31 president [prézidənt]
- 32 CEO [chief executive officer]
- 33 COO [chief operating officer]
- 34 vice president
  ※ vice は「副, 代理」の意味
- 35 company management
- 36 accountant [əkáuntənt]
- 37 auditor [ɔ́ːdɪtər]
- 38 board of directors
- 39 director [diréktər]
- 40 general manager
- 41 deputy branch manager
  ※ deputy は「代理」の意味
- 42 section manager[chief]
- 43 deputy[assistant] manager
- 44 store manager
- 45 position [pəzíʃn]

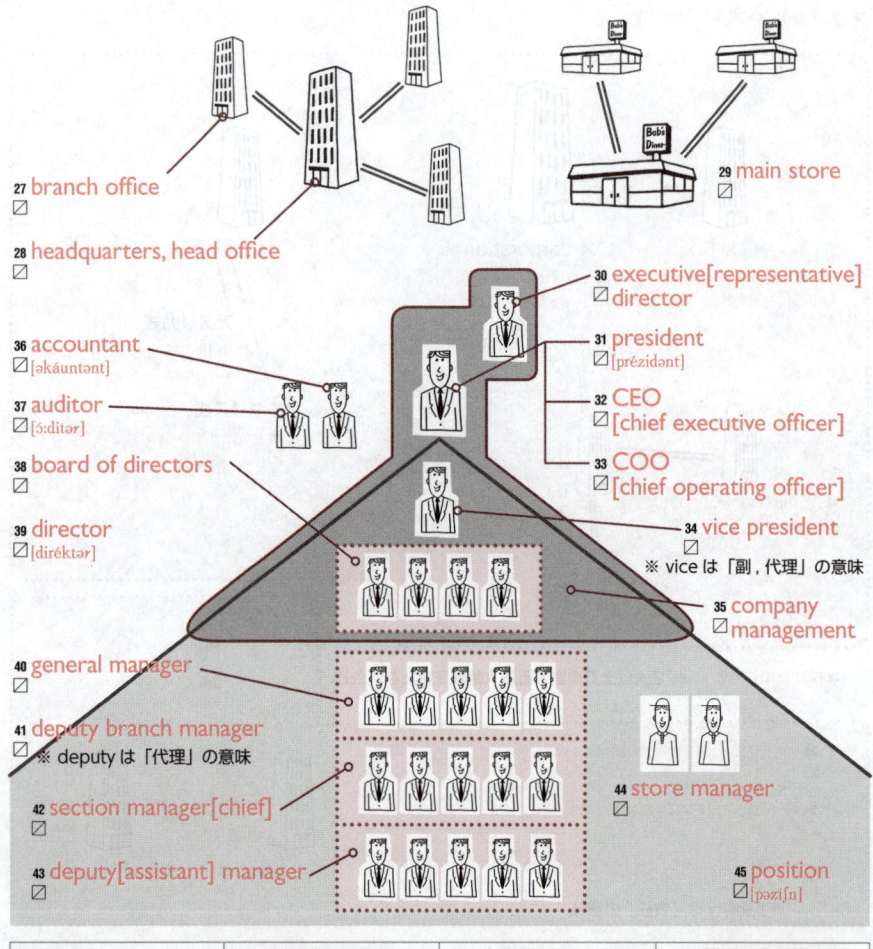

#	Term	訳
27	branch office	支社
28	headquarters, head office	本社, 本部, 本店
29	main store	本店
30	executive [representative] director	代表取締役
31	president	会長, 社長
32	CEO[chief executive officer]	最高経営責任者
33	COO[chief operating officer]	最高執行責任者
34	vice president	副会長, 副社長
35	company management	会社の経営陣
36	accountant	会計士
37	auditor	監査役
38	board of directors	取締役会
39	director	管理職の人, 重役, 取締役
40	general manager	本部長
41	deputy branch manager	副部長, 副支店長
42	section manager[chief]	課長
43	deputy[assistant] manager	係長
44	store manager	店長
45	position	地位, 職

— 76 —

4. 会社の組織

♪ ✲Company organization chart「組織図」✲

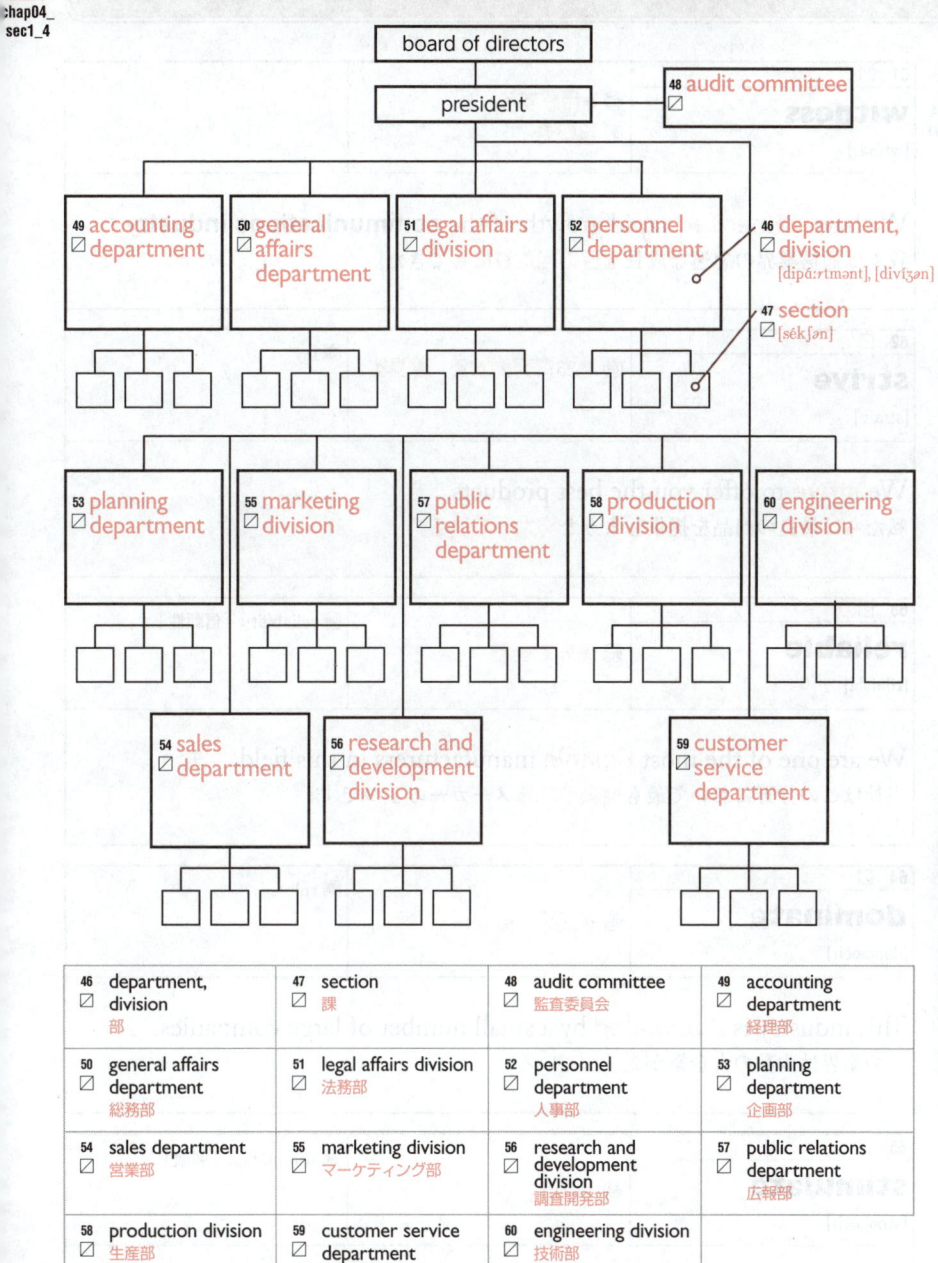

```
                    board of directors
                           │
                       president ─────── 48 audit committee
        ┌──────┬──────────┼──────────┬──────────┐
   49 accounting  50 general    51 legal affairs  52 personnel    46 department,
      department     affairs        division         department      division
                     department                                      [dipá:rtmənt], [divíʒən]
                                                               47 section
                                                                  [sékʃən]

   53 planning  55 marketing  57 public       58 production  60 engineering
      department    division      relations       division       division
                                  department

        54 sales      56 research and              59 customer
           department    development                  service
                         division                     department
```

46	department, division 部	47	section 課	48	audit committee 監査委員会	49	accounting department 経理部
50	general affairs department 総務部	51	legal affairs division 法務部	52	personnel department 人事部	53	planning department 企画部
54	sales department 営業部	55	marketing division マーケティング部	56	research and development division 調査開発部	57	public relations department 広報部
58	production division 生産部	59	customer service department お客様サービス部	60	engineering division 技術部		

— 77 —

Section 2　例文で覚える！

61 witness
[wítnəs]
- 他 を目撃する
- 名 目撃者

We have **witnessed** rapid growth of the **communications industry**.
我々は通信業界の急速な成長を目の当たりにしてきた。

62 strive
[stráiv]
- 自 懸命に努力する, 奮闘する
- 類 try

We **strive** to offer you the best products.
私たちは最良の商品を提供しようと努力している。

63 reliable
[riláiəbl]
- 形 信頼できる
- 派 reliability「信頼性」

We are one of the most **reliable** manufacturers in this field.
当社はこの分野において最も信頼できるメーカーの1つです。

64 dominate
[dámənèit]
- 他 を支配する
- 類 rule

This industry is **dominated** by a small number of large companies.
この業界は少数の大企業が支配している。

65 stimulate
[stímjəlèit]
- 他 を刺激する
- 派 stimulation「刺激」

Job creation will **stimulate** the economy.
雇用の創出は景気を刺激するだろう。

4. 会社の組織

66 struggle [strʌ́gl]
- 自 努力する, 奮闘する
- 名 苦闘
- 類 strive

We are **struggling** to win the competition with other **companies**.
私たちは他社との競争に勝つために努力している。

67 state of chaos
- 混乱状態
- 類 state of confusion

The **construction industry** is in a **state of chaos**.
建設業界は混乱状態にある。

68 work in
- 他〈分野〉で働く

She is **working in** the **manufacturing industry**.
彼女は製造業の分野で働いている。

69 lead [líːd]
- 他 を先導する, リードする
- 名 先導
- 派 leader「リーダー」

The company has been **leading** the world steel market for many years.
その会社は何年もの間, 世界の鉄鋼市場を先導している。

70 take over
- 他 ①を買収する
- ②を引き継ぐ

The company is trying to **take over** one of its **competitors**.
その会社は競合他社の1社を買収しようとしている。

71 found
[fáund]

他 を設立する, 創立する

類 establish

He **founded** a firm specializing in market research.
彼は市場調査を専門とする会社**を設立した**。

72 charge
[tʃáːrdʒ]

他 〈代金〉を請求する
名 料金

The travel **agency charged** me a high service fee.
その旅行代理店は私に高いサービス料**を請求した**。

73 manage
[mǽnidʒ]

他 ①を経営する
②[manage to *do* で]を何とか成し遂げる

類 run

At the seminar she is learning how to **manage** a company.
彼女はそのセミナーで会社**を経営する**方法を学んでいる。

74 control
[kəntróul]

他 を管理する
名 制御

類 regulate

That **parent company** is responsible for **controlling** three subsidiaries.
その親会社には3つの子会社**を管理する**責任がある。

75 approve
[əprúːv]

他 を承認する

派 approval「承認」

The **general manager approved** my plans for a new project.
本部長は私の新しいプロジェクトの計画**を承認した**。

4. 会社の組織

76 promote
[prəmóut] 他
① 〈商品(の販売)〉を促進する
② 〈人〉を昇進させる
反 demote「の地位を下げる」

The **sales department** will start a campaign to **promote** the product.
営業部は，その製品の販売を促進するためのキャンペーンを開始する。

77 underestimate
[ʌ̀ndəréstimèit] 他 を過小評価する
反 overestimate「を過大評価する」

We shouldn't **underestimate** the potential of our young researchers.
私たちは我が社の若い研究者たちの潜在能力を過小評価するべきではない。

78 perfect
[pə́:rfikt] 形
① 最適の，うってつけの
② 完全な，完ぺきな
反 imperfect「不完全な」

He is the **perfect** man for the job.
彼はその仕事にうってつけの男だ。

79 strict
[stríkt] 形 (人・規律などに) 厳しい
類 severe

Although our boss is very **strict** with us, we like her.
上司は私たちにとても厳しいが，私たちは彼女が好きだ。

80 inspire
[inspáiər] 他 〈人〉を奮い立たせる
派 inspiration「刺激」

She **inspired** us to work harder to achieve the goal.
彼女に刺激されて，私たちは目標達成に向けてもっと頑張るようになった。

| 81 **assist** [əsíst] | 他〈人〉を(補助的に)助ける 名 援助 | 類 help |

My job is to **assist** the project manager.
私の仕事はプロジェクトマネージャーを補佐することだ。

| 82 **mature** [mətjúər] | 形 (人・精神が)十分に成長した 他 を成熟させる | 反 immature「未熟な」 |

She is **mature** and responsible enough to hold a higher **position**.
彼女はもっと上の役職に就くのに，十分成長しているし責任感もある。

| 83 **appoint** [əpɔ́int] | 他〈人〉を任命する | 派 appointment「任命」 |

She was **appointed** **president** of the company.
彼女は会社の社長に任命された。

| 84 **assume** [əs(j)úːm] | 他〈責任〉を取る | 派 assumption「引き受け」 |

Top management should **assume** responsibility for that accident.
経営陣はその事故の責任を取るべきだ。

| 85 **ascertain** [æsərtéin] | 他 を確かめる，突き止める | 類 find out |

Each section has to **ascertain** its own financial status.
それぞれの課は，自分の課の財政状態を確認しなければならない。

4. 会社の組織

86 **commit** [kəmít]
他 〈人〉に責任を負わせる
派 commitment「責任」

We are **committed** to the safety of our employees.
社員の安全を守ることは私たちの責務です。

87 **divide** [diváid]
他 を(統一的に)分ける
名 分割
派 division「分割」

The team was **divided** into three groups by the project leader.
そのチームはプロジェクトリーダーにより3つの集団に分けられた。

88 **finalize** [fáinəlàiz]
他 を完成させる, 終了させる
派 final「最後の」

The remodeling of the **main store** has not been **finalized** yet.
本店の改装はまだ終了していない。

89 **hire** [háiər]
他 を雇う
反 fire「を首にする」

We need to **hire** a new **accountant** as soon as possible.
我々はできるだけ早く新しい会計係を雇う必要がある。

90 **attribute** [ətríbjuːt] 動, [ǽtribjùːt] 名
他 〈結果〉を(原因に)帰する
名 特質
類 ascribe

Our boss **attributed** the success to the efforts of the entire staff.
私たちの上司は, その成功はスタッフ全員の努力によるものだとした。

91 overseas
[òuvərsíːz]

形 海外の
副 海外へ, 海外で

類 abroad

We are going to open our first **overseas** **branch office** in Hawaii next year.
我々は来年, ハワイに初の海外支店をオープンするつもりだ。

92 in charge of

を管理して

類 responsible for

She is **in charge of** the **marketing division**.
彼女がマーケティング部の責任者だ〔を管理している〕。

93 assign
[əsáin]

他〈人〉を(地位・部署に)任命する

類 appoint

I was **assigned** to be in charge of that project.
私はその計画の責任者に任命された。

94 state
[stéit]

他 を明言する

類 express

Our company policy **states** employees may not accept gifts from clients.
会社の方針は, 従業員は取引先から贈り物をもらってはいけないと明言している。

95 dedicate
[dédikèit]

他 を専念させる

類 devote

We need to **dedicate** ourselves to providing customers with high-quality products.
私たちはお客さまに高品質な製品を提供することに専念する必要がある。

— 84 —

4. 会社の組織

96　elect
[ilékt]
他〈大統領・議長など〉を（投票で）選ぶ
類 choose

I believe he'll be **elected** as the next president.
彼が次期会長に**選ば**れると思う。

97　critical
[krítikl]
形 危機の
類 dangerous

The company is in a **critical** financial situation.
その会社は**危機的な**財政状態にある。

98　consist of
他 から成り立つ
類 compose

The committee **consists of** eight people, including three executives.
委員会は3名の取締役を含む8名**から成り立つ**。

99　individually
[ìndivídʒuəli]
副 個別に
派 individual「個々の」

The employees have an interview with the president of the company **individually** at the end of each business year.
従業員は，毎年年度末に**個別に**社長の面談を受ける。

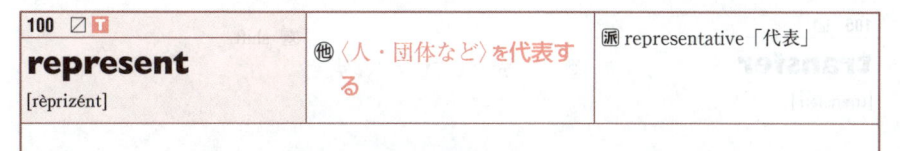

100　represent
[rèprizént]
他〈人・団体など〉を代表する
派 representative「代表」

She **represented** her company at the international conference.
彼女は会社**を代表**してその国際会議に出席した。

101 ☑ T		
temporary [témpərèri]	形 一時的な	反 permanent「永久の」

I work at X Corp. in a **temporary** position as a software engineer.
私はX社でソフトウエアエンジニアの臨時の地位に就いて働いている。

102 ☑		
responsible for	〈人・事〉に責任がある	関 responsibility「責任」

You're **responsible for** the contents of the sales report.
あなたは販売報告書の内容に責任がある。

103 ☑ T		
senior [síːnjər]	形 先輩の 名 年長者	反 junior「年下の」

If you are in trouble, seek the advice of your **senior** colleagues.
困ったときは、先輩社員にアドバイスを求めなさい。

104 ☑		
managerial [mænidʒíəriəl]	形 管理(者)の	派 manager「管理者」

We need someone with extensive **managerial** experience.
管理職の経験を十分に持った人材が必要だ。

105 ☑		
transfer [trænsfə́ːr]	他 〈人〉を転任させる, 移す	類 shift

He was **transferred** to the **head office** last month.
彼は先月本社に転勤になった。

4. 会社の組織

106 initiate
[iníʃièit]
他 を始める
類 start

Our leader suggested that we **initiate** a new sales plan.
私たちのリーダーは新たな販売計画を始めるべきだと提案した。

107 caliber
[kǽləbər]
名 能力

We are pleased to have gotten a person of his **caliber** to lead our organization.
我々は彼のように組織を導いてくれる能力がある人物を採用できて喜んでいる。

108 praise
[préiz]
他 を褒める
名 (言葉による)賞賛
類 admire

The manager **praised** his staff for their outstanding performance.
部長は部下たちの優れた成績を賞賛した。

109 declare
[dikléər]
自 他 (を)宣言する
類 proclaim

The production manager **declared** that they would increase the productivity further.
製造責任者はさらに生産性を高めることを宣言した。

110 outside
[àutsáid, ´-´]
形 外側の
副 外で, 外に
反 inside「内側の」

We decided to have more **outside directors**.
我が社は社外取締役を増やすことを決めた。

chap04 sec2_11

111 capable [kéipəbl]
形 能力がある
反 incapable「能力がない」

We are a team of professionals **capable** of solving any problem.
私たちはどんな問題でも解決する**能力のある**プロ集団です。

112 experienced [ikspíəriənst]
形 経験を積んだ
反 inexperienced「経験不足の」

We have **experienced** web designers who will help you.
我が社にはお客さまの役に立つ**経験を積んだ**ウェブデザイナーがいます。

113 create [kriéit]
他 を創作する, 考案する
派 creation「創造」

Our most popular item was **created** by the **planning department**.
我が社で最も人気のある商品は, 企画部で**作ら**れたものだ。

114 assure [əʃúər]
他 〈人〉に保証する
派 assurance「保証」

The president **assured** us that we'll be in the black next year.
来年は黒字になると社長は私たち**に保証した**。

115 post [póust]
名 地位, 職
類 position

She returned to her **post** as accounts **section manager**.
彼女は会計課長の**職**に戻った。

4. 会社の組織

116 beneficiary
[bènifíʃièri]

名 (年金・保険金などの) 受取人

The benefits office set up a hot line for the pension **beneficiaries**.
福利厚生課は，年金**受給者**のために電話相談サービスを開設した。

117 make a speech
スピーチをする

類 give[deliver] a speech

At the party she **made a speech** as a representative of our company.
彼女は会社の代表として，そのパーティーで**スピーチをした**。

118 suitable
[súːtəbl]

形 ふさわしい

類 appropriate

I believe I'm the most **suitable** candidate for the position.
私がその役職に最も**ふさわしい**候補者だと思う。

119 inspect
[inspékt]

他 を詳しく調べる

派 inspection「検査，観察」

The store manager **inspected** all the floors for slippery areas.
店長は滑りやすい場所はないかすべてのフロア**を詳しく調べた**。

120 on behalf of
〜の代わりに

類 instead of

The **vice president** attended the meeting **on behalf of** the CEO.
CEO **の代わりに**，副社長がその会議に出席した。

Section 3　実際の文書で確認！

NOTICE

In regard to the positions of president, vice president and department heads at our new branch office in Sydney, the following assignments have been made, effective immediately.

President: Gordon Heyward

Vice president: Kent Homes

Customer service department: Emma Smith

Sales department: Ethan Garcia

Planning department: George Miller

Market-research department: William Moore

Public relations department: Michele Wilson

Merchandise department: Robert Lee

General affairs department: Eric Norton

Accounting department: Elizabeth Stewart

*The branch office will open on April 1st.
*All persons listed above will attend the general meeting to be held at the head office on May 15th.
*For more information: Visit the website of the personnel department
http://www.tex.com/123/Office-of-Personnel-Management

Kathy Swan, Manager, personnel department

和訳

お知らせ

シドニーの新支店における社長，副社長，及び各部署のリーダーの職をここに発表します。以下の任務割当が行われました。即日発効します。

社長：ゴードン・ヘイワード

副社長：ケント・ホームズ

お客様サービス部：エマ・スミス

営業部：イーサン・ガルシア

企画部：ジョージ・ミラー

市場調査部：ウィリアム・ムーア

広報部：ミシェル・ウィルソン

商品部：ロバート・リー

総務部：エリック・ノートン

経理部：エリザベス・スチュワート

＊シドニー支店は4月1日から営業します。
＊上にあげたメンバー全員が5月15日に本社で開かれる全体会議に出席します。

＊詳しくは人事部のホームページをご覧ください
　http://www.tex.com/123/Office-of-Personnel-Management

キャシー・スワン　人事部長

※Review Words※

☑ position → Sec.1-45	☑ president → Sec.1-31	☑ vice president → Sec.1-34
☑ department → Sec.1-46	☑ branch office → Sec.1-27	☑ customer service department → Sec.1-59
☑ sales department → Sec.1-54	☑ planning department → Sec.1-53	☑ public relations department → Sec.1-57
☑ general affairs department → Sec.1-50	☑ accounting department → Sec.1-49	☑ head office → Sec.1-28
☑ personnel department → Sec.1-52		

第5章
雇 用

英語で何と言うでしょうか？

boss

☞ 答えは P.96

Section 1 イラストで覚える！

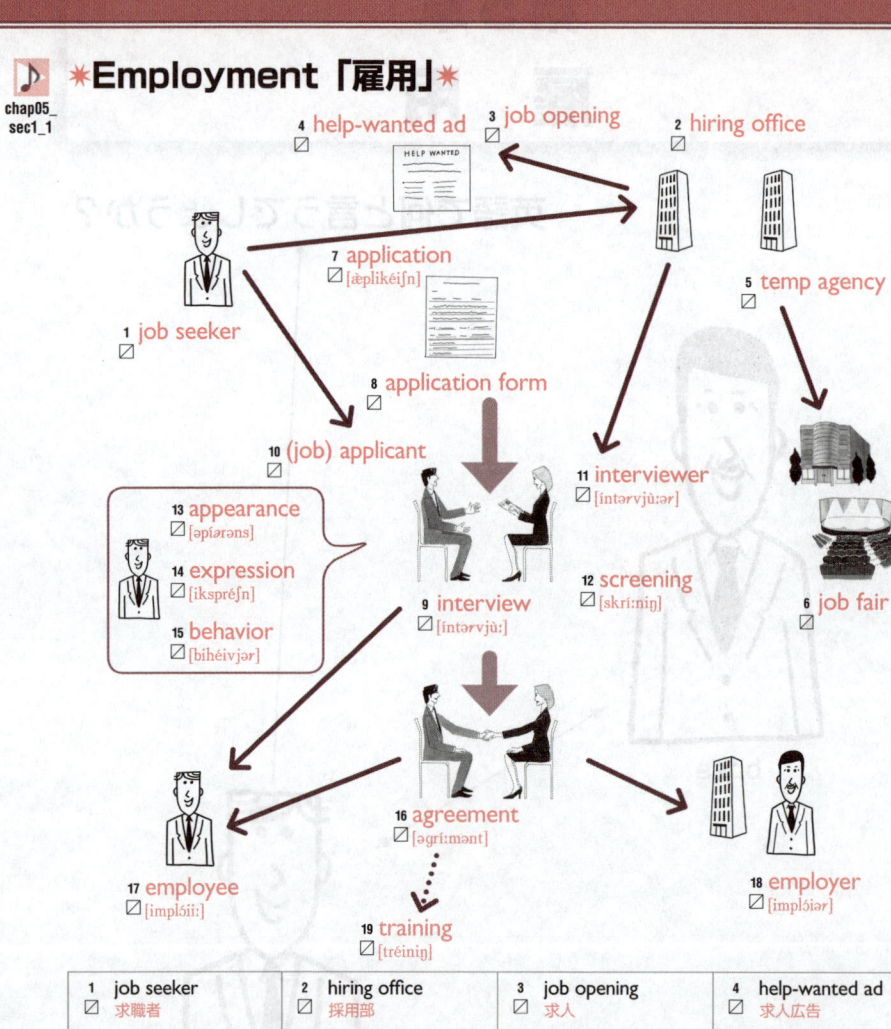

✻Employment「雇用」✻

1. job seeker
2. hiring office
3. job opening
4. help-wanted ad
5. temp agency
6. job fair
7. application [æplikéiʃn]
8. application form
9. interview [íntərvjùː]
10. (job) applicant
11. interviewer [íntərvjùːər]
12. screening [skríːniŋ]
13. appearance [əpíərəns]
14. expression [ikspréʃn]
15. behavior [bihéivjər]
16. agreement [əgríːmənt]
17. employee [implóiíː]
18. employer [implóiər]
19. training [tréiniŋ]

1 job seeker 求職者	2 hiring office 採用部	3 job opening 求人	4 help-wanted ad 求人広告
5 temp agency 人材派遣会社	6 job fair 就職フェア	7 application 申し込み	8 application form 申込書, エントリーシート
9 interview 面接	10 (job) applicant 応募者	11 interviewer 面接官	12 screening 審査
13 appearance 身だしなみ	14 expression 表情	15 behavior ふるまい	16 agreement 同意
17 employee 従業員, 社員	18 employer 雇用者	19 training 研修	

✱Résumé「履歴書」✱

20 qualification [kwɑ̀ləfikéiʃn]

21 expertise [èkspə:rtíːz]

22 experience [ikspíəriəns]

23 accomplishment, achievement [əkɑ́mpliʃmənt], [ətʃíːvmənt]

24 education [èdʒəkéiʃn]

25 reference [réfərəns]

履歴書でよく使うその他の語句

26 career [kəríər]

27 skill [skíl]

28 ability [əbíləti]

29 knowledge [nɑ́lidʒ]

30 specialty [spéʃəlti]

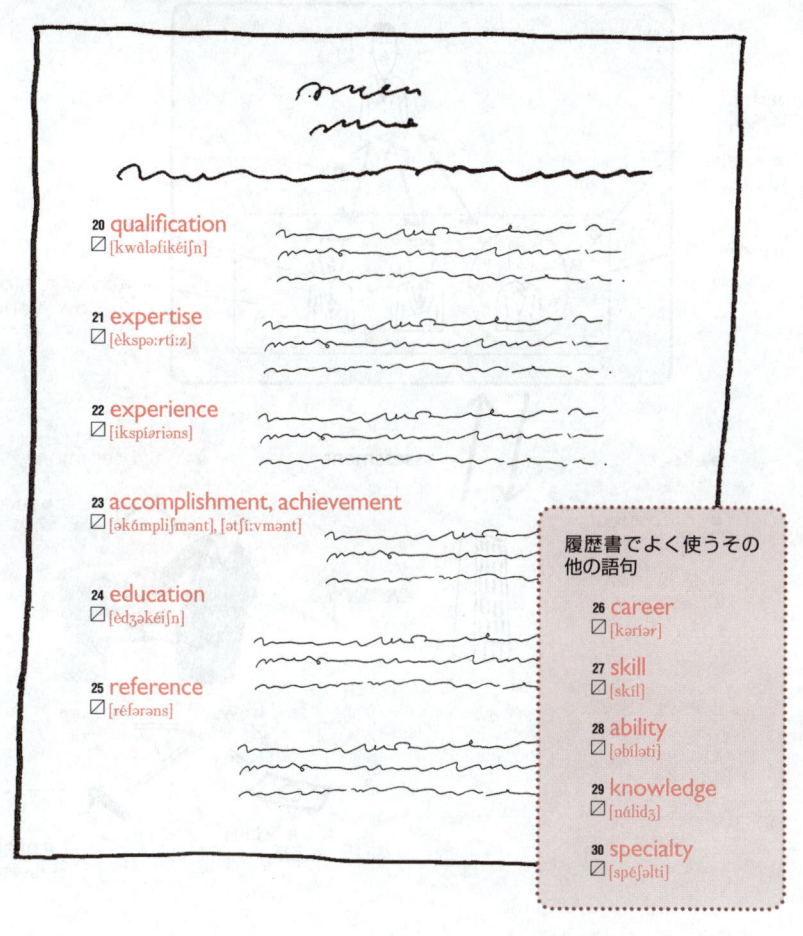

20	qualification 資格	21	expertise 専門知識, 専門技術	22	experience 経験	23	accomplishment, achievement 業績
24	education 教育	25	reference 推薦	26	career キャリア	27	skill 技能
28	ability 能力	29	knowledge 知識	30	specialty 専門, 専攻		

✻ Assessment 「評価」✻

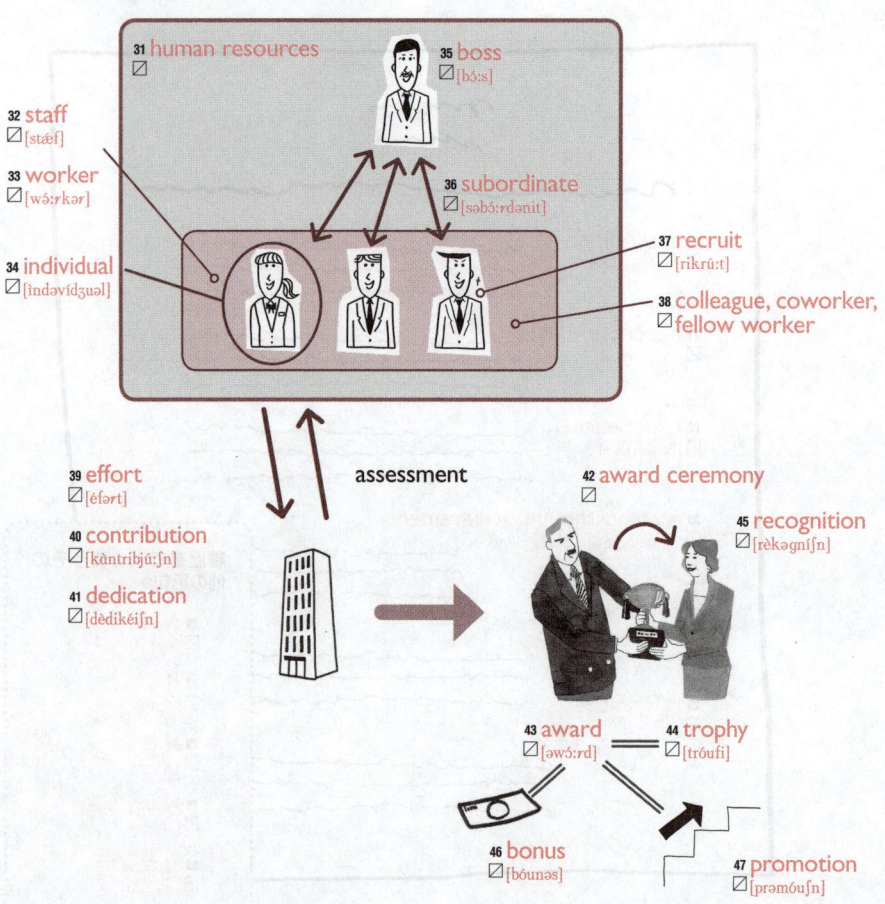

chap05_sec1_3

- 31 human resources
- 32 staff [stæf]
- 33 worker [wə́ːrkər]
- 34 individual [ìndəvídʒuəl]
- 35 boss [bɔ́ːs]
- 36 subordinate [səbɔ́ːrdənit]
- 37 recruit [rikrúːt]
- 38 colleague, coworker, fellow worker
- 39 effort [éfərt]
- 40 contribution [kàntribjúːʃn]
- 41 dedication [dèdikéiʃn]
- 42 award ceremony
- 43 award [əwɔ́ːrd]
- 44 trophy [tróufi]
- 45 recognition [rèkəgníʃn]
- 46 bonus [bóunəs]
- 47 promotion [prəmóuʃn]

assessment

31 human resources 人材	32 staff スタッフ，従業員	33 worker 労働者	34 individual 個人
35 boss 上司	36 subordinate 部下	37 recruit 新入社員	38 colleague, coworker, fellow worker 同僚
39 effort 努力	40 contribution 貢献	41 dedication 献身	42 award ceremony 授賞式
43 award 賞	44 trophy トロフィー	45 recognition 評価，表彰	46 bonus ボーナス
47 promotion 昇進			

— 96 —

5. 雇用

✳Occupation 「職業」✳

- 48 editor [édɪtər]
- 49 engineer [èndʒəníər]
- 50 professor [prəfésər] 
- 51 graphic designer 
- 52 journalist, reporter [dʒə́:rnəlɪst], [rɪpɔ́:rtər] 
- 53 chef [ʃéf] 
- 54 salesperson [séɪlzpə̀:rsn] 
- 55 specialist [spéʃəlɪst] 
- 56 clerk [klə́:rk]
- 57 secretary [sékrətèri] 
- 58 market researcher 
- 59 consultant [kənsʌ́ltənt] 

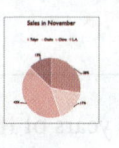

48	editor	49	engineer	50	professor	51	graphic designer
	編集者		エンジニア，技術者		教授		グラフィックデザイナー
52	journalist, reporter	53	chef	54	salesperson	55	specialist
	報道記者		シェフ		販売員		専門家
56	clerk	57	secretary	58	market researcher	59	consultant
	事務員		秘書		市場調査員		相談役，顧問

— 97 —

Section 2　例文で覚える！

60
undergo
[Àndərgóu]
他〈試練など〉を受ける
関 experience「を経験する」

You will **undergo** special **training** over the next two weeks.
これから2週間特別研修を受けてもらいます。

61
accept
[əksépt, æk-]
他 を受け入れる
反 reject「を断る」

Applications will also be **accepted** by e-mail.
申し込みはメールでも受け付ける。

62
hands-on
[hǽndzάn, -ɔ́n]
形 実務の，実際的な

Applicants are supposed to have three years of **hands-on** experience.
応募者は3年の実務経験があるものとする。

63
notify
[nóutəfài]
他 に通知する
類 inform

The **hiring office notified** me of the change in date.
採用部は私に日程変更を通知した。

64
possess
[pəzés]
他〈才能・富など〉を持っている
派 possession「所有」

Applicants must **possess knowledge** of computer programming and software development.
応募者はコンピュータ・プログラミングとソフトウエア開発の知識を持っていなければならない。

5. 雇用

65. intensive
[inténsiv]
形 集中的な

We can offer an **intensive** course in business English if you wish.
希望者はビジネス英語の集中コースを受けることができます。

66. apply for
他 に申し込む，志願する

I'd like to **apply for** the position of restaurant manager that is posted on your website.
御社のウェブサイトに掲載されている，レストランの店長職に申し込みたいのですが。

67. seek
[síːk]
他 を探す
関 job seeker「求職者」

We're **seeking** someone who has management **experience**.
当社は管理職の経験がある人を探している。

68. specific
[spəsífik]
形 特定の
名 細目
類 particular

Specific skills and **abilities** are required for this job.
この仕事には特定の技術と能力が必要だ。

69. current
[kə́ːrənt]
形 最新の，今の
名 流れ
類 up-to-date

They tried to find **current** job openings at the company.
彼らはその会社の最新の求人を探そうとした。

70 on-the-job
[ɑ́nðədʒɑ̀b]

形 実地の

We will receive **on-the-job** training this summer.
我々はこの夏，実地研修を受ける。

71 verbal
[vɚ́ːrbl]

形 ①言葉の
②口頭の

関 verbal promise「口約束」

Excellent **verbal** communication **skills** are a must for this job.
この仕事には優れた言語コミュニケーション能力が必須です。

72 one-on-one
[wʌ́nɑnwʌ́n, -ɔn-]

形 1対1の

類 one-to-one

I had a **one-on-one** interview with the sales manager.
私は販売部長と1対1の面接を受けた。

73 lack
[lǽk]

名 不足していること
他 を欠く

類 shortage

Her enthusiasm made up for her **lack** of experience.
彼女は経験不足を熱意で補った。

74 believe
[bilíːv]

他 自 (を)信じている

反 doubt「を疑う」

I **believe** you'll play an important role in our company.
あなたが当社で重要な役割を果たすことを信じている。

— 100 —

5. 雇用

75 informative
[ínfɔ́ːrmətiv]
形 有益な
類 beneficial

The **job fair** at the Central Hotel was **informative**.
セントラルホテルで開かれた就職フェアは有益だった。

76 search for
他〈仕事・人・物など〉を探す
類 look for

There are a lot of **job seekers searching for** new jobs.
新しい仕事を探す求職者がたくさんいる。

77 certain
[sə́ːrtn]
形 ①ある程度の ②確かな
関 certainly「確かに」

Every job comes with a **certain** amount of stress.
どんな仕事にもある程度のストレスはつきものだ。

78 recruit
[rikrúːt]
他 を募集する，補充する
名 新入社員
関 recruiter「採用担当者」

We need to **recruit** more sales reps.
営業の社員をもっと補充する必要がある。

79 put out
他 を出す，発表する
関 publish「を出版する」

We need to **put out** a **help-wanted ad** as soon as possible.
我々はなるべく早く求人広告を出す必要がある。

80 graduate
[grǽdʒuèit] 動, [grǽdʒuit] 名

自 (大学を) 卒業する
名 卒業生

反 enter「に入学する，入る」

He **graduated** from a foreign university.
彼は外国の大学を卒業した。

81 require
[rikwáiər]

他 ①を必要とする
　 ②を(人に)要求する

類 need

What kind of **education** is **required** to become a bank clerk?
銀行員になるために必要とされている教育は何ですか。

82 field
[fí:ld]

名 ①分野
　 ②野原

類 area

What is your **field** of **expertise**?
あなたの専門分野は何ですか？

83 demonstrate
[démənstrèit]

他 〈能力など〉を発揮する，表に出す
自 デモをする

派 demonstration「デモ(行進)，実演説明」

He **demonstrated** his language ability.
彼は語学の能力を発揮した。

84 eager
[í:gər]

形 [eager to do で]を熱望して

派 eagerly「熱心に」

I'm **eager** to engage in the sales promotion activities.
私は販売促進活動に従事することを熱望している。

5. 雇用

85 skilled [skíld] 形 熟練した 類 proficient

We are looking for **individuals** who are **skilled** in repairing cameras.
我々はカメラの修理に熟練した人を探している。

86 additionally [ədíʃənəli] 副 その上 類 in addition

Additionally, I speak French fluently and Italian at a basic level.
その上，私はフランス語を流ちょうに話し，基本レベルのイタリア語もできます。

87 fluent [flúːənt] 形 流ちょうな 派 fluently「流ちょうに」

Applicants should be **fluent** in English and have a minimum of two years of accounting experience.
応募者は英語が流ちょうで2年以上の経理の経験がなければならない。

88 specialize in 他 を専攻する 関 specialized「専門的な」

I **specialized in** space engineering at Tokyo University.
私は東京大学で宇宙工学を専攻した。

89 dynamic [dainǽmik] 形 活動的な 名 原動力 類 active

I am a **dynamic** person who enjoys learning new things.
私は新しいことを学ぶのが好きな活動的な人間です。

— 103 —

90

fortunate [fɔ́ːrtʃənit]

形 幸運な

派 fortunately「幸運にも」

We are really **fortunate** to have gotten acquainted with a capable person like you.
あなたのような有能な方と知り合えて私たちは本当に幸運だ。

91

enclose [inklóuz]

他 を同封する, 封入する

派 enclosure「同封のもの」

Be sure to **enclose** your résumé.
必ず履歴書を同封してください。

92

minimum [mínəməm]

形 最低限の

反 maximum「最大限の」

What is the **minimum** qualification for the job?
この仕事に最低限必要な資格は何ですか。

93

diverse [divə́ːrs, dai-]

形 多様な

派 diversify「を多様化する」

I have 10 years of **diverse** work experience in information technology.
私は10年間, IT分野で多様な仕事の経験があります。

94

professional [prəféʃənl]

形 ①職業の
　②本格的な, プロの

反 amateur「アマチュアの」

What is your greatest **professional** accomplishment?
あなたの業務上の一番の業績は何ですか。

5. 雇用

95. pursue [pərsúː]
他 ①を続ける
②を追う、追跡する
類 chase

She is **pursuing** a **career** in the financial industry.
彼女は金融業界でのキャリアを積んでいる。

96. bestow [bistóu]
他〈名誉・賞など〉を授ける
類 confer

The French government **bestowed** a decoration on our president.
フランス政府は我が社の社長に勲章を授けた。

97. congratulate [kəngrǽtʃəlèit]
他〈人〉を祝う
関 Congratulations!「おめでとう」

The president **congratulated** her on her outstanding sales performance.
社長は優れた営業成績を上げたことで彼女を祝った。

98. achieve [ətʃíːv]
自他 ①〈目的など〉(を)成し遂げる
②〈名声など〉(を)獲得する
派 achievement「達成」

Without your cooperation, we couldn't have **achieved** this great success.
皆さんの協力がなければ、私たちはこの素晴らしい成功を得ることはできなかったでしょう。

99. contribute [kəntríbjuːt]
自 寄与する
他〈金など〉を(人に)与える
派 contribution「寄付、貢献」

As you know, Mr. Brown has **contributed** greatly to our success.
ご存じのように、ブラウン氏は当社の成功に大いに寄与してきました。

100 join [dʒɔ́in]
他 に参加する，加わる
類 participate in ～

It is nearly four decades since he **joined** the company.
彼がこの会社に入社して40年になろうとしています。

101 make use of
他 を活用する，利用する
類 utilize

We should **make** the best **use of** our **human resources**.
我が社の人材を最大限に活用しなければならない。

102 deserve [dizə́ːrv]
他 に値する
類 be worthy of

He **deserves** a **promotion** and a huge raise.
彼は昇進と大幅な昇給に値する。

103 competent [kɑ́mpitənt]
形 有能な
反 incompetent「無能な，役に立たない」

He is one of our most **competent** employees.
彼は最も有能な従業員の1人だ。

104 tend [ténd]
自 [tend to do で] …する傾向がある
派 tendency「傾向，風潮」

Employee evaluations **tend** to be subjective.
人事考課は主観的になる傾向がある。

5. 雇用

105 remarkable
[rimá:rkəbl]
形 注目すべき, 際立った
類 notable

The new employees have made **remarkable** progress over the last six months.
新入社員たちはこの半年で, 際立った進歩をしてきている。

106 evaluate
[ivæljuèit]
他 を評価する
派 evaluation「評価」

We'll **evaluate** the period you've worked and offer you a company pension.
当社は勤務期間を評価して企業年金を支給する。

107 reward
[riwɔ́:rd]
他 に報酬を与える, 報いる
名 報酬
関 in reward for「〜の報酬として」

We'll **reward** you for your **efforts** during the past three years.
私たちはあなたのこの3年間の努力に報酬を与えるつもりだ。

108 celebrate
[séləbrèit]
他 を祝う
派 celebration「祝賀会」

We **celebrated** her promotion to personnel manager.
私たちは彼女の人事部長への昇進を祝った。

109 incentive
[inséntiv]
名 刺激, 動機
類 stimulation

A **bonus** gives employees a financial **incentive**.
ボーナスは社員に対する経済的な刺激になる。

110 distinguished
[distíŋgwiʃt]

形 顕著な, 優れた

類 outstanding

Your **distinguished** contribution helped our business spread worldwide.
あなたの優れた貢献で私たちの事業が世界中に広がった。

111 analytical
[ǽnəlítikl]

形 分析的な

Market researchers should have **analytical** abilities.
市場調査員は分析的な能力を持っているべきだ。

112 enable
[inéibl]

他 [enable + 名 + to do で] 〜が…することを可能にする

類 allow 〜 to do

Her **dedication** to the work **enabled** us to meet the deadline.
彼女のその仕事への献身のおかげで私たちは締め切りに間に合わせることができた。

113 desirable
[dizáiərəbl]

形 望ましい

反 undesirable「望ましくない」

The ability to speak a second language is highly **desirable**.
第二言語を話す能力があることが非常に望ましい。

114 appreciate
[əprí:ʃièit]

他 を感謝する, ありがたく思う

派 appreciation「感謝, 評価」

I really **appreciate** the opportunity for an interview.
面接の機会を設けていただいたことを本当に感謝します。

5. 雇用

115 proud [práud]
形 誇りに思う, 自慢する
反 ashamed「恥じて」

I am **proud** to present this award of **recognition** to Mr. Smith.
スミスさんにこの表彰状を授与することを誇りに思います。

116 proofread [prú:frì:d]
他 を校正する

The **editor** **proofread** the materials carefully.
その編集者は原稿を注意深く校正した。

117 focus [fóukəs]
自 重視する, 重点的に取り扱う
名 焦点
類 concentrate

That **graphic designer** is **focusing** on the advertising industry.
そのグラフィックデザイナーは広告業界に着目している。

118 dispatch [dispætʃ]
他 を派遣する

We **dispatched** three **salespersons** to the branch office.
我々は3名の販売員をその支店に派遣した。

119 unique [ju:ní:k]
形 独特の, 比類のない
類 incomparable

The **chef** is famous for his **unique** menu.
そのシェフは類を見ないメニューで有名だ。

Section 3　実際の文書で確認！

MICHIKO LEE
1-2-3, Shinjuku-ku, Tokyo 162-****　Phone/Fax (03)1234-5678
michiko@letmeknow.com

OBJECTIVE
　　A position in an international trading company

EXPERTISE
　　· Good knowledge of the German market
　　· Excellent communication skills in English and German
　　· Hands-on experience in international trade

EDUCATION
　　· BS degree in economics, Nihon Boueki University (graduated in 2006)
　　· Completed course in advanced German, Berlin Language School(2010)

QUALIFICATIONS
　　· Pre-1st grade, Test of English Proficiency
　　· 1st grade, Test of German Proficiency

ACTIVITIES
　　· Campus English Newspaper Club: Made a major contribution as an editor
　　· Debate club: Won 3rd-place award at Germany national debate competition in 2009

WORK EXPERIENCE
　　International Medicine Times Ltd., Tokyo as a part-time employee 2002-2006
　　· As an assistant market researcher
　　Germany Trade Ltd., Berlin as a temporary staff member 2006-2010
　　· As a secretary to the manager, international trade section

REFERENCES　Available on request

和訳

ミチコ・リー

162-**** 東京都新宿区 1-2-3　電話 / ファックス (03)1234-5678
michiko@letmeknow.com

希望職種
　　　国際貿易会社での職務

専門知識
　　　・ドイツ市場に関する十分な知識
　　　・英語とドイツ語での優れたコミュニケーション能力
　　　・国際貿易の実務経験

学歴
　　　・日本貿易大学　経済学士号　（2006 年卒業）
　　　・ベルリン言語学校　上級ドイツ語課程修了（2010 年）

資格
　　　・英検準一級
　　　・独検一級

活動
　　　・大学英語新聞部：編集者として大いに寄与
　　　・ディベートクラブ：2009 年度　ドイツ全国ディベートコンクール 3 位入賞

職歴
　　　国際医学タイムズ株式会社　東京，パートタイム社員として　2002 年-2006 年
　　　・市場調査員アシスタント
　　　ドイツ貿易株式会社　ベルリン，派遣社員として　2006 年-2010 年
　　　・国際貿易部部長秘書

推薦
　　　請求がありしだい可能

☀Review Words☀

☐ expertise ➡ Sec.1-21	☐ knowledge ➡ Sec.1-29	☐ skill ➡ Sec.1-27
☐ hands-on ➡ Sec.2-62	☐ experience ➡ Sec.1-22	☐ education ➡ Sec.1-24
☐ graduate ➡ Sec.2-80	☐ qualification ➡ Sec.1-20	☐ contribution ➡ Sec.1-40
☐ editor ➡ Sec.1-48	☐ award ➡ Sec.1-43	☐ employee ➡ Sec.1-17
☐ market researcher ➡ Sec.1-58	☐ staff ➡ Sec.1-32	☐ secretary ➡ Sec.1-57
☐ reference ➡ Sec.1-25		

第6章
勤務スタイル・福利厚生

英語で何と言うでしょうか？

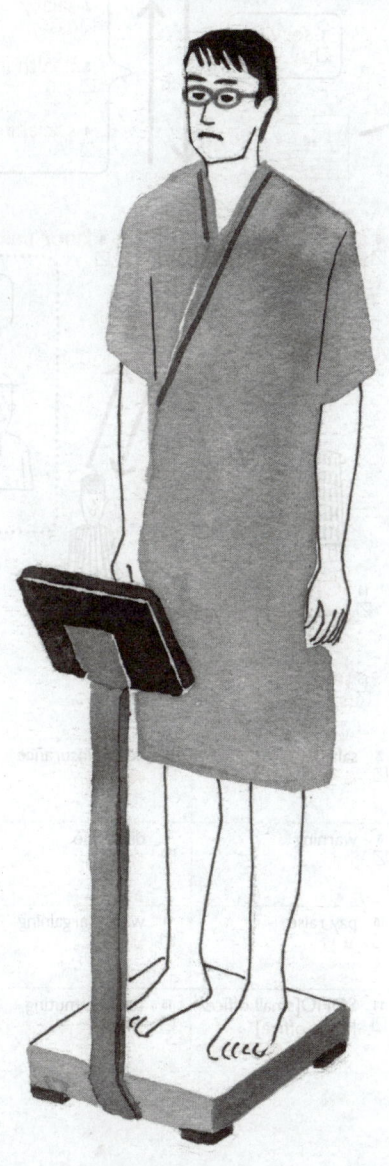

☞答えは P.116

Section 1 イラストで覚える！

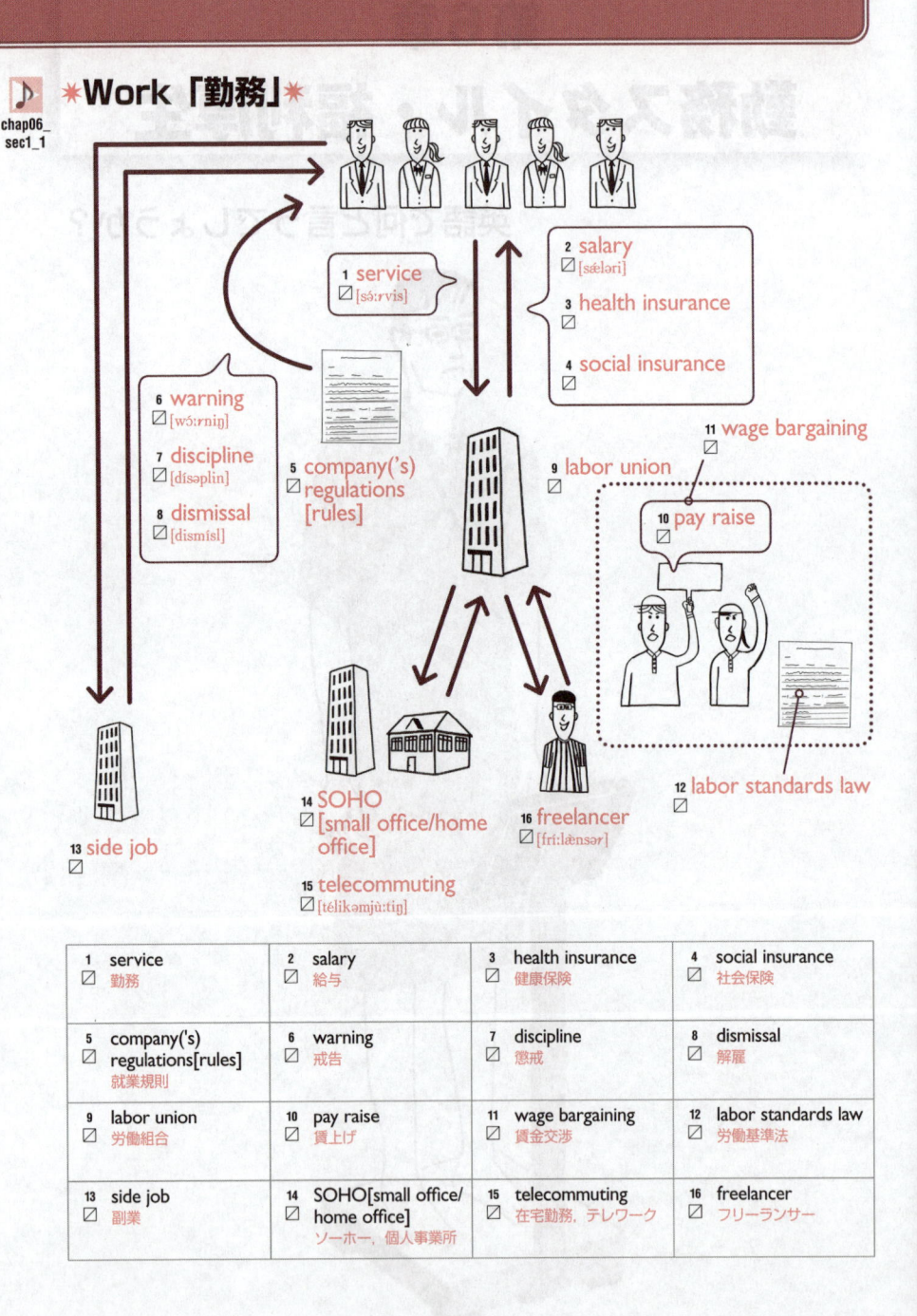

Work「勤務」

1. service [sə́ːrvis]
2. salary [sǽləri]
3. health insurance
4. social insurance
5. company('s) regulations [rules]
6. warning [wɔ́ːrniŋ]
7. discipline [dísəplin]
8. dismissal [dismísl]
9. labor union
10. pay raise
11. wage bargaining
12. labor standards law
13. side job
14. SOHO [small office/home office]
15. telecommuting [téləkəmjùːtiŋ]
16. freelancer [fríːlænsər]

#	語	訳
1	service	勤務
2	salary	給与
3	health insurance	健康保険
4	social insurance	社会保険
5	company('s) regulations[rules]	就業規則
6	warning	戒告
7	discipline	懲戒
8	dismissal	解雇
9	labor union	労働組合
10	pay raise	賃上げ
11	wage bargaining	賃金交渉
12	labor standards law	労働基準法
13	side job	副業
14	SOHO[small office/home office]	ソーホー，個人事業所
15	telecommuting	在宅勤務，テレワーク
16	freelancer	フリーランサー

Terms of employment 「雇用条件」

- 17 working pattern :
- 24 duration : [djuəréiʃn]
- 25 annual salary :
  - 26 monthly salary
  - 27 hourly wage
  - 28 piece [píːs]

- 18 regular employee
- 19 permanent job
- 20 part-time worker
- 21 contract employee
- 22 temporary worker
- 23 temporary employee

- 29 annual leave :
- work days :
- work hours :
- 36 endorsement [indɔ́ːrsmənt]
- 35 shift [ʃíft]

- 30 leave, time off
- 31 (un)paid vacation
- 32 maternity leave
- 33 childcare leave
- 34 nursing (care) leave

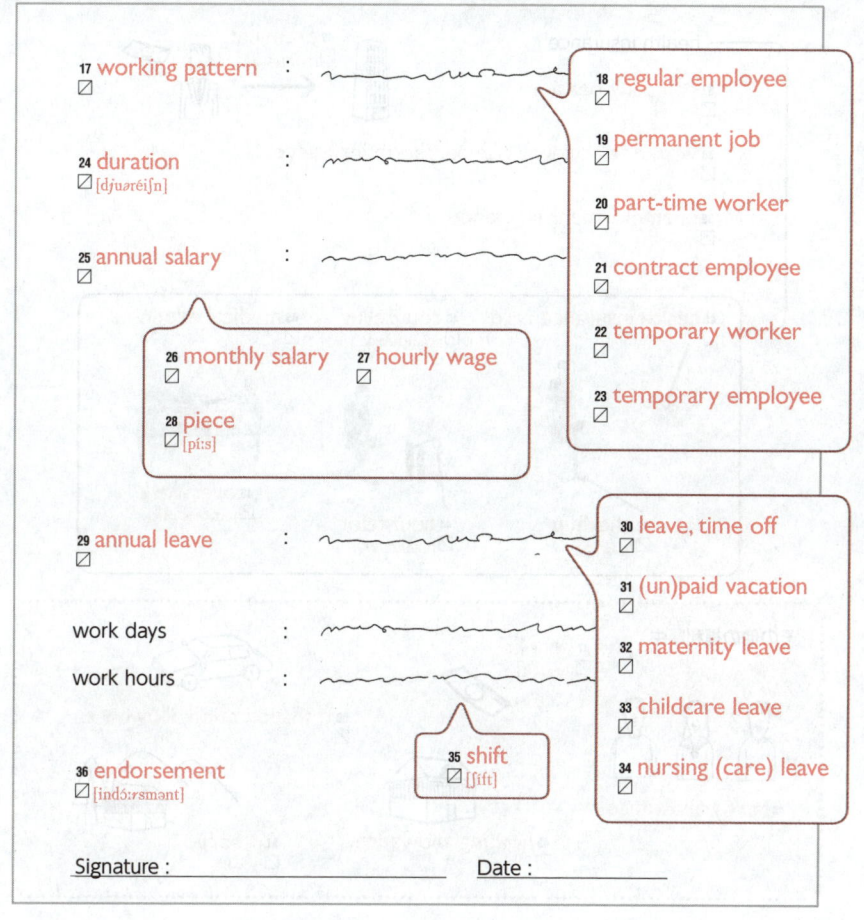

Signature :　　　　　　　　　　Date :

17 working pattern 勤務形態	18 regular employee 正社員	19 permanent job 常勤職	20 part-time worker パートタイマー
21 contract employee 契約社員	22 temporary worker 派遣社員	23 temporary employee 嘱託社員	24 duration 雇用期間
25 annual salary 年俸	26 monthly salary 月給	27 hourly wage 時給	28 piece 出来高
29 annual leave 年次休暇	30 leave, time off 休暇	31 (un)paid vacation 有（無）給休暇	32 maternity leave 出産休暇
33 childcare leave 育児休暇	34 nursing (care) leave 介護休暇	35 shift シフト，交代勤務時間	36 endorsement 是認

♪ ✱Welfare program 「福利厚生」✱

- health insurance
  - 37 company pension
  - 38 worker's accident compensation insurance
  - 39 unemployment insurance
  - 40 premium [príːmiəm]
  - 41 health insurance card
  - 42 checkup [tʃékʌp]
  - 43 counseling [káunsəliŋ]
  - 44 counselor [káunsələr]
  - 45 medical expenses
  - 46 overwork [óuvərwə̀ːrk]

その他の福利厚生
- 47 benefit [bénəfit]
- 48 family allowance
- 49 housing allowance
- 50 transportation allowance
- 51 resort [rizɔ́ːrt]

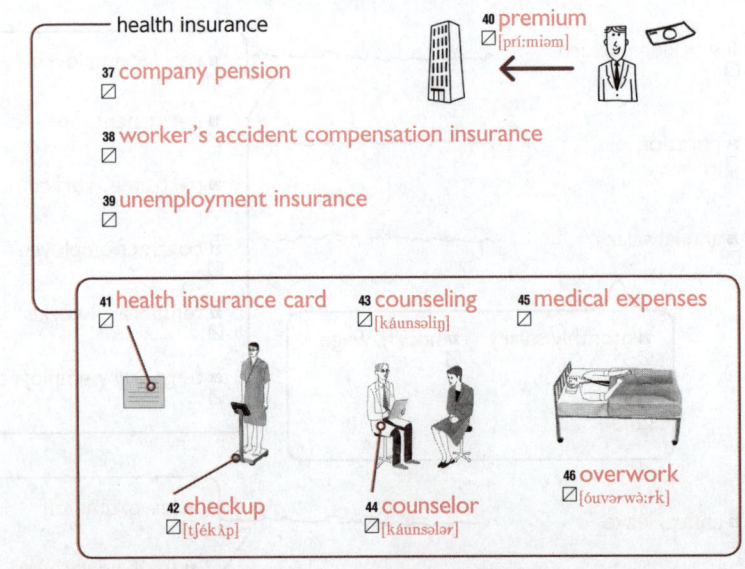

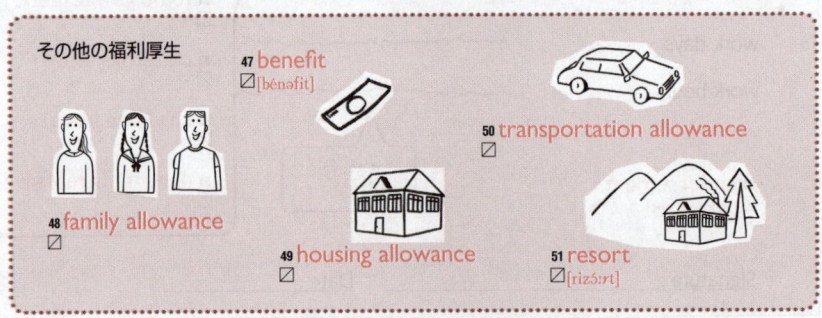

37 company pension 厚生年金	38 worker's accident compensation insurance 労災保険	39 unemployment insurance 失業保険	40 premium 保険料
41 health insurance card 健康保険証	42 checkup 健康診断	43 counseling カウンセリング	44 counselor カウンセラー
45 medical expenses 医療費	46 overwork 過労	47 benefit 給付金	48 family allowance 扶養手当
49 housing allowance 住宅手当	50 transportation allowance 通勤手当	51 resort 保養地	

6. 勤務スタイル・福利厚生

✱Personnel change「人事異動」✱

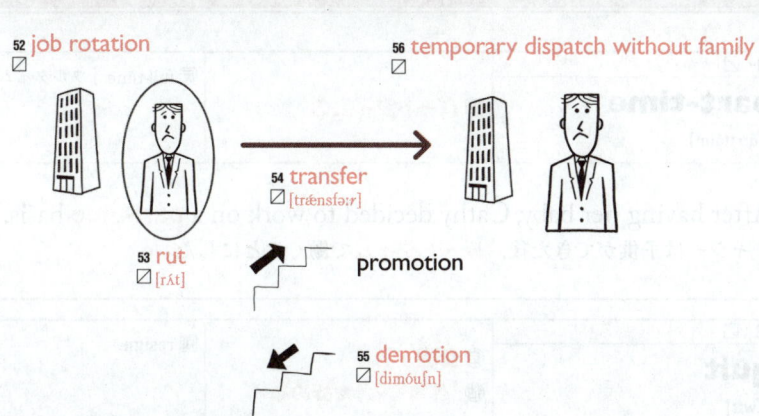

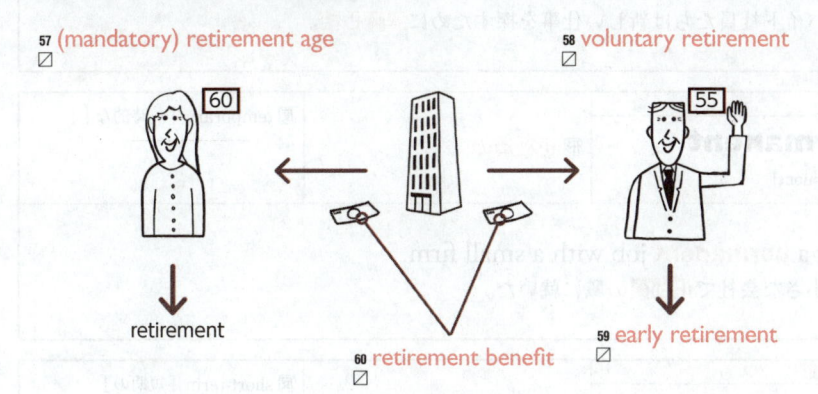

52 job rotation
53 rut [rʌt]
54 transfer [trænsfər]
55 demotion [dimóuʃn]
56 temporary dispatch without family

promotion

✱Retirement「退職」✱

57 (mandatory) retirement age
58 voluntary retirement
59 early retirement
60 retirement benefit

retirement

52	job rotation	53	rut	54	transfer	55	demotion
	配転		マンネリに陥った状態		転勤		降格
56	temporary dispatch without family	57	(mandatory) retirement age	58	voluntary retirement	59	early retirement
	単身赴任		定年		希望退職		早期退職
60	retirement benefit						
	退職金						

– 117 –

Section 2　例文で覚える！

61. part-time [páːrttáim]
形 パートタイムの
反 full-time「フルタイムの」

After having her baby, Cathy decided to work on a **part-time** basis.
キャシーは子供ができた後、パートタイムで働くことにした。

62. quit [kwít]
自 辞職する
他〈仕事など〉を辞める
類 resign

The **part-time workers quit** to look for new jobs.
アルバイト社員たちは新しい仕事を探すために辞職した。

63. permanent [páːrmənənt]
形 正社員の
反 temporary「一時的な」

I got a **permanent** job with a small firm.
私は小さな会社で正社員の職に就いた。

64. long-term [lɔ́ːŋtə́ːrm]
形 長期の
反 short-term「短期の」

In the past, **long-term** employment was ensured at our company.
当社ではかつて長期雇用が保証されていた。

65. afford [əfɔ́ːrd]
他 [afford to *do* で] …する余裕がある
派 affordable「入手可能な」

The company can't **afford** to give a **pay raise**.
その会社には賃上げをする余裕はない。

6. 勤務スタイル・福利厚生

66 **increase** [inkríːs]
- 他 を上げる，増やす
- 自 上がる，増える
- 反 decrease「を下げる，減らす」

The management agreed to **increase** his base **salary** to $50,000.
経営陣は彼の基本給を 50000 ドルに上げることに同意した。

67 **initial** [iníʃl]
- 形 最初の，初期の
- 反 last「最後の」

Mr. Sato received an **initial annual salary** of $50,000.
佐藤さんは最初の年俸として 5 万ドルを受け取った。

68 **inevitable** [inévitəbl]
- 形 ①避けられない ②いつもの
- 反 avoidable「回避できる」

A wage cut is **inevitable** in this depression.
この不景気では賃金カットは避けられない。

69 **after tax**
- 税引きで，手取りで
- 反 before tax「税込みで」

Approximately how much is the annual salary **after tax**?
年収は税抜きでだいたいどれくらいになりますか。

70 **inadequate** [inædikwit]
- 形 不適当な，不十分な
- 類 insufficient

My **monthly salary** is **inadequate** to support my family.
私の月給は家族を養うには不十分だ。

– 119 –

71 retain
[ritéin]

他 を保つ, 維持する

類 keep

Attracting and **retaining** skilled staff is essential to the success of our business.
熟練したスタッフを引き付けて維持することは，我々のビジネスの成功にとって不可欠だ。

72 call for

他 を要求する

類 demand

The **labor union** is **calling for** higher wages.
労働組合は賃上げを要求している。

73 substantial
[səbstǽnʃl]

形 相当な

類 considerable

After I was certified as an accountant, I got a **substantial** salary raise.
会計士の資格を取った後，相当給料が上がった。

74 pay
[péi]

他 〈代金など〉を払う

関 pay back「〈金〉を払い戻す」

The employees are **paid** by the **piece** instead of by the hour.
従業員たちは時給ではなく，出来高で支払われている。

75 maximum
[mǽksəməm]

名 最大
形 最大限の

反 minimum「最小」

The travel allowance is limited to a **maximum** of 20,000 yen per month.
通勤手当は最大月2万円に限定されている。

6. 勤務スタイル・福利厚生

76 exhausted [iɡzɔ́ːstid]
形 疲れ果てた
派 exhaust「を疲れ果てさせる」

Every worker was **exhausted** from many hours of overtime.
労働者は皆，何時間もの残業で疲れ果てていた。

77 in accordance with
（規則など）に従って
関 according to「〜に従って」

The bonuses will be paid **in accordance with** the terms of employment.
賞与は雇用条件に従って支払われる。

78 adopt [ədápt]
他 を採用する，取り入れる
派 adoption「採用」

Many large firms have **adopted** a flextime policy.
多くの大企業がフレックスタイム制を採用している。

79 implement [ímplimènt]
他 を実行する
関 carry out

We won't survive if we don't **implement** this restructuring plan.
このリストラ計画を実行しなければ，我が社は生き残れない。

80 earn [ə́ːrn]
他〈金〉を稼ぐ

You **earn** overtime pay by working more than eight hours a day.
1日8時間以上働けば残業代が稼げる。

― 121 ―

| 81 **stability** [stəbíləti] | 名 安定(性) | 派 stable「安定した」 |

Many people need the security and **stability** of a **permanent job**.
多くの人が定職の安心と安定を必要としている。

| 82 **be entitled to** | 〜を受ける資格〔権利〕がある | |

Ms. Sawai **is entitled to** three months of **maternity leave**.
澤井さんには3カ月の出産休暇を取る権利があります。

| 83 **conform** [kənfɔ́ːrm] | 自 (慣習・規則などに) 従う
他 〈人・言動〉を(法・型などに) 順応させる | 類 obey |

Every employee should **conform** to the company's rules of employment.
すべての従業員は就業規則に従わなければならない。

| 84 **compromise** [kɑ́mprəmàiz] | 自 (人と〜について) 妥協する, 和解する
名 妥協 | 類 concede |

The management **compromised** on the issue with the striking workers.
経営陣はストライキをしている労働者とその問題について和解した。

| 85 **overall** [òuvərɔ́ːl] | 形 全体の, 全般的な | 類 entire |

They are monitoring the **overall** condition of the facilities.
彼らは施設の全体的な状況を監視している。

6. 勤務スタイル・福利厚生

86 **permission**
[pərmíʃn]
名 許可, 許し
派 permit「を許可する」

My boss gave me **permission** to take **time off**.
上司は私が休暇を取るのを許可した。

87 **enact**
[inækt]
他〈法律〉を制定する
類 establish

The Labor Standards Law was **enacted** in 1947.
労働基準法は1947年に施行された。

88 **inclusive**
[inklú:siv]
形 含めた

This pay rate is **inclusive** of **annual leave**.
この賃金には、年次休暇が含まれている。

89 **cost-cutting**
[kɔ́:stkʌ̀tiŋ]
形 経費削減の
類 budget-cutting

As a **cost-cutting** measure, working more than 200 hours a month is prohibited.
経費削減策の1つとして、1カ月に200時間以上働くことは禁止されている。

90 **comprehensive**
[kàmprihénsiv]
形 包括的な
反 exclusive「排他的な」

Our terms of employment are in need of a **comprehensive** revision.
当社の労働条件は包括的な改正が必要である。

— 123 —

91 weekday [wíːkdèi]	名 平日	
The woman had children and preferred the early **weekday** shift. その女性には子供がいて，平日の早いシフトを希望していた。		

92 eligibility [èlidʒəbíləti]	名 適性, 有資格	派 eligible「資格のある，ふさわしい」
The age of **eligibility** for pension benefits is sixty in that country. その国では年金の受給資格年齢は60歳だ。		

93 introduce [ìntrədjúːs]	他 ①を導入する ②を紹介する	派 introduction「導入」
Our company **introduced** childcare leave a few years ago. うちの会社は数年前に育児休暇制を導入した。		

94 adhere to	他〈規則など〉に忠実に従う，を順守する	類 abide by
All employees are requested to **adhere to** the terms of this policy. すべての従業員は，この方針の条件に従うことを要求されている。		

95 renew [rinjúː]	他 ①〈契約・免許など〉を更新する，継続する ②を再開する	派 renewal「更新，書き換え」
The English conversation school refused to **renew** the contracts of some teachers. その英会話学校は，何人かの教師との契約更新を拒否した。		

6. 勤務スタイル・福利厚生

96 modify [mádəfài]
他〈計画・意見など〉を(部分的に)修正する，変更する
類 adjust

The company rules were **modified** to permit more flexible work hours.
就業規則は，労働時間にもっと融通が利くように**修正**された。

97 successive [səksésiv]
形 ①連続的な ②歴代の
類 consecutive

She has been absent from work for three **successive** days without any notice.
彼女は3日**続けて**無断欠勤をしている。

98 violate [váiəlèit]
他 ①〈法律・条約など〉に違反する ②〈権利など〉を侵害する
派 violation「違反，妨害」

He was fired for **violating** a company policy.
彼は会社の方針**に背いた**として解雇された。

99 enroll [inróul]
他〈人〉を登録する，加入させる
類 register

Companies must **enroll** their employees in the **social insurance** program.
企業は従業員**を**社会保険に**加入**させなければならない。

100 provide [prəváid]
他〈人〉に提供する，を提供する
派 provider「供給者」

They **provide** employees with an additional **benefit**.
会社は従業員たちに追加の給付金**を与える**。

101	fire [fáiər]	他〈人〉を解雇する 自 発射する	類 dismiss

Even if you are **fired**, you can receive unemployment benefits.
解雇された場合でも失業保険は受け取れる。

102	actual [ǽktʃuəl]	形 実際の	派 actually「実際は」

We pay the **actual** travel expenses.
当社は交通費として実費を支払う。

103	rigid [rídʒid]	形 ①厳格な, 柔軟性のない ②堅い, こわばった	反 flexible「柔軟な」

The existing **rigid** welfare system should be improved.
融通の利かない現状の福祉制度は改善されるべきだ。

104	approximately [əpráksəmitli]	副 およそ	類 around

This year's unemployment rate will be **approximately** 5 percent.
今年の失業率はおよそ5パーセントになるでしょう。

105	collapse [kəlǽps]	自（疲労などで）倒れる,（建物が）倒壊する	反 endure「持ちこたえる, 持続する」

She **collapsed** from **overwork** and was sent to the hospital.
彼女は過労で倒れ, 病院に運ばれた。

6. 勤務スタイル・福利厚生

106 deduct [didʌ́kt]
他 を控除する，差し引く
派 deduction「差引高，控除額」

You can **deduct** your **medical expenses** on your income tax return.
医療費は確定申告時に控除することができる。

107 annual [ǽnjuəl]
形 年1回の，年次の
名 年報，年鑑
類 yearly

The **annual** **checkup** will be conducted on June 4.
年次健康診断は6月4日に行われる。

108 consult [kənsʌ́lt]
他 〈専門家〉に相談する，〈医者〉にかかる
派 consultant「コンサルタント，相談相手」

You should **consult** a professional **counselor** for advice.
専門のカウンセラーに相談してアドバイスをもらうべきです。

109 retire [ritáiər]
自 退職する
他 〈人〉を（定年などで）解雇する
派 retirement「退職」

Employees who **retire** early will receive extra employment benefits.
早期に退職する社員は，退職金を割り増しされる。

110 compensate [kɑ́mpənsèit]
自 償う，補う，補償する
他 〈人〉に補償する
類 make up

This plan aims to **compensate** for rising **health insurance** costs.
このプランは上昇を続ける健康保険費を補うことを目的としている。

― 127 ―

111 slight
[sláit]

形 わずかな
名 軽視

類 small

There was a **slight** decline in the unemployment rate.
失業率は**わずかに**減少した。

112 recover
[rikʌ́vər]

自 回復する

派 recovery「回復」

He took two months off work to **recover** fully.
彼は完全に**回復する**まで2カ月会社を休んだ。

113 sound
[sáund]

他 ①〈警報など〉を発する
②〈ベル・らっぱなど〉を鳴らす

関 signal「を合図で知らせる」

The strike **sounded** a **warning** to all laborers in the country.
そのストライキは国中の労働者たちに警告**を発した**。

114 abide by

他 〈法律など〉に従う

類 adhere to

All the employees have to **abide by** the company's regulations.
全従業員が会社の規則**に従わ**なければならない。

115 risk
[rísk]

他 〈命・財産など〉を危険にさらす

関 risk management「危機管理」

Mr. Ono **risks** disciplinary **dismissal** if he breaks the company's regulations once again.
小野さんは，もう一度会社の規則を破ると，懲戒免職**の恐れがある**。

6. 勤務スタイル・福利厚生

116. eliminate [ilímineit]
他 を排除する、なくす
類 exclude

They are trying to **eliminate** sexual harassment in the workplace.
彼らは職場でのセクハラの撲滅に取り組んでいる。

117. announce [ənáuns]
他 を発表する
派 announcement「発表」

Yesterday the company **announced** Bob's **transfer** to the New York office.
会社は昨日、ボブのニューヨーク支社への転勤を発表した。

118. inform [infɔ́ːrm]
他 〈人〉に知らせる、通知する
派 information「情報」

Have they already **informed** employees of the personnel change next month?
社員はもう来月の人事異動について知らされているのですか。

119. encourage [inkə́ːridʒ]
他 ①を促進する
   ②を励ます、勇気づける
類 promote

The automaker **encouraged voluntary retirement** from the company.
その自動車メーカーは社内から希望退職者を募った。

120. raise [réiz]
他 ①〈程度・率・料金など〉を高くする
   ②〈資金など〉を集める
類 increase

The company **raised** its **mandatory retirement age** to 65.
その会社は定年を65歳に引き上げた。

— 129 —

Section 3　実際の文書で確認！

Employment Agreement

Employment agreement, between ___S & C Ltd.___ and ___Michiko Lee___ .

The company agrees to employ Michiko Lee as a **temporary employee** and Michiko Lee hereby agrees to work for the company on the following terms and conditions of employment.

1. Commencement date: April 1st, 2011

2. Location:　　Tokyo head office (at the time of hiring)
3. Work hours:　Flextime: 8 hours a day (Core time: 11:00-15:00)
　　　　　　　　Daily **time off**: 1 hour (from 12:30-13:30)
4. Work days：　Monday through Friday except national holidays
5. **Duration**:　The term of employment shall be 3 years.
6. **Salary**:　　Base salary　　Yen 2 hundred thousand /month
　　　　　　　　Bonus　　Seasonal bonus shall be **paid** in June and December.
7. Deduction from base salary for tax and **social insurance** will be made **in accordance with** Japanese law.
8. **Transportation allowance**: Up to yen 30 thousand/month
9. Overtime work between the hours of 22:00 and 5:00 the following day: will be recomposed at 160% of the hourly rate.
　　　All other overtime work: 130% of the hourly rate
　　　Holiday work: 130% of the hourly rate
10. **Paid vacation**: 20 days of paid vacation per year in each of the three years of employment

All other terms and conditions shall be governed by current **company rules** and any rules or regulations that may be **introduced** by the Company from time to time.

Signed this April 1st, 2011

S & C Ltd　　　　　　　　_Michiko Lee_
Company　　　　　　　　　Employee

和訳

雇用契約書

　　　S＆C 株式会社　　　と　　　ミチコ・リー　　　との雇用契約

本社は嘱託社員としてミチコ・リーを雇うことに同意し，本被雇用者は以下の雇用条件に従い本社にて就労することに同意する。

1. 開始日：　　2011年4月1日

2. 場所：　　東京本社(雇用開始時)
3. 就労時間：　フレックスタイム制：1日8時間(コアタイム：11:00-15:00)
　　　　　　　休憩：1時間(12:30-13:30)
4. 勤務日：　月―金　祝日を除く
5. 雇用期間：　3年間
6. 給与：　　基本給　20万円/月
　　　　　　特別手当　6月と12月に支給
7. 税金と社会保険のための基本給からの控除は日本の法律に基づいて行われる。

8. 通勤手当：　3万円/月　まで
9. 22:00 から 翌日 5:00 の残業：時給換算の160％
　　その他の残業：時給換算の130％
　　休日勤務：時給換算の130％

10. 有給休暇：　3年の雇用期間の各年次につき20日の有給休暇

その他のすべての条件は，現行の社則及び本社において適時導入される社則や規則によって規定される。

署名期日　　2011　年　4　月　1　日

　　　S＆C 株式会社　　　　　　　ミチコ・リー
　会社　　　　　　　　　　　　　被雇用者

✱Review Words✱

☐ temporary employee ➡ Sec.1-23	☐ time off ➡ Sec.1-30	☐ duration ➡ Sec.1-24
☐ salary ➡ Sec.1-2	☐ pay ➡ Sec.2-74	☐ social insurance ➡ Sec.1-4
☐ in accordance with ➡ Sec.2-77	☐ transportation allowance ➡ Sec.1-50	☐ paid vacation ➡ Sec.1-31
☐ company rule ➡ Sec.1-5	☐ introduce ➡ Sec.2-93	

第7章
会 議

英語で何と言うでしょうか？

☞ 答えは P.135

Section 1　イラストで覚える！

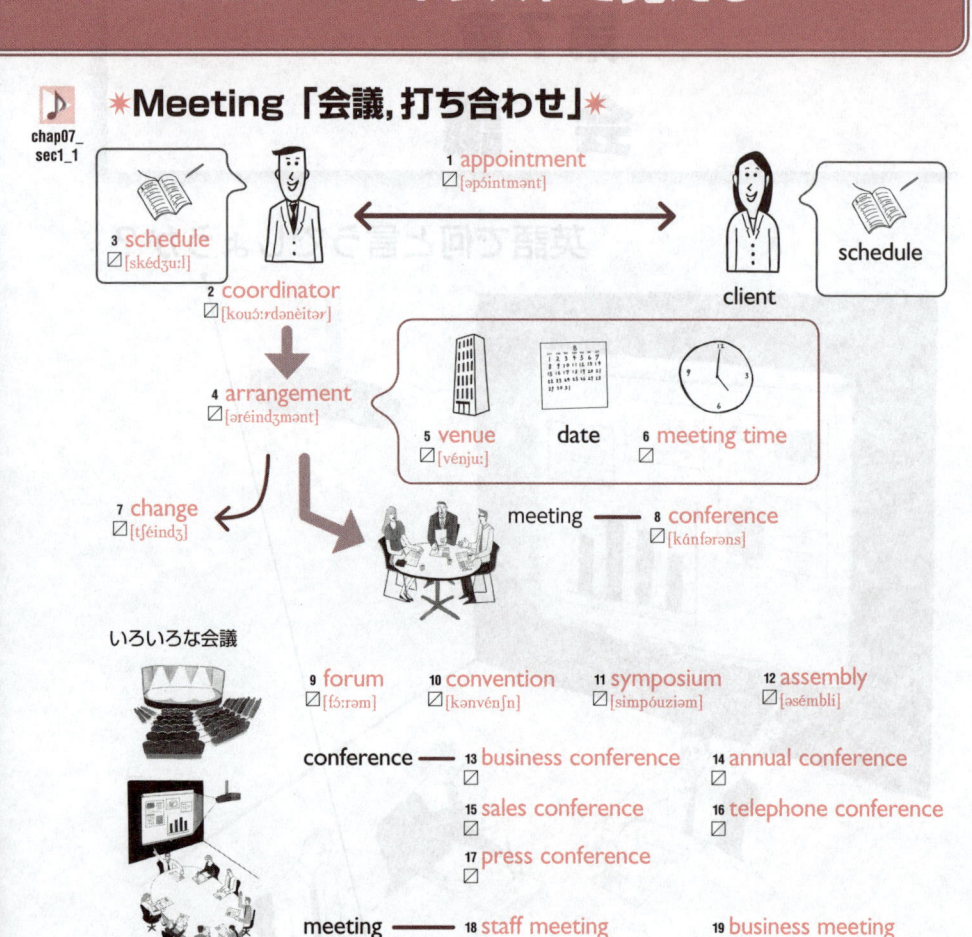

✳ Meeting「会議, 打ち合わせ」✳

1 appointment [əpɔ́intmənt]
2 coordinator [kouɔ́ːrdənèitər]
3 schedule [skédʒuːl]
4 arrangement [əréindʒmənt]
5 venue [vénjuː]
6 meeting time
7 change [tʃéindʒ]
8 conference [kánfərəns]

client

いろいろな会議

9 forum [fɔ́ːrəm]
10 convention [kənvénʃn]
11 symposium [simpóuziəm]
12 assembly [əsémbli]

conference ─
13 business conference
14 annual conference
15 sales conference
16 telephone conference
17 press conference

meeting ─
18 staff meeting
19 business meeting

1	appointment (人と会う)約束, アポ	2	coordinator 取りまとめ役	3	schedule スケジュール	4	arrangement 準備, 手配
5	venue 開催場所	6	meeting time 打ち合わせの時間	7	change 変更	8	conference 会議
9	forum 公開討論会	10	convention 大会	11	symposium 公開討論会	12	assembly 会合, 集会
13	business conference 営業会議	14	annual conference 年次会議	15	sales conference 販売会議	16	telephone conference 電話会議
17	press conference 記者会見	18	staff meeting スタッフミーティング	19	business meeting 営業会議, 商談		

7. 会議

✲ Meeting [Conference] room 「会議室」✲

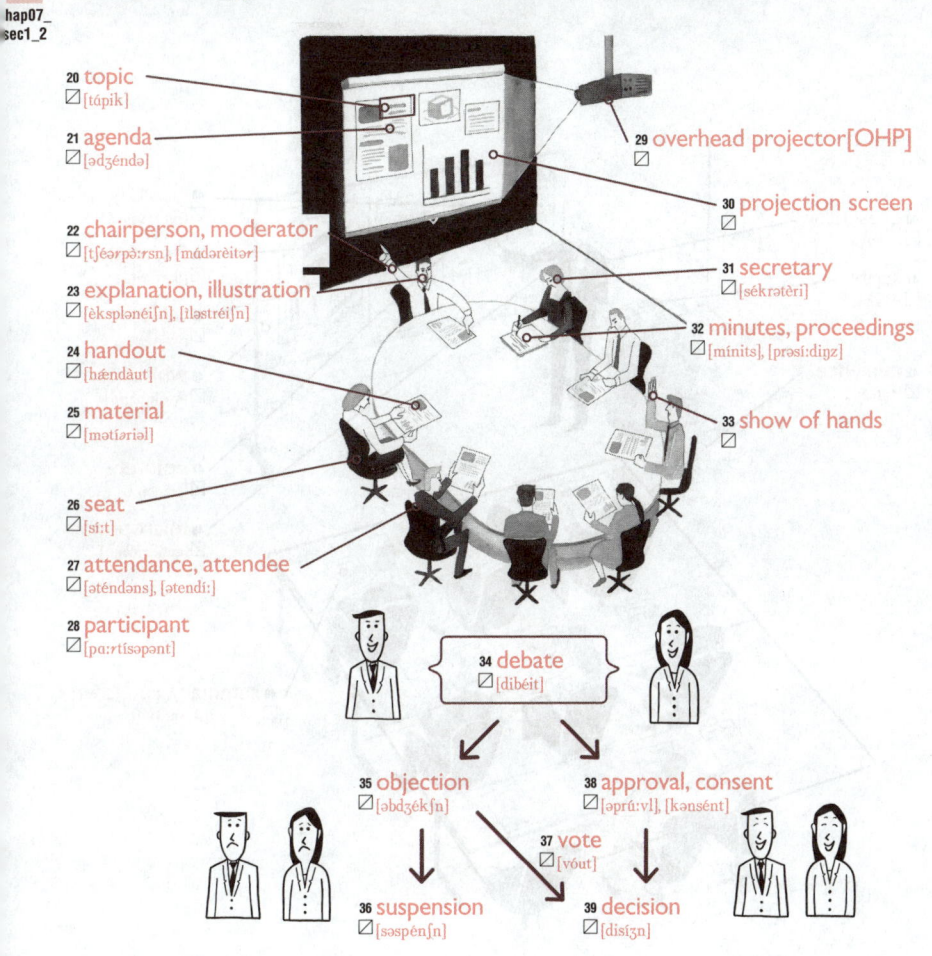

20 topic [tápik]
21 agenda [ədʒéndə]
22 chairperson, moderator [tʃéərpə̀ːrsn], [mɑ́dərèitər]
23 explanation, illustration [èksplənéiʃn], [ìləstréiʃn]
24 handout [hǽndàut]
25 material [mətíəriəl]
26 seat [síːt]
27 attendance, attendee [əténdəns], [ətendíː]
28 participant [pɑːrtísəpənt]
29 overhead projector [OHP]
30 projection screen
31 secretary [sékrətèri]
32 minutes, proceedings [mínits], [prəsíːdiŋz]
33 show of hands
34 debate [dibéit]
35 objection [əbdʒékʃn]
36 suspension [səspénʃn]
37 vote [vóut]
38 approval, consent [əprúːvl], [kənsént]
39 decision [disíʒn]

20 topic 主題	21 agenda 検討課題	22 chairperson, moderator 議長，司会者	23 explanation, illustration 説明（後者は図や絵などによる説明）
24 handout プリント，印刷物	25 material 資料	26 seat 席	27 attendance, attendee 出席者
28 participant 参加者	29 overhead projector [OHP] 投影機，プロジェクター	30 projection screen 映写幕	31 secretary 書記
32 minutes, proceedings 議事録	33 show of hands 挙手	34 debate 討論	35 objection 反対
36 suspension 保留	37 vote 採決	38 approval, consent 同意	39 decision 決定

✳Presentation 「プレゼンテーション」✳

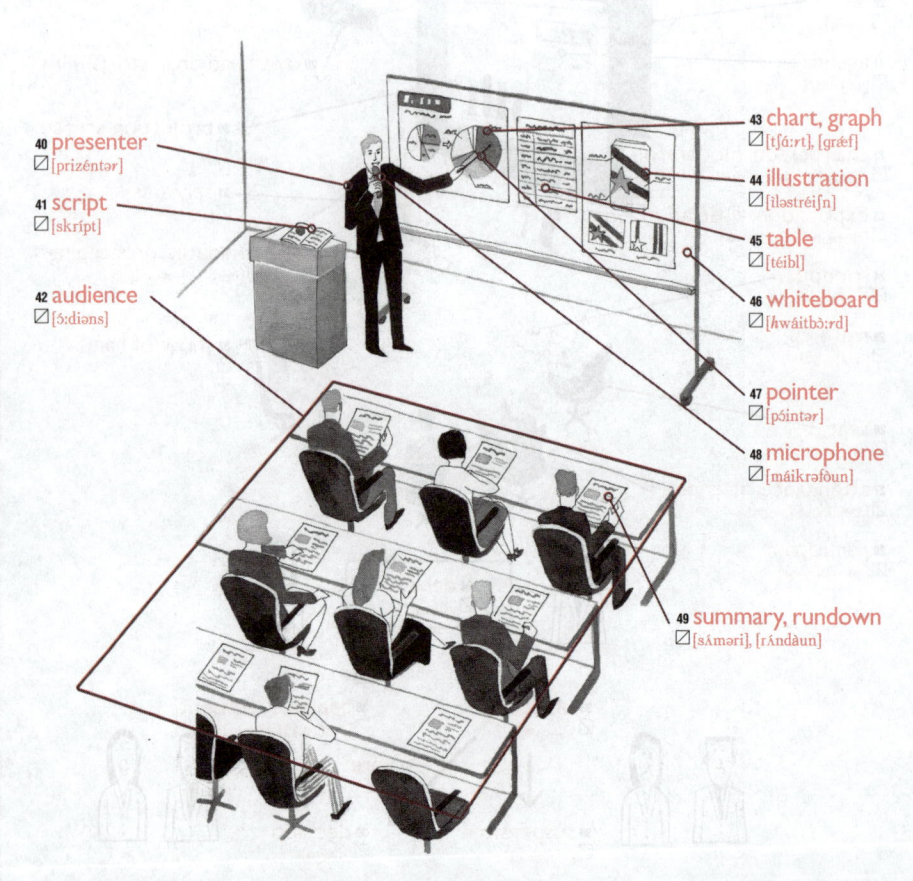

chap07_sec1_3

- **40 presenter** [prizéntər]
- **41 script** [skrípt]
- **42 audience** [ɔ́ːdiəns]
- **43 chart, graph** [tʃɑːrt], [grǽf]
- **44 illustration** [ìləstréiʃn]
- **45 table** [téibl]
- **46 whiteboard** [hwáitbɔ̀ːrd]
- **47 pointer** [pɔ́intər]
- **48 microphone** [máikrəfòun]
- **49 summary, rundown** [sʌ́məri], [rʌ́ndàun]

40	presenter 発表者, プレゼンター	41	script 台本	42	audience 聴衆	43	chart, graph 図表
44	illustration 図, 絵	45	table 表	46	whiteboard ホワイトボード	47	pointer 指示棒
48	microphone マイク	49	summary, rundown 要約				

— 136 —

7. 会議

✴ Chart, Graph 「図表」 ✴

50 bar chart[graph]

51 vertical axis

52 horizontal axis

53 pie chart[graph]

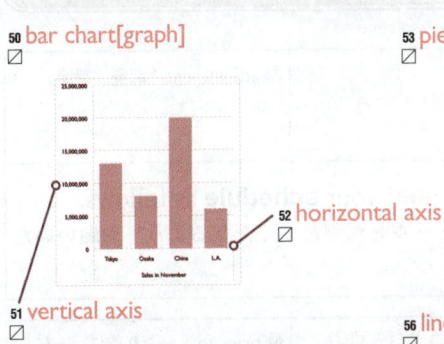

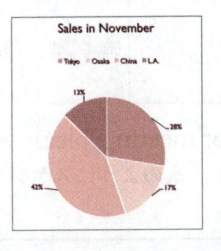

table

S&C Co. Sales Price April to September					
	April	May	June	July	August	September
Tokyo	15,000	12,000	12,500	13,000	15,500	15,500
Beijing	20,000	19,000	18,500	18,000	21,000	21,000
L.A.	12,000	10,000	11,500	11,500	12,500	13,000

54 column [kάləm]

55 row [róu]

56 line graph

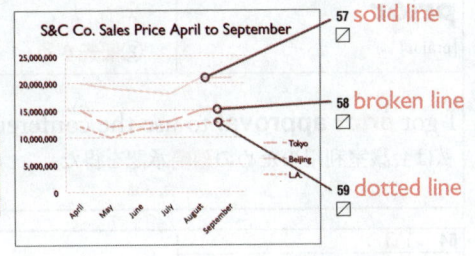

57 solid line

58 broken line

59 dotted line

60 Pareto chart

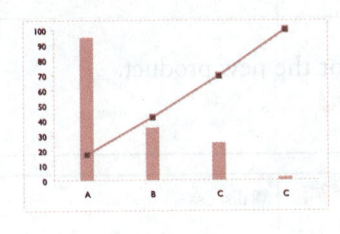

61 scatter graph[chart]

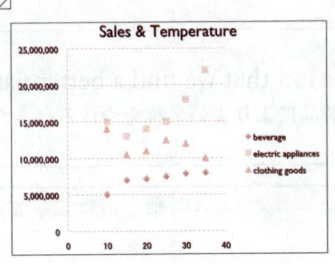

50	bar chart[graph] 棒グラフ	51	vertical axis 縦軸	52	horizontal axis 横軸	53	pie chart[graph] 円グラフ
54	column 縦列, 列	55	row 横列, 行	56	line graph 折れ線グラフ	57	solid line 実線
58	broken line 破線	59	dotted line 点線	60	Pareto chart パレート図	61	scatter graph[chart] 散布図

— 137 —

Section 2 例文で覚える！

62 adjust [ədʒʌ́st]
他 を調整〔調節〕する
派 adjustment「調整，調節」

As for the time of meeting, please **adjust** your **schedule** as follows.
会議の時間に関して，次のようにスケジュールを調整してくださるよう，お願いいたします。

63 prior [práiər]
形 ①（時間・順序が）前の，先の
②優先する
関 prior to「～より前に，～に先立って」

I got **prior** approval to use the conference room.
私は会議室利用のための事前承認を得た。

64 suggest [səgdʒést]
他 を提案する
類 propose

He **suggested** that we find a better name for the new product.
彼はその新製品によりよい名称をつけるべきだと提案した。

65 debate [dibéit]
他 について議論する，討論する
名 討論
類 discuss

That issue was extensively **debated** at the last meeting.
その件は前回の会議で徹底的に議論された。

66 constructive [kənstrʌ́ktiv]
形 建設的な
派 construct「を建てる」

He has a **constructive** opinion on the future of the IT industry.
彼はIT業界の将来について建設的な考えを持っている。

7. 会 議

67. concrete
[kánkriːt, -ˊ-]
- 形 具体的な
- 名 コンクリート
- 反 abstract「抽象的な」

You should make a more **concrete** proposal on how to advertise this product.
この製品の広告の仕方に関するより**具体的な**提案を行うべきだ。

68. general
[dʒénərəl]
- 形 ①全体の ②一般の
- 派 generally「一般に」

A **general** meeting is held annually, attended by all the employees.
全体会議は年1回，すべての従業員が出席して行われる。

69. unanimous
[ju(ː)nǽnəməs]
- 形 満場一致の
- 派 unanimously「満場一致で」

The proposal was accepted by a **unanimous** vote.
その提案は採決の結果，**満場一致で**可決された。

70. apologize
[əpálədʒàiz]
- 自 謝る，わびる

We **apologize** for the inconvenience due to the change in the plan.
計画の変更により，ご不便をおかけしたことを**おわび申し上げ**ます。

71. summarize
[sʌ́məràiz]
- 他 を要約する
- 派 summary「概要」

This graph **summarizes** the results of our research.
このグラフは我々の調査結果**を要約した**ものです。

72 oppose
[əpóuz]
他 に反対する
反 agree「賛成する」

Do you have a good reason for **opposing** the plan?
その計画に反対する十分な理由がありますか？

73 convenient
[kənvíːniənt]
形 都合がよい，便利な
派 convenience「好都合，便利」

Please let us know what would be a **convenient** date and time for the next meeting.
次回の打ち合わせについて，ご都合のよい日時をお教えください。

74 proceed
[prəsíːd]
自 進む，前進する
類 advance

Let's **proceed** to the last item on the **agenda**.
検討課題の最後の項目に進みましょう。

75 schedule
[skédʒuːl]
他 を予定する，スケジュールに入れる
関 reschedule「の計画を変更する」

The **conference** is **scheduled** for 3 p.m. today.
会議は今日の午後3時に予定されている。

76 alternative
[ɔːltə́ːrnətiv]
形 代わりの
派 alternate「（会議などの）代理人」

Let's set up an **alternative** meeting time.
代わりの打ち合わせ時間を設定しましょう。

7. 会議

77 depend on 他 次第である, に頼る 類 rely on

The success of a meeting **depends** largely **on** the preparations made for it.
会議の成否の多くは準備にかかっている。

78 dispute [dispjúːt] 動, [dispjúːt, ́ ́] 名
他 に反論する, 異議を唱える
名 口論, 論争

I don't **dispute** what you say, but I want to make one thing clear.
おっしゃることに異議を唱えるつもりはありませんが, 1つはっきりさせたいことがあります。

79 alteration [ɔːltəréiʃn] 名 変更
派 alter「を変える, 変更する」

We need to make minor **alterations** to our existing marketing method.
我々は, 現行の販売手段に多少の変更を加える必要がある。

80 confident [kánfidənt] 形 自信のある, 確信した
派 confidence「自信, 信頼」

We are **confident** that this project will bring considerable profit to your company.
今回のプロジェクトが御社にかなりの利益をもたらすことに確信を持っております。

81 confirm [kənfə́ːrm] 他 を確認する
派 confirmation「確認」

He called Mr. White to **confirm** the **appointment** for Monday afternoon.
彼は, 月曜日の午後のアポを確認するためにホワイト氏に電話した。

82 ongoing
[ángòuiŋ]

形 進行中の, 継続している

反 finished「終えた, 完成した」

There is an **ongoing** debate about the matter among economists.
その件に関しては経済学者の間で議論が続いている。

83 change
[tʃéindʒ]

他 を変える
名 取り替え, 異動

Would it be possible to **change** our appointment to next Friday?
約束の日を今度の金曜日に変えていただくことは可能でしょうか？

84 present
[prézənt]

形 出席して

反 absent「欠席して」

The documents were given to everyone **present** at the sales meeting.
その書類は, 営業会議に出席していた人全員に配られた。

85 controversial
[kàntrəvə́ːrʃl]

形 論議を呼ぶ, 賛否両論のある

We tried to avoid the **controversial** topic in that meeting.
私たちはその会議で物議をかもす話題を避けようとした。

86 reach
[ríːtʃ]

他 に達する, 届く

関 come up to「に達する」

We **reached** a decision on the subject.
私たちはその問題について決定に至った。

7. 会議

87 clarify [klǽrəfài]
- 他 を明らかにする
- 類 reveal

We need to **clarify** the problems we're having with our sales methods.
我々は販売方法の問題点を明らかにする必要がある。

88 defend [difénd]
- 他 を弁護する, 正しいと主張する

You must be strong-willed if you want to **defend** your ideas to the end.
最後まで自分の考えを弁護しようと思うなら, 強い意志が必要だ。

89 comment [kάment]
- 自 コメントする, 解説する
- 名 コメント, 批評
- 類 remark

Mr. Honda **commented** on the present economic situation at the **press conference**.
本田氏は記者会見で現在の経済状況についてコメントした。

90 postpone [poustpóun]
- 他 を延期する
- 類 put off

The meeting was **postponed** because of the heavy traffic jam.
会議はひどい交通渋滞のため延期された。

91 thorough [θə́ːrou]
- 形 徹底的な, 完全な
- 類 extensive

They made a **thorough** investigation into the failure of the project.
彼らはその計画の失敗に対し徹底的な調査をした。

92 adjourn
[ədʒə́ːrn]

他 を延期する, 休会にする

類 postpone

That **convention** was **adjourned** until 2:15.
その大会は2時15分まで休会になった。

93 miss
[mís]

他 ①に出席しない
② 〈列車・飛行機など〉に乗り遅れる

反 attend「に出席する」

Due to illness, I **missed** the **forum** yesterday.
病気のため、私は昨日の公開討論会を欠席した。

94 arrange
[əréindʒ]

他 を手配する

派 arrangement「準備」

We **arranged** a **business meeting** with an executive from ABC Corp.
私たちはABC社の重役との商談を手配した。

95 reschedule
[rìːskédʒul]

他 の予定を変更する

関 schedule「を予定する」

We can **reschedule** tomorrow's **staff meeting** to 3 p.m.
明日のスタッフ・ミーティングは午後3時に変更できる。

96 register
[rédʒistər]

自 登録する

派 registration「登録」

Mr. Endo **registered** to attend the **annual conference**.
遠藤さんは年次会議への出席を登録した。

7. 会議

97. participate in
他 に参加する
類 take part in

How many members **participated in** that **sales conference**?
何人のメンバーがその販売会議に参加したのですか。

98. organize
[ɔ́ːrɡənàiz]
他 を準備する, 編成する
派 organization「組織, 団体」

We are supposed to **organize** the next month's **business conference**.
私たちが来月の営業会議を準備することになっている。

99. detailed
[díteild, ditéild]
形 詳細な
類 precise

A **detailed** agenda helps a meeting run smoothly.
詳細な議題リストは会議の円滑な進行を助ける。

100. assign
[əsáin]
他 を割り当てる
類 allocate

Please sit in your **assigned** seat.
割り当てられた席にお座りください。

101. overwhelming
[òuvərhwélmiŋ]
形 圧倒的な
関 overwhelming majority「圧倒的多数」

The conference room was too small for the **overwhelming** number of attendees.
会議室は, 圧倒的な数の出席者に対して小さすぎた。

— 145 —

102 hand out

他 を配る

類 distribute

She **handed out** the **material** before the meeting.
彼女は会議の前に資料を配った。

103 reserve [rizə́ːrv]

他 を予約する

派 reservation「予約」

I have already **reserved** the conference room for the meeting next week.
私はすでに来週の打ち合わせのために会議室を予約してある。

104 serve as

他 として仕える, 働く

He has **served as chairperson** of the conference for many years.
彼は長年, その会議の議長を務めている。

105 brief [bríːf]

形 簡潔な, 手短な

関 in brief「手短に言えば, 要するに」

He gave a **brief** explanation of the new project.
彼は新しい企画の簡単な説明をした。

106 sufficient [səfíʃnt]

形 十分な

類 enough

Although she had **sufficient** time to prepare, her presentation ended in failure.
十分な準備時間があったにもかかわらず, 彼女のプレゼンは失敗に終わった。

7. 会議

107 recognize [rékəgnàiz]
他 を認める, 認知する
派 recognition「認識」

She is **recognized** for her outstanding presentations.
彼女は優れたプレゼンを行うことで認められている。

108 work on
他 に取り組む

I **worked on** a **summary** of their speeches after the conference.
私は会議の後に彼らのスピーチの要約に取り組んだ。

109 impress [imprés]
他 に感銘を与える
派 impression「印象」

Her presentation **impressed** most of those present.
彼女のプレゼンは, 出席者の多くに感銘を与えた。

110 engage [ingéidʒ]
他 ①〈人〉を(会話などに)引き入れる
②〈人〉を従事させる
派 engagement「約束」

Mr. Matsui's passionate speech **engaged** the **audience**.
松井氏の情熱的なスピーチは聴衆を引きつけた。

111 hand [hǽnd]
他 を手渡す
類 pass

I was **handed** the **microphone** by the chairperson.
私は議長からマイクを手渡された。

112 cancel
[kǽnsl]
他 を中止する，取り消す
派 cancellation「キャンセル」

Mr. Green's presentation was **canceled** because his flight was badly delayed.
飛行機が大幅に遅れたため，グリーン氏のプレゼンテーションは中止となった。

113 highlight
[háilàit]
他 を強調する，目立たせる
類 emphasize

His presentation **highlighted** the efficiency of product management at his company.
彼はプレゼンで，自社の製品管理の効率のよさを強調した。

114 discuss
[diskʌ́s]
他 について話し合う，討論する
派 discussion「討論」
類 debate

The **presenters discussed** some important matters.
プレゼンターたちは，いくつかの重要な問題について話し合った。

115 compile
[kəmpáil]
他 を収集してまとめる
類 collect

We **compiled** our past sales data for inclusion in this brochure.
私たちは，この冊子に加えるための過去の販売データを収集した。

116 indicate
[índikèit]
他 を示す
派 indication「兆候」

This **bar chart indicates** the amount of imported bananas.
この棒グラフはバナナの輸入量を示している。

7. 会議

117 refer [rifə́ːr]
- 自 ①参照する
- ②言及する
- 派 reference「参照（文），言及」

Please **refer** to the graph above.
上のグラフをご**参照**ください。

118 intricate [íntrikit]
- 形 複雑な，難解な
- 類 complex

The explanation with the **pie chart** made the **intricate** problem comprehensible.
円グラフを使った説明で，**複雑**な問題はわかりやすくなった。

119 complicated [kάmplikèitid]
- 形 複雑な
- 反 simple「簡単な，シンプルな」

The graph is too **complicated** to understand.
そのグラフは**複雑**すぎて理解するのが難しい。

120 average [ǽvəridʒ]
- 形 平均の
- 名 平均，平均値
- 類 normal

This **line graph** shows the **average** temperatures in Beijing.
この折れ線グラフは北京の**平均**気温を示している。

121 following [fάlouiŋ]
- 形 次の
- 反 previous「前の」

Please look at the **following pareto chart**.
次のパレート図をご覧ください。

− 149 −

Section 3 実際のスクリプトで確認！

Presentation

W: Good morning, everybody. Please take your seats. My name is Kate Atkins. I'm from the sales department, and I will chair today's meeting. Thank you for attending our monthly meeting today. First, we apologize to you for the abrupt change of meeting room and meeting time. Now, Tim Rogers, who leads our sales department, will make today's presentation.

M: OK. Oh, is my microphone working? Good. Now, I'll begin my presentation.

W: Oh, we still have several participants who don't have all the handouts yet. If you'll wait just one minute, Tim, I'll hand the materials out to them. OK, that's all, I think ... Tim, please.

M: Thanks, Kate. Now, the topic of today's presentation is "the N-series." We released the series at the end of last year. All the products of the series were selling well, almost at the same rate, for the first half of the year. But from the beginning of July, the products began selling at different rates. Please look at the data on the first page of the material marked Data Group A.

W: Data Group A is the volume with a yellow cover.

M: This data shows last month's sales activity for N-3. And now please see the pie chart on the whiteboard, projected by the OHP. This graph shows the sales of each N-series product for the last month, including N-3. As you see, the sales of N-3 account for almost all sales of the N-series. In the beginning each one of the N-series' products represented about 30 percent of the total, but at the end of last month, the remarkable growth of N-3 changed the proportion completely.

— 150 —

和訳

プレゼンテーション

W：皆さん，おはようございます。席についてください。ケイト・アトキンスと申します。営業部からまいりました。本日の会議の司会を務めさせていただきます。本日は月例会議にお集まりくださりありがとうございます。まずはじめに，会議室と会議時間の急な変更がございましたことをお詫びします。では，営業部を指揮するティム・ロジャーズが本日のプレゼンテーションを行います。

M：はい。さて，マイクは入っているかな？　よしと。ではプレゼンテーションを始めます。

W：あら，まだプリントを全部もらっていない参加者がいらっしゃる。ちょっと待って，ティム。資料を彼らに配るから。いいわ，これで全部みたいね…ティム，ではどうぞ。

M：ありがとう，ケイト。さて，本日のプレゼンテーションのトピックは，「Nシリーズ」です。我が社は昨年末にそのシリーズを発売しました。そのシリーズの製品はすべて上半期の間よく売れ，売り上げの割合もほぼ同じでした。しかし，7月の初めから，その売り上げ率が変わり始めました。資料分類Aの最初のページのデータをご覧ください。

W：資料分類Aは黄色い表紙の冊子です。

M：このデータが表しているのは先月のN-3の販売動向です。そして今度はOHPで映したホワイトボード上の円グラフをご覧ください。このグラフは，N-3を含むNシリーズ製品それぞれの先月の売り上げを表しています。N-3の売り上げがNシリーズの売り上げのほとんど全部を占めていることがわかります。当初，Nシリーズ製品はそれぞれ，全体のおよそ30パーセントの割合を占めていましたが，先月の終わりには，N-3の驚くべき成長が売り上げの割合を完全に変えました。

— 151 —

✻Review Words✻

☐ seat ➡ Sec.1-26	☐ apologize ➡ Sec.2-70	☐ meeting time ➡ Sec.1-6
☐ microphone ➡ Sec.1-48	☐ participant ➡ Sec.1-28	☐ handout ➡ Sec.1-24
☐ hand out ➡ Sec.2-102	☐ material ➡ Sec.1-25	☐ topic ➡ Sec.1-20
☐ pie chart ➡ Sec.1-53	☐ whiteboard ➡ Sec.1-46	☐ OHP ➡ Sec.1-29
☐ graph ➡ Sec.1-43	☐ change ➡ Sec.2-83	

第8章
企画・開発

英語で何と言うでしょうか？

☞答えは P.156

Section 1 イラストで覚える！

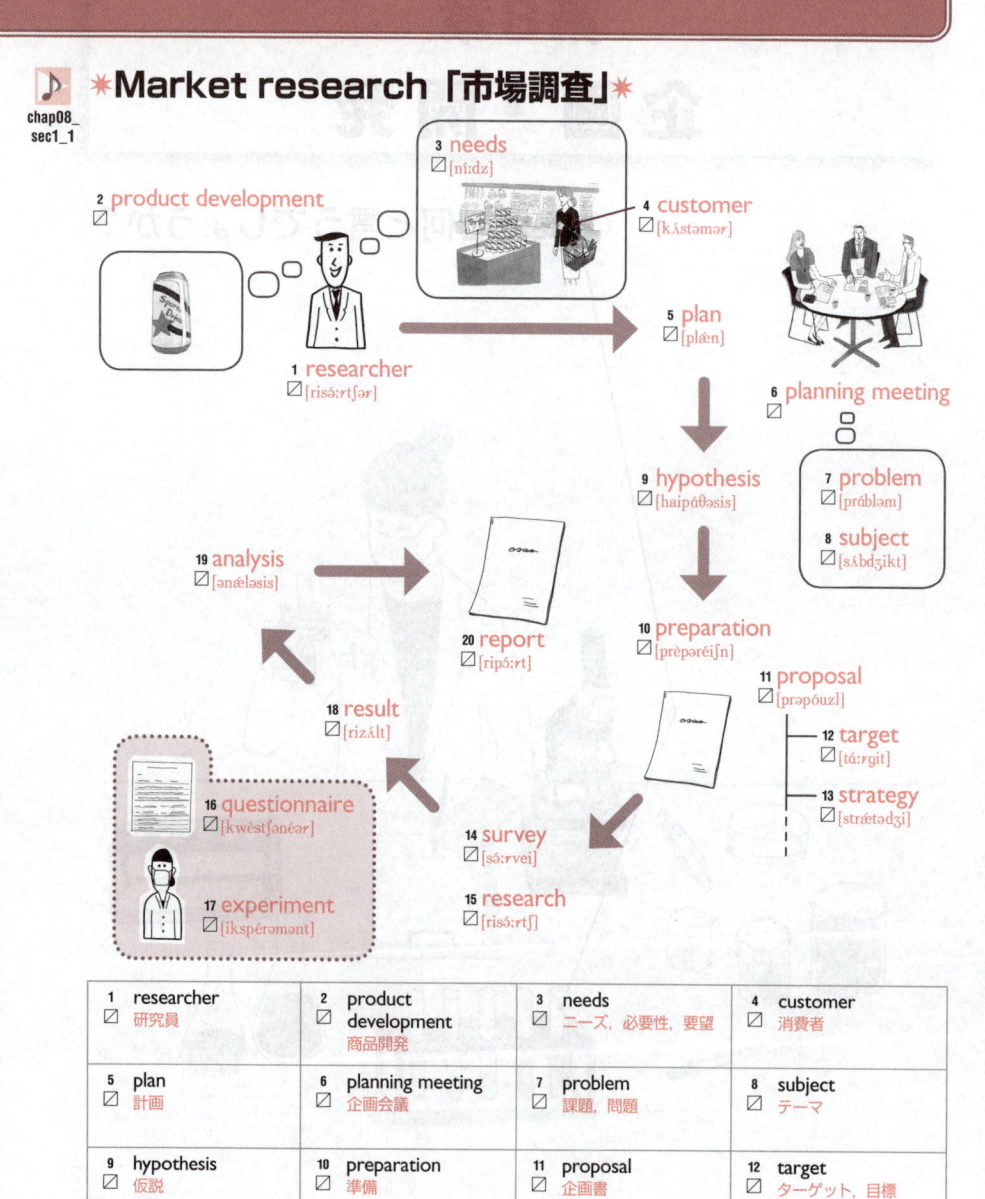

✳ Market research「市場調査」✳

- 1 researcher [rísɚːrtʃɚr]
- 2 product development
- 3 needs [níːdz]
- 4 customer [kʌ́stəmɚr]
- 5 plan [plǽn]
- 6 planning meeting
- 7 problem [prɑ́bləm]
- 8 subject [sʌ́bdʒikt]
- 9 hypothesis [haipɑ́θəsis]
- 10 preparation [prèpəréiʃn]
- 11 proposal [prəpóuzl]
- 12 target [tɑ́ːrgit]
- 13 strategy [strǽtədʒi]
- 14 survey [sɚ́ːrvei]
- 15 research [rísɚːrtʃ]
- 16 questionnaire [kwèstʃənéɚr]
- 17 experiment [ikspérəmənt]
- 18 result [rizʌ́lt]
- 19 analysis [ənǽləsis]
- 20 report [ripɔ́ːrt]

1	researcher 研究員	2	product development 商品開発	3	needs ニーズ，必要性，要望	4	customer 消費者
5	plan 計画	6	planning meeting 企画会議	7	problem 課題，問題	8	subject テーマ
9	hypothesis 仮説	10	preparation 準備	11	proposal 企画書	12	target ターゲット，目標
13	strategy 戦略	14	survey （たくさんの人や組織を対象とした）調査	15	research （専門的な）研究	16	questionnaire アンケート
17	experiment 実験	18	result 結果	19	analysis 分析	20	report 報告（書），レポート

8. 企画・開発

Survey 「調査」

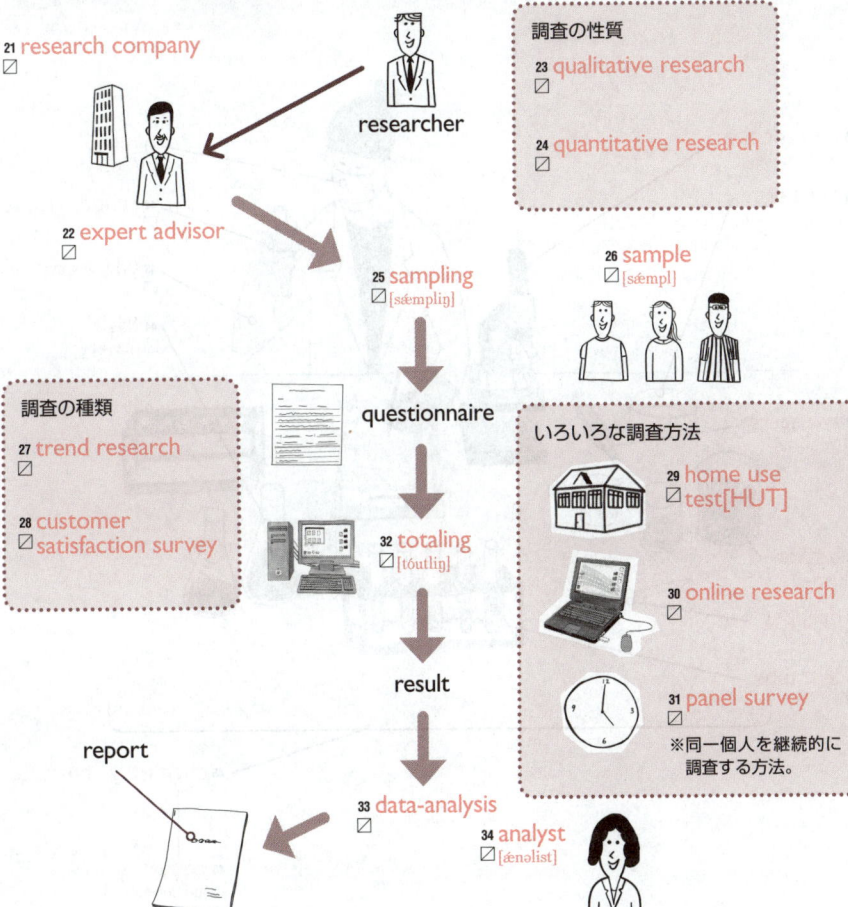

- 21 research company — 調査会社
- 22 expert advisor — 専門相談員
- researcher

調査の性質
- 23 qualitative research — 定性調査, 質的調査
- 24 quantitative research — 定量調査, 量的調査

- 25 sampling [sǽmpliŋ] — 見本抽出
- 26 sample [sǽmpl] — 標本, 抽出標本
- questionnaire
- 32 totaling [tóutliŋ] — 集計
- result
- 33 data-analysis — データ解析
- 34 analyst [ǽnəlist] — アナリスト, 分析専門家
- report

調査の種類
- 27 trend research — トレンド調査
- 28 customer satisfaction survey — 顧客満足度調査

いろいろな調査方法
- 29 home use test [HUT] — ホームユーステスト
- 30 online research — ネットリサーチ, オンライン調査
- 31 panel survey — パネル調査
  ※同一個人を継続的に調査する方法。

21	research company	調査会社
22	expert advisor	専門相談員
23	qualitative research	定性調査, 質的調査
24	quantitative research	定量調査, 量的調査
25	sampling	見本抽出
26	sample	標本, 抽出標本
27	trend research	トレンド調査
28	customer satisfaction survey	顧客満足度調査
29	home use test [HUT]	ホームユーステスト
30	online research	ネットリサーチ, オンライン調査
31	panel survey	パネル調査
32	totaling	集計
33	data-analysis	データ解析
34	analyst	アナリスト, 分析専門家

Laboratory 「研究室」

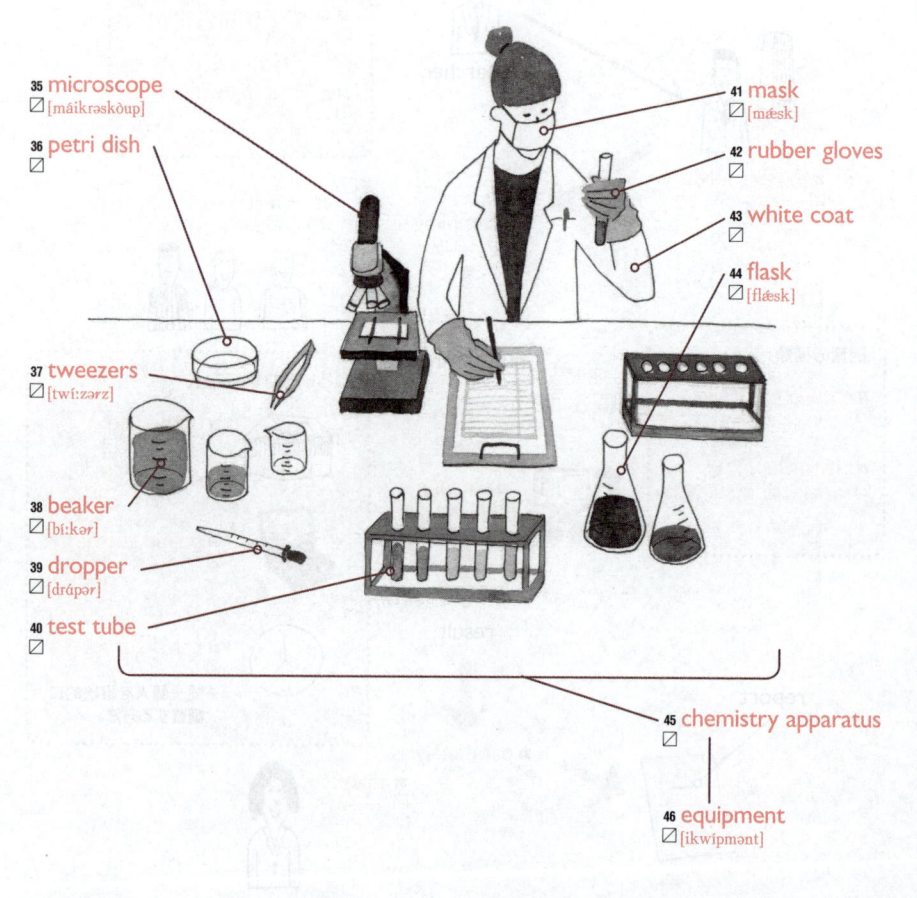

- 35 microscope [máikrəskòup]
- 36 petri dish
- 37 tweezers [twíːzərz]
- 38 beaker [bíːkər]
- 39 dropper [drápər]
- 40 test tube
- 41 mask [mæsk]
- 42 rubber gloves
- 43 white coat
- 44 flask [flæsk]
- 45 chemistry apparatus
- 46 equipment [ikwípmənt]

35	microscope 顕微鏡	36	petri dish シャーレ	37	tweezers ピンセット	38	beaker ビーカー
39	dropper スポイト	40	test tube 試験管	41	mask マスク	42	rubber gloves ゴム手袋
43	white coat 白衣	44	flask フラスコ	45	chemistry apparatus 実験道具	46	equipment 機器

8. 企画・開発

✳Proposal「企画書」✳

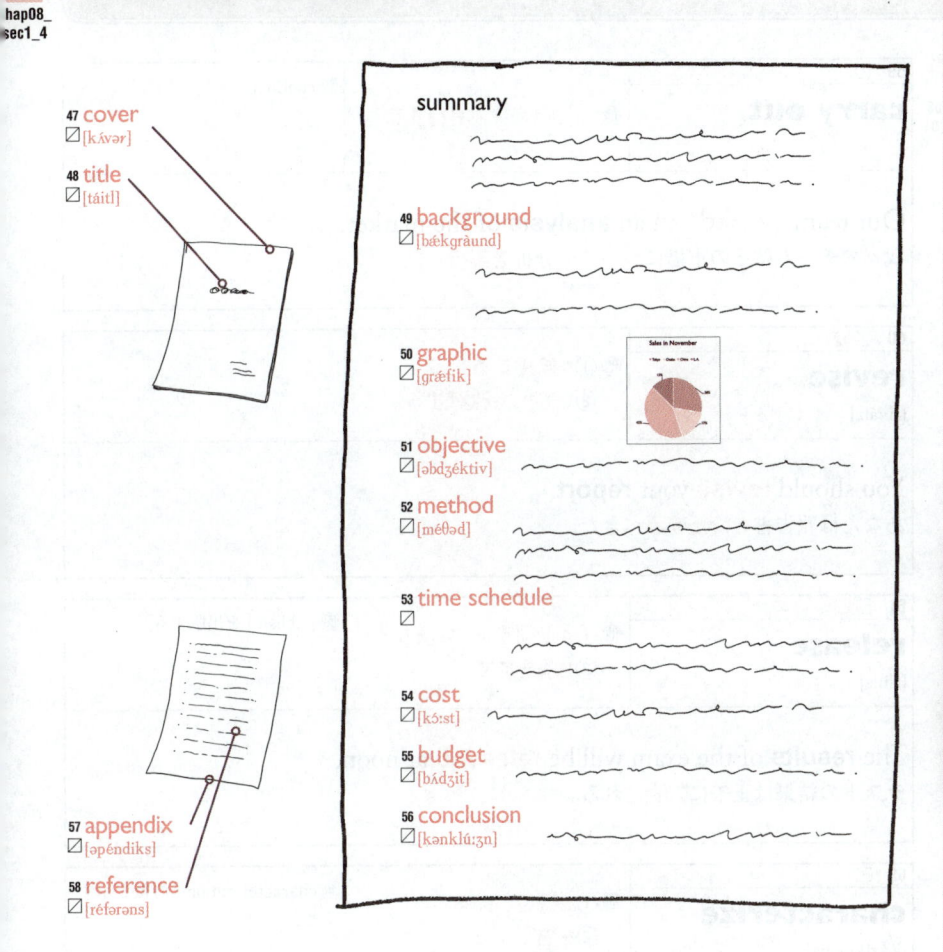

- 47 cover [kʌ́vər]
- 48 title [táitl]
- 49 background [bǽkgràund]
- 50 graphic [grǽfik]
- 51 objective [əbdʒéktiv]
- 52 method [méθəd]
- 53 time schedule
- 54 cost [kɔ́ːst]
- 55 budget [bʌ́dʒit]
- 56 conclusion [kənklúːʒn]
- 57 appendix [əpéndiks]
- 58 reference [réfərəns]

47 cover 表紙	48 title タイトル	49 background 背景	50 graphic 図形
51 objective 目的	52 method 方法	53 time schedule 工程表	54 cost 費用
55 budget 予算	56 conclusion 結論	57 appendix 巻末資料	58 reference 参考文献

– 157 –

Section 2　例文で覚える！

59 carry out
他〈計画など〉を**実行する**　　類 conduct

Our team **carried out** an **analysis** of the market.
我々のチームはその市場についての分析**を実行した**。

60 revise [riváiz]
他 ①**を修正する**
　 ②〈書物〉を改訂する

You should **revise** your **report**.
あなたは報告書**を修正する**べきだ。

61 release [rilí:s]
他 ①**を公開する，公表する**
　 ②を解き放つ

関 publish「を出版する」

The **results** of the exam will be **released** at noon.
テストの結果は正午に**公表**される。

62 characterize [kǽriktəràiz]
他 ①**を特色づける**
　 ②を描写する

派 characterization「特徴を示すこと」

High-tech products are **characterized** by their short life cycles.
ハイテク製品は寿命が短いことが**特徴**だ。

63 solve [sálv]
他〈問題など〉**を解く，解決する**

派 solution「解決（策）」

He easily **solved** the **problem**.
彼はその問題を容易に**解決した**。

8. 企画・開発

64 extensive [iksténsiv]
形 広範な, 〈場所が〉広大な
反 intensive「集中的な」

We did **extensive** research on female students' choice of clothing.
我々は女子学生の服装の好みについて広範な調査を行った。

65 feasible [fí:zəbl]
形 実行できる
類 possible

I don't think that is a **feasible** plan in this recession.
この不景気において、それが実行できる計画だとは思わない。

66 potential [pəténʃl]
形 潜在的な
類 possible

We should focus on the **potential** customers.
我々は、潜在的な顧客にターゲットを絞るべきです。

67 cutting-edge [kʌ́tiŋédʒ]
形 最先端の
関 state-of-the-art「最新式の」

Those engineers are working on **cutting-edge** technology.
その技術者たちは最先端の科学技術に取り組んでいる。

68 alternate [ɔ́:ltə:rnit]
形 代わりの, どちらか一方の
名 代わりをする人, 代理人
派 alternative「代わりの」

You should always have an **alternate** plan in case things don't go as planned.
予定通りに物事が運ばなかった場合に備えて、いつも代わりの計画を用意しておいた方がよい。

69 innovate
[ínəvèit]
⾃ 革新する

派 innovation「革新，一新」

Our industry must **innovate** and market new technologies as quickly as possible.
我々の産業はできるだけ早く革新し，新しい技術を市場に出さなければならない。

70 draw up
他〈計画〉を立てる

類 draft

We **drew up** a yearly sales plan.
我々は年次販売計画を立てた。

71 propose
[prəpóuz]
他 を提案する

類 suggest

He **proposed** a **hypothesis** to explain the condition.
彼はその状況を説明するために，仮説を提案した。

72 invent
[invént]
他 を発明する

類 contrive

A device aimed at reducing noise pollution has been **invented**.
騒音公害を減らすための装置が発明された。

73 conduct
[kəndʌ́kt]
他 を行う

派 conductor「案内人，ガイド」

The company **conducted** a public opinion **survey**.
その会社は世論調査を行った。

8. 企画・開発

74 focus on
他 を重点的に取り扱う

The manufacturer is **focusing on product development** this year.
そのメーカーは今年度，商品開発を重点的に取り扱っている。

75 latest
[léitist]
形 最新の
関 up-to-date「最新式の」

This laboratory has the **latest equipment** for DNA testing.
この実験室にはDNA検査用の最新の機器がある。

76 appropriate
[əpróupriit]
形 適切な
類 proper

We need to create an **appropriate** marketing **strategy** for this product.
我々はこの製品について適切なマーケティング戦略を立てる必要がある。

77 test-market
[téstmà:rkit]
他 をテスト販売する

These new products will be **test-marketed** in some areas of the EU.
これらの新製品はEUの一部地域でテスト販売される。

78 put ~ into practice
～を実行する
関 conduct「を実行する」

Countless **experiments** were conducted before the idea was **put into practice**.
そのアイデアが実行されるまで，無数の実験が行われた。

— 161 —

| 79 | allot [əlάt] | 他 を割り当てる | 類 assign |

We **allotted** one week for the **preparation** of the meeting.
我々はその会議の準備のために一週間を割り当てた。

| 80 | result in | 他 をもたらす，に終わる | 関 end up「結局〜になる」|

The measure **resulted in** quick improvement in sales.
その処置は売り上げの急速な改善につながった。

| 81 | determine [ditə́ːrmin] | 他 を決定する | 類 decide |

It is the market that **determines** the true value of goods.
商品の真の価値を決めるのは市場である。

| 82 | deliberate [dilíbərèit]動, [dilíbərit]形 | 自 熟考する / 形 慎重な | 派 deliberately「慎重に」|

The president **deliberated** for a few minutes and gave the green light to the project.
社長は数分間熟考してからプロジェクトにゴーサインを出した。

| 83 | evident [évidənt] | 形 明白な | 類 obvious |

It is **evident** that this price will be accepted in the US.
この価格がアメリカで受け入れられることは明白である。

8. 企画・開発

84 abandon
[əbǽndən]
他 を途中であきらめる，断念する
類 give up

They **abandoned** the plan to build a plant in China.
彼らは中国に工場を造る計画**を断念した**。

85 competitive
[kəmpétitiv]
形 競争力のある

We need to reduce production **costs** to remain **competitive**.
競争力を持ち続けるためには，生産コストを下げる必要がある。

86 anticipate
[æntísəpèit]
他 を予想する
類 expect

Companies must be able to **anticipate** customer **needs**.
企業は顧客のニーズ**を予想する**ことができなくてはならない。

87 careful
[kéərfl]
形 ①念入りな
②注意深い
派 carefully「注意深く」

Our **careful** market research produced some very interesting results.
入念な市場調査により，とても興味深い結果が出た。

88 influence
[ínfluəns]
名 影響力
他 に影響を及ぼす
類 effect

Customer feedback has a great **influence** on product development.
顧客の声は商品開発に大きな**影響力**を持っている。

― 163 ―

89 target
[tá:rgit]

他 をターゲットにする
名 的, 標的

類 focus

This series of cosmetics **targets** working women in their 30's.
この化粧品シリーズは，30代の働く女性をターゲットにしている。

90 identify
[aidéntəfài]

他 を明らかにする

源 identification「身分証明（書）」

We have to **identify** the cause of the product's failure.
その商品が失敗した原因を明らかにしなければならない。

91 predict
[pridíkt]

他 を予測する, 予言する

類 foretell

The analyst **predicted** the fall of the dollar.
そのアナリストはドルの下落を予測した。

92 prove
[prúːv]

自 （結果的に）～となる

類 come out

The product **proved** to be a huge success, far exceeding our expectations.
その製品は我々の予想をはるかに超える大ヒットとなった。

93 fill out

他 〈書類など〉に必要事項を書き入れる

類 fill in

Please **fill out** the **questionnaire**.
アンケートに必要事項を書き入れてください。

8. 企画・開発

94 investigate
[invéstigèit]
- 他 を(詳細に)調べる
- 自 調査〔研究〕する
- 類 look into

You should thoroughly **investigate** the market before entering it.
市場に参入する前には徹底的に**調査する**べきだ。

95 disagree with
- 他 に同意できない
- 反 agree with「に同意する」

I **disagree with** your assessment of the situation.
私はあなたの状況判断**に同意しかねる**。

96 compare
[kəmpéər]
- 他 ①を比べる
- ②を例える
- 派 comparable「匹敵する，相当する」

In this **home use test**, two products are to be **compared**.
このホームユーステストでは，2つの製品が**比べ**られる。

97 look into
- 他 を調査する，調べる
- 関 investigate「を調査する」

The company is **looking into** the possibility of expanding its business overseas.
その会社は事業を海外に拡大する可能性について**調査**している。

98 execute
[éksikjù:t]
- 他 を実行する
- 類 conduct

How can we **execute** our business strategy more effectively?
どうすれば我が社のビジネス戦略**を**もっと効果的に**実行**できるでしょうか。

| 99 | observe [əbzə́ːrv] | 他 ①を観察する ②〈法律など〉を守る | 派 observant「注意深い，観察力の鋭い」 |

We continue to **observe** market trends to determine the right time to introduce a new product.
新製品を投入する適切なタイミングを決めるため，私たちは市場のトレンドを観察し続けている。

| 100 | analyze [ǽnəlàiz] | 他 を分析する | |

We conducted market research to **analyze** consumer behavior.
消費者の行動を分析するため，私たちは市場調査を行った。

| 101 | explore [iksplɔ́ːr] | 他 を探す | 類 probe |

The purpose of this research is to **explore** the relationship between customer satisfaction and brand loyalty.
この研究の目的は，顧客の満足度とブランドへの忠誠心の関係を探ることだ。

| 102 | examine [igzǽmin] | 他 を調査する | 派 examination「試験，検査」 |

The **samples** of the goods are to be **examined** at random.
商品の抽出見本は無作為に調査される。

| 103 | define [difáin] | 他 を定義する | 派 definable「定義できる」 |

Marketing has many aspects and is difficult to **define** briefly.
マーケティングには多くの側面があり，手短に定義するのは難しい。

8. 企画・開発

104 obvious
[ábviəs]
形 明らかな
類 clear

It's **obvious** that consumers are cutting back on luxury items.
消費者がぜいたく品への支出を減らしているのは**明らか**だ。

105 at random
無作為に

We conducted a customer survey, whose participants were chosen **at random**.
我々は顧客調査を行ったが，その参加者は**無作為**に選ばれた。

106 continue
[kəntínjuː]
他 を続ける
反 cease「を止める，終える」

The **online research** will be **continued** for another six months.
そのオンライン調査はあと半年間**続けられる**。

107 select
[silékt]
他 (多くのものから)を選ぶ
類 choose

These are samples **selected** for examination.
これらは検査のために**選ば**れたサンプルです。

108 respondent
[rispɑ́ndənt]
名 回答者
関 answer「に解答する」

The company chose **respondents** to the panel survey based on age and sex.
その会社は年齢と性別に基づいてパネル調査の**回答者**を選んだ。

109 collect
[kəlékt]
他 を集める
派 collector「収集家」

Researchers collected data on more than 1,000 subjects.
研究者たちは1000人以上の被験者に関するデータを集めた。

110 develop
[divéləp]
他 を開発する
派 development「開発，発展」

Researchers at this company are developing recycling methods.
この会社の研究員はリサイクル方法を開発している。

111 protective
[prətéktiv]
形 保護する

We have to wear this protective mask in this room.
この部屋ではこの保護マスクを着けなければなりません。

112 prepare
[pripéər]
他 を用意する
派 preparation「準備（すること）」

She is now preparing a report on the results of the seminar.
彼女は今，セミナーの結果についてのレポートを準備している。

113 alphabetically
[ælfəbétikli]
副 アルファベット順に
類 in alphabetical order

The appendix is ordered alphabetically.
その巻末資料はアルファベット順に並んでいる。

8. 企画・開発

114
ultimate [ʌ́ltəmit]
形 最終的な, 究極の
派 ultimately「最後に, 究極的に」

The committee's **ultimate** conclusion pleased almost everyone.
委員会の最終的な結論に, ほぼ全員が喜んだ。

115
exceed [iksíːd]
他 を超える
類 surpass

The **budget** for this project should not **exceed** $100,000.
このプロジェクトの予算は10万ドルを超えてはならない。

116
above-mentioned [əbʌ́vménʃnd]
形 前述の
類 aforementioned

The **above-mentioned** method will not work in this case.
前述の方法はこの場合は機能しないだろう。

117
turn out
自 〜であることが判明する
関 end up「結局〜になる」

Our desperate efforts to succeed in the plan **turned out** to be in vain.
その計画の成功のための我々の必死の努力は, 結局無駄であった。

118
list [líst]
名 表, リスト
他 を一覧表にする

This is the **list** of **references** for his thesis.
これは彼の論文の参考文献のリストだ。

Section 3　実際の文書で確認！

Customer Survey　2011

The target group of this market research is our female customers aged over 20 who regularly use our product "Superduper." The results and analysis of the questionnaire will be used for future product development and a fuller understanding of your needs.

Please fill out the questions below.

1 What is the most important factor when you choose cosmetic products?
　☐ quality　☐ price　☐ publicity　☐ others _____

2 How long have you used Superduper?
　☐ 3 years　☐ 2 years　☐ 1 year　☐ less than 1 year

3 Have you ever tried a similar product made by any of the following companies?
　☐ TTP　☐ NNF　☐ C & T　☐ others _____

3' If you checked any of the above, why do you select our Superduper now?

　..
　..
　..

4 Have you encountered any problem(s) when using Superduper?
　☐ Yes　　　　　　　☐ No

4' If Yes, please state the problem(s).

　..
　..

We will not use the contents of this research or your personal information for any other purpose. Thank you for your cooperation.

Tanner Hopkins, *Chief* Researcher
Research and Development

> 和訳

顧客調査 2011

この市場調査は，私どもの製品"スーパーデューパー"をご愛用いただいている20歳より上の女性のお客さまを対象にしております。アンケートの結果と分析は今後の商品開発やお客さまのニーズをよりよく把握するために使われます。

以下の質問にお答えください。

1　化粧品をお選びになるときにどの要素が最も重要ですか？
　　□品質　　□価格　　□知名度　　□その他 _____

2　どのくらいスーパーデューパーをご使用ですか？
　　□3年　　□2年　　□1年　　□1年未満

3　今までに以下の他社の類似製品を試したことはありますか？
　　□TTP社　　□NNF社　　□C＆T社　　□その他 _____

3'　上記の欄のいずれかに印をつけた方にお聞きします。現在スーパーデューパーをお選びになられている理由は？
_____
_____
_____

4　スーパーデューパーをお使いになられて，何か問題はございますか？
　　□はい　　　　　　　□いいえ

4'「はい」をお選びになられた方は，その問題をお聞かせください。
_____
_____
_____

私どもはこれらの調査内容とあなたの個人情報を他の目的に使用することは一切ありません。
ご協力ありがとうございました。

主任研究員　タナー・ホプキンス
研究開発部

☀ Review Words ☀

☐ customer ➡ Sec.1-4	☐ survey ➡ Sec.1-14	☐ target ➡ Sec.2-89
☐ result ➡ Sec.1-18	☐ analysis ➡ Sec.1-19	☐ questionnaire ➡ Sec.1-16
☐ product development ➡ Sec.1-2	☐ needs ➡ Sec.1-3	☐ fill out ➡ Sec.2-93
☐ select ➡ Sec.2-107	☐ problem ➡ Sec.1-7	☐ research ➡ Sec.1-15
☐ researcher ➡ Sec.1-1		

第9章
製　造

→ それぞれ英語で何と言うでしょうか？

☞ 答えは P.175

Section 1　イラストで覚える！

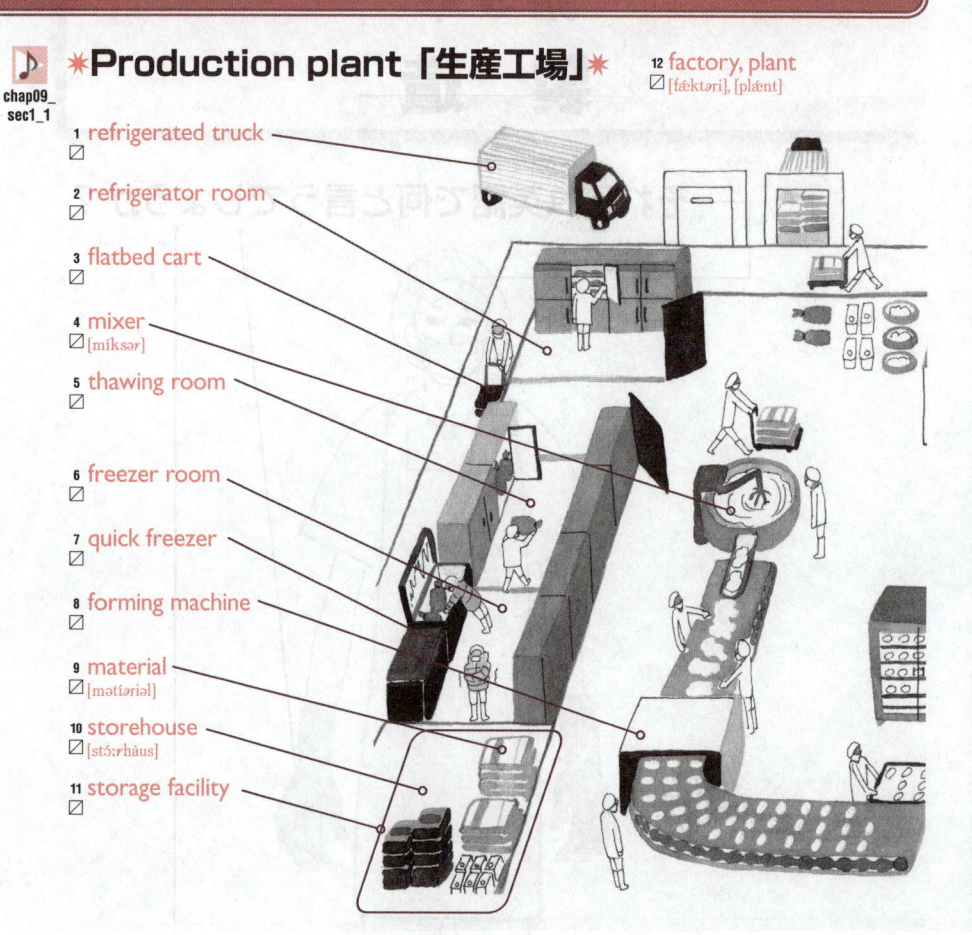

✴ Production plant「生産工場」✴

1. refrigerated truck
2. refrigerator room
3. flatbed cart
4. mixer [míksər]
5. thawing room
6. freezer room
7. quick freezer
8. forming machine
9. material [mətíəriəl]
10. storehouse [stɔ́ːrhàus]
11. storage facility
12. factory, plant [fǽktəri], [plǽnt]

1 refrigerated truck 冷蔵トラック	2 refrigerator room 冷蔵室	3 flatbed cart 台車	4 mixer ミキサー
5 thawing room 解凍室	6 freezer room 冷凍室	7 quick freezer 急速冷凍機	8 forming machine 成形機
9 material 材料	10 storehouse 倉庫	11 storage facility 保存設備	12 factory, plant 工場

9. 製造

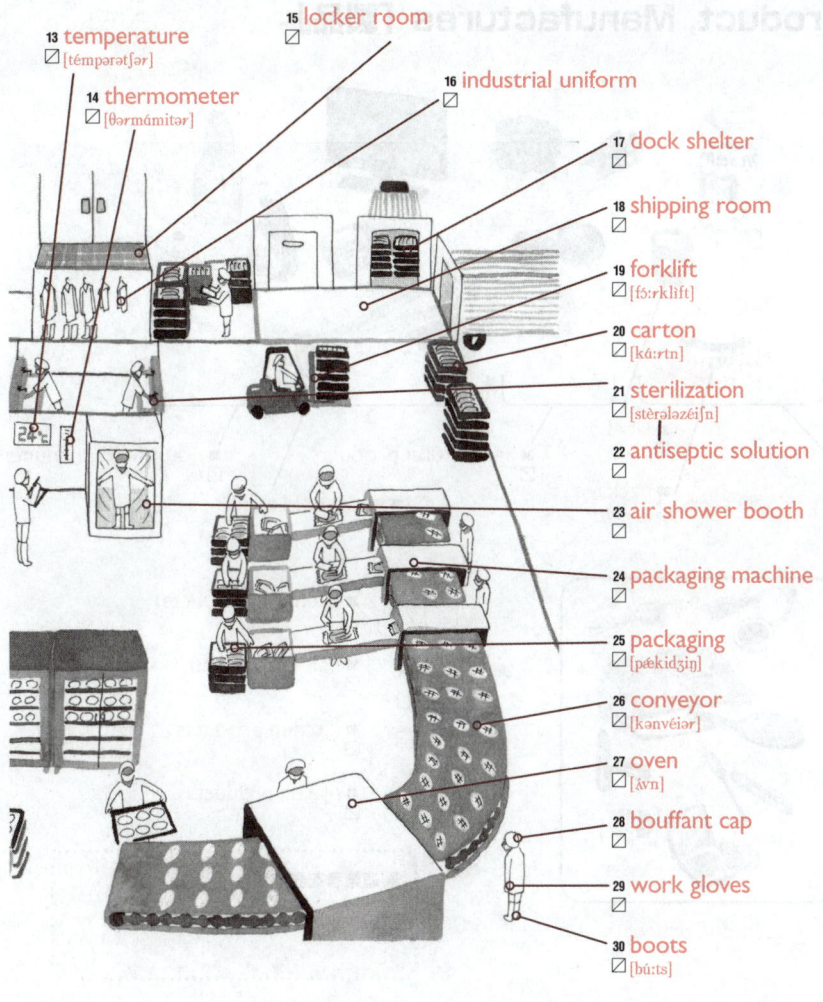

- 13 temperature [témpərətʃər]
- 14 thermometer [θərmámitər]
- 15 locker room
- 16 industrial uniform
- 17 dock shelter
- 18 shipping room
- 19 forklift [fɔ́ːrklìft]
- 20 carton [káːrtn]
- 21 sterilization [stèrələzéiʃn]
- 22 antiseptic solution
- 23 air shower booth
- 24 packaging machine
- 25 packaging [pǽkidʒiŋ]
- 26 conveyor [kənvéiər]
- 27 oven [ʌ́vn]
- 28 bouffant cap
- 29 work gloves
- 30 boots [búːts]

13	temperature 温度, 気温	14	thermometer 温度計	15	locker room 更衣室	16	industrial uniform 作業着
17	dock shelter ドックシェルター	18	shipping room 出荷室	19	forklift フォークリフト	20	carton 容器, 箱
21	sterilization 殺菌	22	antiseptic solution 消毒液	23	air shower booth エアーシャワー室	24	packaging machine 包装機
25	packaging 梱包	26	conveyor ベルトコンベア	27	oven オーブン	28	bouffant cap 衛生帽
29	work gloves 軍手	30	boots 長靴				

✵ Product, Manufactures 「製品」 ✵

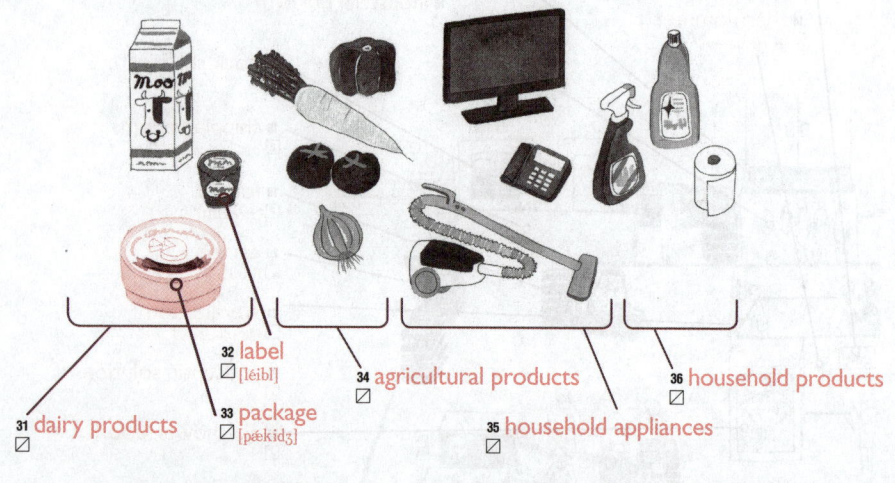

31 dairy products
32 label [léibl]
33 package [pǽkidʒ]
34 agricultural products
35 household appliances
36 household products
37 cosmetic products
38 chemical products
39 hair-care products
40 kitchen products
41 plastic products

製造業者を表す語
42 manufacturer [mǽnjəfæktʃərər]
43 producer [prədjúːsər]

31 dairy products 酪農生産物，乳製品	**32** label 商標，ラベル	**33** package （商品などの）包装	**34** agricultural products 農産物
35 household appliances 家電	**36** household products 家庭用品	**37** cosmetic products 化粧品	**38** chemical products 化学製品
39 hair-care products ヘアケア製品	**40** kitchen products 台所製品	**41** plastic products プラスチック製品	**42** manufacturer 製造業者，メーカー
43 producer メーカー			

9. 製造

✱ Out of order 「故障して」✱

- 44 failure [féiljər]
- 45 malfunction [mælfʌ́ŋkʃn]
- 46 maintenance [méintənəns]
- 47 parts, components [pɑ́ːrts], [kəmpóunənts]
- 48 machinery [məʃíːnəri]
- 49 specification, spec [spèsəfikéiʃn], [spék]

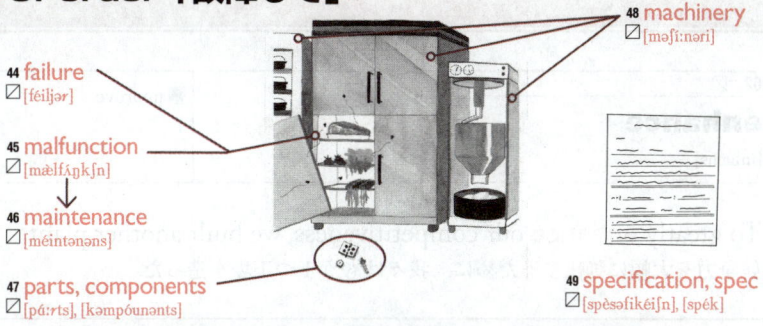

✱ Quality management 「品質経営, 品質管理」✱

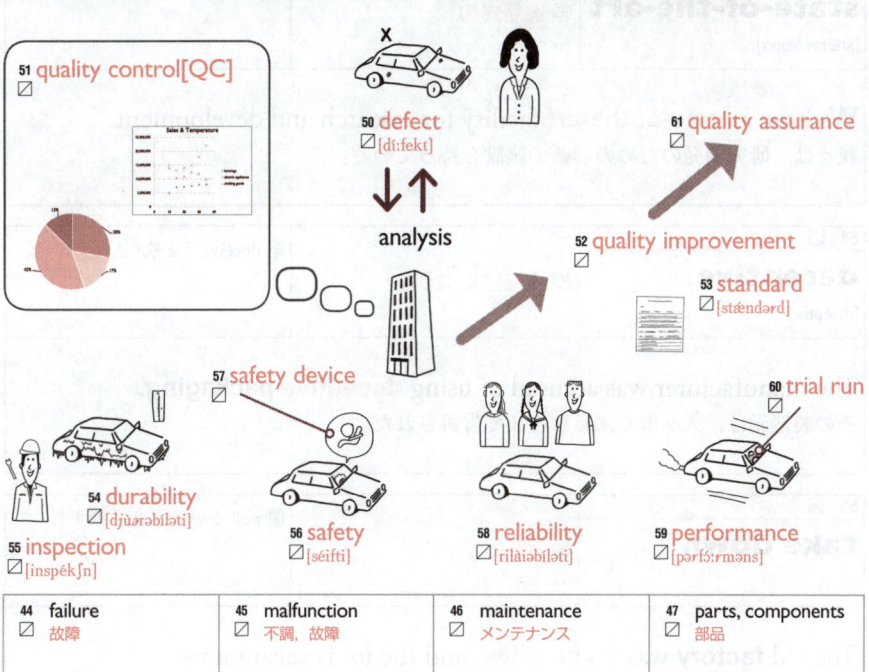

- 51 quality control [QC]
- 50 defect [dɪfékt]
- ↓↑ analysis
- 52 quality improvement
- 53 standard [stǽndərd]
- 61 quality assurance
- 57 safety device
- 60 trial run
- 54 durability [djùərəbíləti]
- 55 inspection [inspékʃn]
- 56 safety [séifti]
- 58 reliability [rilàiəbíləti]
- 59 performance [pərfɔ́ːrməns]

44	failure 故障	45	malfunction 不調, 故障	46	maintenance メンテナンス	47	parts, components 部品
48	machinery 機械類	49	specification, spec 詳細事項, 仕様書	50	defect 欠陥	51	quality control[QC] 品質管理
52	quality improvement 品質改善	53	standard 標準, 規格	54	durability 耐久性	55	inspection 検査
56	safety 安全性	57	safety device 安全装置	58	reliability 信頼性	59	performance 性能
60	trial run 試行, 試運転	61	quality assurance 品質保証				

Section 2　例文で覚える！

62　enhance [inhǽns]　他〈質など〉を強化する　類 improve

To greatly **enhance** our competitiveness, we built another plant.
競争力を大幅に強化するために，我々はもう1つ工場を造った。

63　state-of-the-art [stéitəvðiáːrt]　形 最新式の　類 up-to-date

We have a **state-of-the-art** facility for research and development.
我々は，研究開発のための最新の施設を持っている。

64　deceptive [diséptiv]　形 人を欺くような　派 deceive「を欺く」

The manufacturer was accused of using **deceptive** packaging.
その製造元は，人を欺くような包装で告訴された。

65　take down　他 を解体する　関 pull down「を取り壊す」

The old **factory** was **taken down** and the lot is vacant now.
古い工場は取り壊され，今は更地になっている。

66　downsize [dáunsàiz]　他 を削減する，縮小する　関 minimize「を最小にする」

The company **downsized** some of their factories due to the recession.
その企業は不況のため，工場のいくつかを縮小した。

9. 製造

67 resume
[riz(j)úːm]
他 を再開する

Our plant **resumes** its operation by this Friday.
我々の工場は今週の金曜日までには操業を再開する。

68 shut down
他 を閉鎖する
類 close

We'll have to **shut down** our assembly line for **maintenance**.
我々は整備のために，組み立てラインを閉鎖しなければならない。

69 warm
[wɔ́ːrm]
他 を温める
形 温かい
反 cool「を冷やす」

The factory has some large **ovens** to **warm** the products.
その工場には，製品を温めるための大きなオーブンがいくつかある。

70 pack
[pǽk]
他 を(箱などに)入れる，詰める
名 包み
関 pack a bag「かばんに荷物を詰める」

That machine **packs** bottles into **cartons**.
あの機械は，びんを箱に入れる。

71 preserve
[prizə́ːrv]
他 を保つ，保存する
類 conserve

All the raw **materials** are **preserved** in the warehouse.
すべての原料が倉庫に保存されている。

– 179 –

72 ☐ **leak** [líːk]	圁 〈水・ガスなどが〉漏れる 他 〈秘密・情報など〉を漏らす	

The factory floor was flooded with oil **leaking** from a pipe.
工場の床はパイプから漏れた油でまみれていた。

73 ☐ **fluctuate** [flʌ́ktʃuèit]	圁 〈相場・熱などが〉変動する, 上下する	類 vary

The **temperature** in the room **fluctuates** depending on the air outside.
室内の気温は, 外気によって変動する。

74 ☐ **abundant** [əbʌ́ndənt]	形 豊富な, 大量の	類 plentiful

This factory uses the area's **abundant** sunlight as an energy source.
この工場では地域の豊富な太陽光をエネルギー源の1つとして使っている。

75 ☐ **recall** [rikɔ́ːl]	他 ①〈欠陥商品〉を回収する ②を思い出す	

The car **manufacturer recalled** more than 15,000 vehicles.
その自動車メーカーは, 15000台以上の車を回収した。

76 ☐ **leading** [líːdiŋ]	形 主要な	類 main

The company is the **leading producer** of medical devices.
その企業は, 医療機器の主要メーカーである。

9. 製造

77 disposable
[dispóuzəbl]
形 使い捨ての

There is a growing demand for **disposable** diapers.
使い捨ておむつの需要が増えている。

78 place
[pléis]
他 を置く
名 場所, 立場
関 place an order「注文する」

Please **place** the **label** on this box.
この箱にラベルを張ってください。

79 equip
[ikwíp]
他 を備え付ける, 装備する
類 fix

The factory is **equipped** with state-of-the-art facilities.
その工場には最新の設備が備えられている。

80 break down
自 壊れる, 故障する
関 out of order「故障中で」

The **packaging machine** suddenly **broke down**.
その梱包機は突然故障した。

81 soak
[sóuk]
他 を十分に湿らせる, たっぷり浸す
自 浸る, つかる
類 immerse

The textile is **soaked** in the dye around the clock.
織物は一昼夜その染料に浸される。

82 freeze
[fríːz]

- 他 を凍らせる
- 自 凍る

反 melt「を溶かす」

The fish was **frozen** in the **quick freezer** to maintain its freshness.
魚は新鮮さを保つため，急速冷凍機で凍らせてあった。

83 coincide
[kòuinsáid]

- 自 ①同時に起こる
- ②一致する

派 coincident「同時に起こる，完全に一致した」

The construction of a new factory **coincided** with the start of an economic boom.
新工場の建設が好景気の始まりと重なった。

84 stand at

他（温度計などが）を示す

The **thermometer** in the large freezer **stood at** minus thirty degrees.
大型冷凍庫内の温度計は，マイナス30度を示していた。

85 pick up

- 他 ①〈人〉を(車などに)乗せる，〈物〉を取りに行く
- ②を拾う

They **pick up** packages at several factories.
彼らは，いくつかの工場で荷物を集荷する。

86 furnish
[fə́ːrniʃ]

他 を供給する

類 supply

The company **furnishes** raw materials to the processed food industry.
その会社は，加工食品業界に原材料を供給している。

9. 製造

87 assess
[əsés]

他 ①〈価値・性質など〉を評価する, 判断する
②を査定する

類 evaluate

We constantly **assess** our production processes to reduce costs.
コストを下げるために, 我々は常に製造過程**の評価をしている**。

88 innovative
[ínəvèitiv]

形 革新的な

派 innovate「革新する」

We must create an **innovative** product in the field of information technology.
我々はIT分野で**革新的な**製品を生み出さなくてはならない。

89 durable
[djúərəbl]

形 耐久力のある, 長持ちする

反 fragile「壊れやすい」

This bag is **durable** enough to hold a laptop.
このバッグは**耐久力がある**ので, ノートパソコンを収納しても大丈夫です。

90 review
[rivjúː]

他 ①を批評する
②を再検討する

関 criticize「を批評する, 非難する」

Sign in to **review** our **cosmetic products**.
当社の化粧品**のレビューを書く**にはサインインしてください。

91 such as

〜のような

関 for example「例えば」

The farm sells **dairy products such as** milk, cheese and yogurt.
その農場では, 牛乳, チーズ, ヨーグルト**のような**乳製品を売っている。

― 183 ―

92 manufacture
[mænjəfǽktʃər]

他 を生産する, 製造する

類 produce

The company **manufactures** various kinds of **chemical products**.
その会社は, さまざまな種類の化学製品を製造している。

93 be known for

～で知られている, 有名である

関 well-known「よく知られた」

The company **is known for** high-quality **kitchen products**.
その企業は, 質の高い台所製品で知られている。

94 ahead of the times

時代に先駆けて

The company's **household appliances** are **ahead of the times**.
その会社の家電製品は, 時代の先を行っている。

95 portable
[pɔ́ːrtəbl]

形 持ち運びできる, 携帯用の

類 mobile

The market for **portable** computing devices continues to expand.
携帯用コンピュータ機器の市場は拡大し続けている。

96 guarantee
[gærəntíː]

他 を保証する
名 保証

類 certify

We **guarantee** that the **agricultural products** are safe.
その農産物が安全であると保証します。

9. 製造

97 **defective** [dıféktıv]
形 欠陥のある
派 defect「欠陥」

The **defective** parts were soon returned to the plant.
その欠陥のある部品は，すぐに工場に返品された。

98 **because of**
〜のために
類 due to

The conveyor stopped **because of** the **failure** of the electrical system.
電気系統の故障のためにコンベヤーが止まった。

99 **suspend** [səspénd]
他 〈活動・営業など〉を一時停止する
反 resume「を再開する」

The factory will **suspend** its operations from August 15.
その工場は8月15日から操業を一時停止する。

100 **assemble** [əsémbl]
他 を集める，組み立てる

We use robots to **assemble** parts.
部品の組み立てにはロボットを使っています。

101 **repair** [rıpéər]
他 を修理する，修繕する
自 (物が) 修理が利く
類 mend

Sometimes it costs more to **repair** an old computer than to buy a new one.
古いパソコンを修理する方が，新品を買うより高くつくこともある。

chap09 sec2_09

102 spend ~ on
他 に〈金〉を費やす

We prepared a large amount of money to **spend on** the latest **machinery**.
我々は，最新の機械に費やすための多額の金を用意した。

103 due to
〜のために

同 because of

The room was hot **due to** the **malfunction** of the air conditioner.
エアコンの故障のため，部屋は暑かった。

104 operate
[ápərèit]

他〈機械など〉を操作する
自（機械などが）作動する

派 operation「作動，運営」

All the machines in the factory are **operated** by computer.
工場内の機械はすべて，コンピュータによって操作されている。

105 temporarily
[tèmpərérəli]

副 一時的に

反 permanently「永久に」

This machine is **temporarily** out of order.
この機械は一時的に故障している。

106 efficient
[ifíʃnt]

形 能率的な，有能な

反 inefficient「能率の悪い」

Examining the parts beforehand is an **efficient** way to reduce **defects** in products.
部品を前もって点検しておくのは，不良品を減らす能率的な方法だ。

– 186 –

9. 製造

107 overhaul
[òuvərhɔ́ːl] 動, [óuvərhɔ̀ːl] 名

- 他 を分解点検する, 精査する
- 名 分解点検, 整備

The conveyers are **overhauled** once a year.
コンベヤーは年に1回, 分解点検される。

108 wrap
[rǽp]

- 他 を包む
- 名 ラップ

類 pack

This machine can **wrap** 2,000 packages per hour.
この機械は1時間に2000パックを包装できる。

109 be concerned

- ① 心配する
- ② 関わる

関 be anxious「心配する」

Many people **are concerned** about the **safety** of food.
多くの人が食の安全を気に掛けている。

110 monitor
[mánitər]

- 他 を監視する
- 名 モニター

He **monitors** the safety **standards** of the factory.
彼はその工場の安全基準を監視している。

111 artificial
[àːrtəfíʃl]

- 形 人工の

反 natural「自然の」

No **artificial** colors, sweeteners or preservatives.
人工着色料, 甘味料, 保存料は一切使われておりません。

112

improve [imprúːv]

- 他 を改善する
- 自 (商売などが)よくなる

派 improvement「改良, 進歩」

We are always working to **improve** the **reliability** of our products.
私たちは製品の信頼性を高めるため, いつも努力しています。

113

crucial [krúːʃl]

- 形 欠くことのできない, 重要な

類 essential

Quality is **crucial** to a product's success.
品質は製品が成功するために決定的に重要だ。

114

decline [dikláin]

- 名 下落, 落ち込み
- 自 (価値などが)低下する

類 decrease

Maintain the machine well in order to prevent a **decline** in **performance**.
機械の性能が低下しないように, しっかりメンテナンスしなさい。

115

warrant [wɔ́ːrənt]

- 他 を保証する

類 certify

This table is **warranted** against defects in materials and workmanship for 1 year.
このテーブルは素材や仕上がりの欠陥に対して1年間の保証が付いている。

116

essential [isénʃl]

- 形 不可欠の, 極めて重要な

類 crucial

Gaining consumer trust is **essential** to increasing sales.
売り上げを伸ばすには消費者の信頼を得ることが不可欠だ。

9. 製造

117 **standardize** [stǽndərdàiz]
他 の規準を統一する
類 regulate

The company **standardized** the operations process on their assembly line.
その会社は組み立てラインにおける作業工程の規準を統一した。

118 **doubt** [dáut]
名 疑い
他 を疑う
関 without a doubt「疑いなく」

I have no **doubt** about the reliability of this product.
この製品の信頼性に疑いはない。

119 **go through**
他 を通過する, 経る
類 get though

Those items must **go through** a strict **inspection**.
それらの商品は, 厳しい検査を通過しなければならない。

120 **perform** [pərfɔ́ːrm]
他 〈仕事など〉を行う
派 performance「成績, (機械の) 性能」

They **performed** an elaborate **trial run** before releasing their new product.
彼らは新製品の発表前に, 念入りな試運転を行った。

121 **out of order**
(機械が) 故障して
関 break down「故障する」

The packaging machine in our factory is **out of order** again.
我々の工場の梱包機はまた故障している。

– 189 –

Section 3　実際のウェブサイトで確認！

♪
chap09_
sec3

Please join our S&C factory tour
To be held from July 1 through 7, 2011

The tour of our production plant will be held for the first time.
We established a new factory on April 1st, including many state-of-the-art machines to improve our products and productivity.

Here is some brief information about the new facilities and devices that you will see during the tour.

★ Freezer room (the lowest temperature here is －55°! You can experience the temperature yourself)
★ Packaging conveyor (You will be surprised at the high speed of the packaging process)
★ High-performance inspection sensor (The sensor can immediately detect any defect of the product)
★ High-powered mega mixer (The power of this mixer is 300HP!)
★ Eco-friendly forklifts (They are powered by electricity and emit no CO_2)

If you wish to visit our factory, kindly fill in the registration form on the last web page ⇐ CLICK HERE and send it to us by June 28th. The number of participants is limited.

If you have any questions, please feel free to contact us by e-mail at: openhouse@S_and_C.com.
Our Welcoming Team is very much looking forward to seeing you at Open House 2011.

During the tour, please observe the following guidelines.
　#1 Follow the tour guide's instructions.
　#2 Always wear the cap and face mask that you will be given.
　#3 Clean your hands with antiseptic solution as instructed.
　#4 At the air shower booth, stay there till the light turns to green.
　#5 Refrain from speaking to the staff members wearing a blue industrial uniform.
　#6 For your safety, don't touch the machinery and devices without permission.

The next page ⇐ CLICK HERE

和訳

Ｓ＆Ｃ工場見学ツアーにご参加ください
2011年7月1〜7日開催

我が社の生産工場にて第1回目の工場見学ツアーが催されます。
当社は4月1日，製品と生産性の向上のために，多くの最新式の機器を備えた新しい工場を設立しました。

以下はツアーでご覧になれる，新しい設備と機器の簡単な情報です。

★冷凍室（最低温度は−55度！　この温度を体感いただけます）

★梱包コンベアー（梱包工程のスピードの速さに驚くことでしょう）

★高性能検査センサー（このセンサーは製品のどんな欠陥もただちに検知します）

★ハイパワーメガミキサー（ミキサーの力は300馬力！）
★エコフレンドリーフォークリフト（電気駆動なので二酸化炭素を排出しません）

工場を訪れたい方は，最後のページ⇐ここをクリックの申し込みフォームにご記入の上，6月28日までに私どもへお送りください。参加人数には限りがございます。

お問い合わせは，メールでopenhouse@S_and_C.comへお気軽にどうぞ。

ウェルカムチームは2011年一般公開であなたに会えることを楽しみにしております。

ツアーの間は以下のガイドラインをお守りください。
  1　ガイドの指示に従うこと。
  2　与えられる帽子とマスクを着用すること。
  3　指示通りに消毒液で手を洗うこと。
  4　エアーシャワー室にはライトが緑色に変わるまでとどまること。
  5　青色の作業服を着ているスタッフに話しかけないこと。
  6　安全のため，許可なしに機械や設備に触れないこと。

次のページへ⇐ここをクリック

✴ Review Words ✴

☐ factory ➡ Sec.1-12	☐ state-of-the-art ➡ Sec.2-63	☐ improve ➡ Sec.2-112
☐ freezer room ➡ Sec.1-6	☐ temperature ➡ Sec.1-13	☐ packaging ➡ Sec.1-25
☐ conveyor ➡ Sec.1-26	☐ performance ➡ Sec.1-59	☐ inspection ➡ Sec.1-55
☐ defect ➡ Sec.1-50	☐ mixer ➡ Sec.1-4	☐ forklift ➡ Sec.1-19
☐ antiseptic solution ➡ Sec.1-22	☐ air shower booth ➡ Sec.1-23	☐ industrial uniform ➡ Sec.1-16
☐ safety ➡ Sec.1-56	☐ machinery ➡ Sec.1-48	

第10章
宣伝・広報

英語で何と言うでしょうか？

☞ 答えは P.195

Section 1 イラストで覚える！

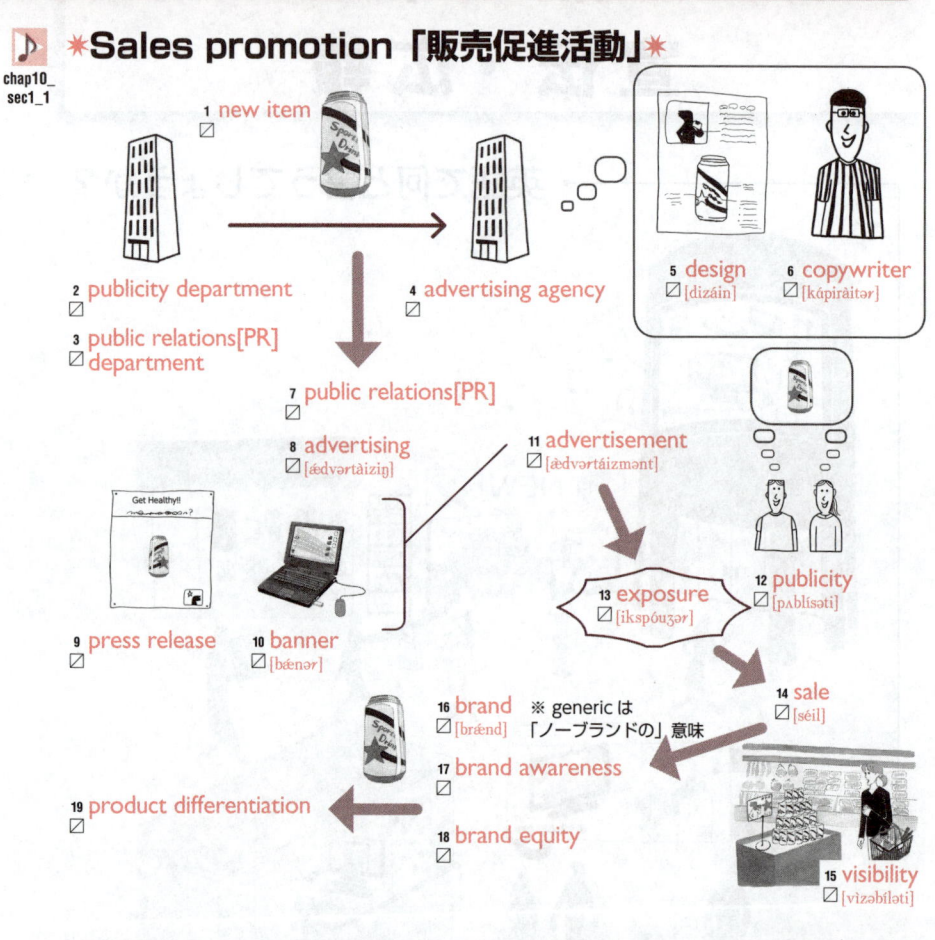

✳Sales promotion「販売促進活動」✳

1. new item
2. publicity department
3. public relations[PR] department
4. advertising agency
5. design [dizáin]
6. copywriter [kάpiràitər]
7. public relations[PR]
8. advertising [ǽdvərtàiziŋ]
9. press release
10. banner [bǽnər]
11. advertisement [ædvərtáizmənt]
12. publicity [pʌblísəti]
13. exposure [ikspóuʒər]
14. sale [séil]
15. visibility [vìzəbíləti]
16. brand [brǽnd] ※ generic は「ノーブランドの」意味
17. brand awareness
18. brand equity
19. product differentiation

1 new item 新商品	2 publicity department 宣伝部	3 public relations[PR] department 広報部	4 advertising agency 広告代理店
5 design デザイン	6 copywriter コピーライター	7 public relations[PR] 広報活動	8 advertising 広告，宣伝（すること）
9 press release プレスリリース	10 banner バナー広告	11 advertisement 広告，宣伝	12 publicity 注目度
13 exposure マスコミに取り上げられること，露出	14 sale 発売	15 visibility 認知度，注目度	16 brand ブランド
17 brand awareness ブランド認知	18 brand equity ブランド資産	19 product differentiation 製品差別化	

10. 宣伝・広報

✴Advertisement「広告, 宣伝」

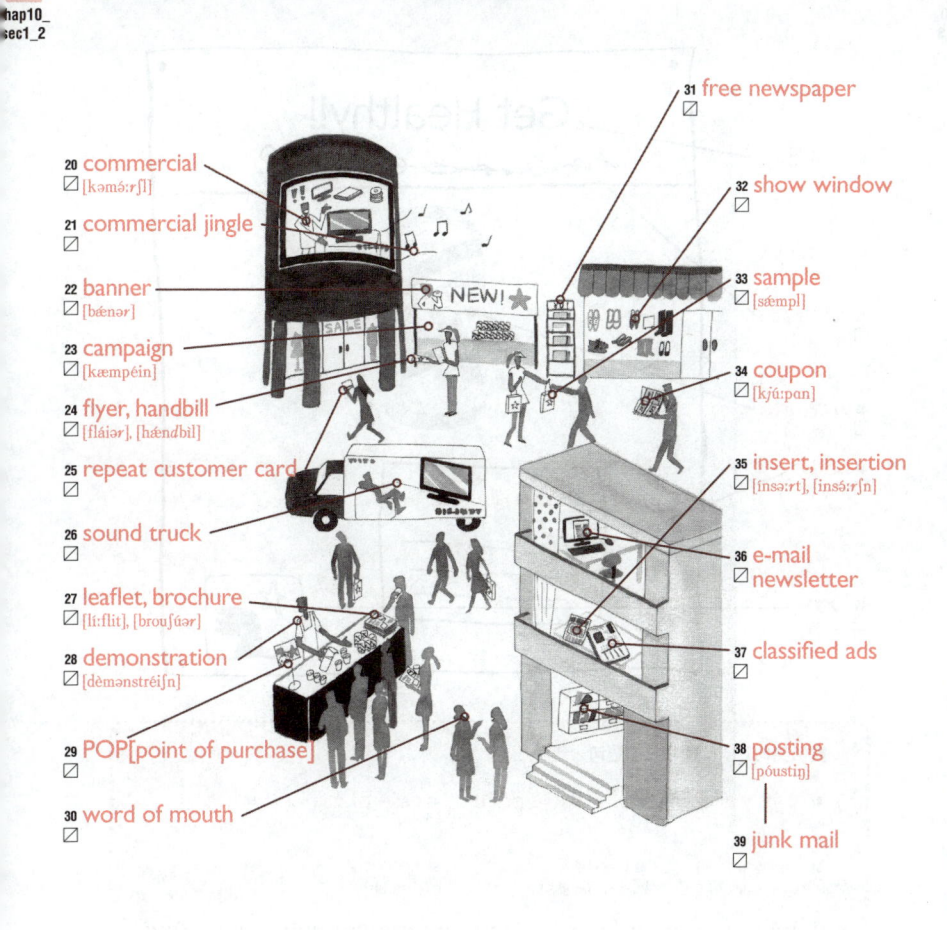

- 20 commercial [kəmə́ːrʃl]
- 21 commercial jingle
- 22 banner [bǽnər]
- 23 campaign [kæmpéin]
- 24 flyer, handbill [fláiər], [hǽndbil]
- 25 repeat customer card
- 26 sound truck
- 27 leaflet, brochure [líːflit], [brouʃúər]
- 28 demonstration [dèmənstréiʃn]
- 29 POP [point of purchase]
- 30 word of mouth
- 31 free newspaper
- 32 show window
- 33 sample [sǽmpl]
- 34 coupon [kjúːpɑn]
- 35 insert, insertion [ínsəːrt], [insə́ːrʃn]
- 36 e-mail newsletter
- 37 classified ads
- 38 posting [póustiŋ]
- 39 junk mail

20 commercial コマーシャル	21 commercial jingle コマーシャルソング	22 banner 横断幕	23 campaign キャンペーン
24 flyer, handbill 宣伝ビラ	25 repeat customer card ポイントカード	26 sound truck 宣伝カー	27 leaflet, brochure パンフレット
28 demonstration 実演販売	29 POP [point of purchase] ポップ	30 word of mouth 口コミ	31 free newspaper フリーペーパー
32 show window ショーウィンドー	33 sample 見本品, サンプル	34 coupon クーポン	35 insert, insertion 折り込み広告
36 e-mail newsletter メールマガジン	37 classified ads 新聞広告	38 posting ポスティング	39 junk mail ダイレクトメール

Poster「ポスター」

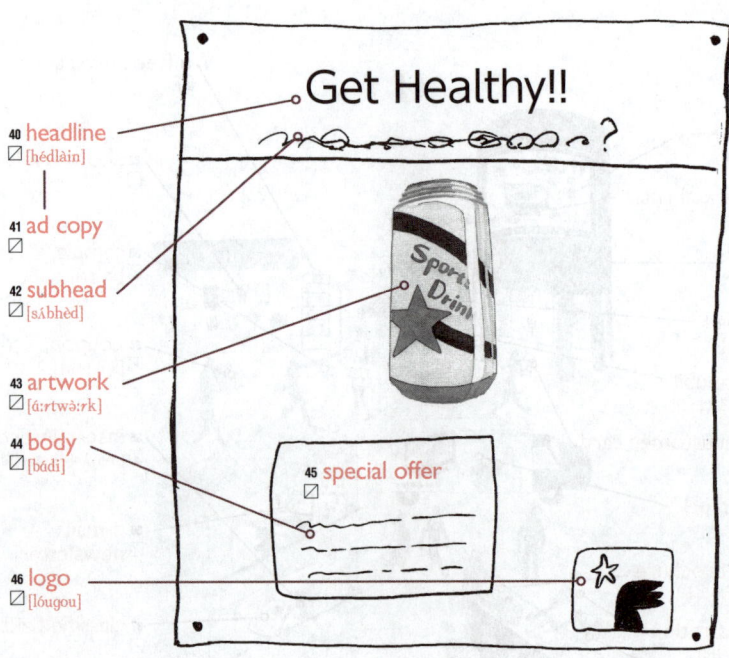

40 headline [hédlàin]
41 ad copy
42 subhead [sʌ́bhèd]
43 artwork [ɑ́ːrtwə̀ːrk]
44 body [bɑ́di]
45 special offer
46 logo [lóugou]

宣伝文句でよく使われる語句

47 high quality
48 affordable price
49 ease of use
50 fresh [fréʃ]
51 memorable [mémərəbl]
52 handmade [hǽndméid]
53 colorful [kʌ́lərfl]
54 friendly [fréndli]

40 headline 見出し	**41** ad copy 宣伝文句	**42** subhead 小見出し	**43** artwork アートワーク，図版
44 body 本文	**45** special offer 特別提供	**46** logo ロゴ	**47** high quality 高品質
48 affordable price 手ごろな価格	**49** ease of use 使いやすさ	**50** fresh 新鮮な	**51** memorable 印象的な
52 handmade 手作りの	**53** colorful 色彩に富んだ，カラフルな	**54** friendly 〜に優しい，親切な	

10. 宣伝・広報

✳ Press[Media] conference 「記者会見」

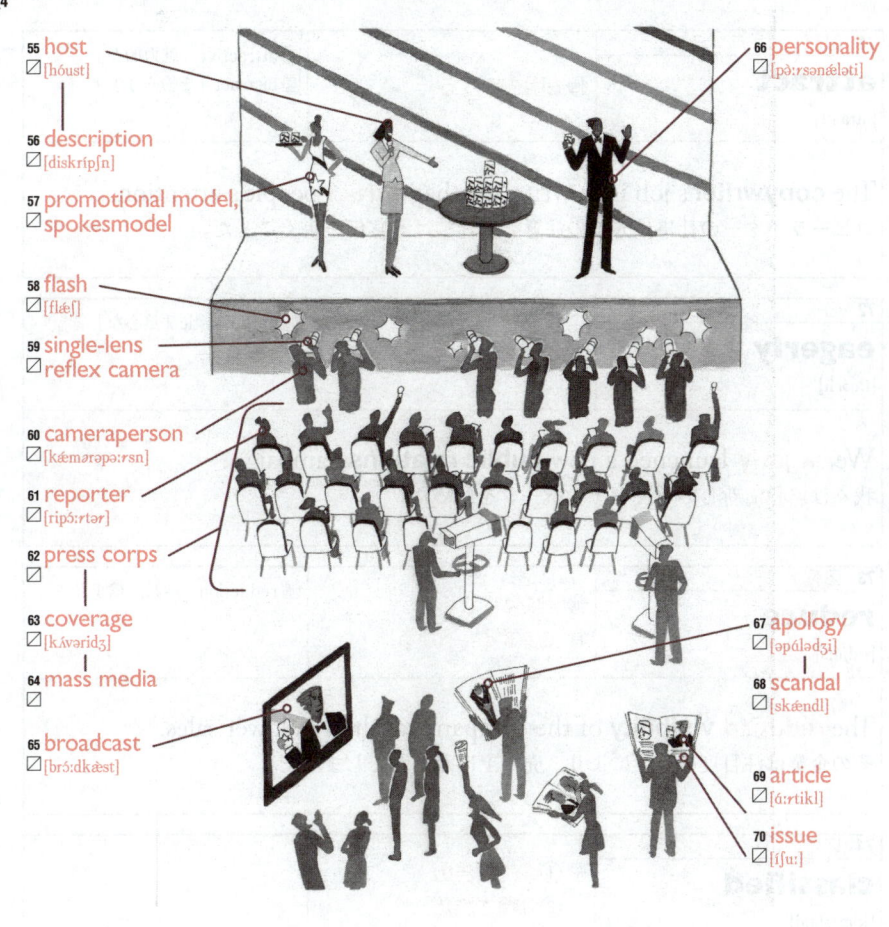

- 55 host [hóust]
- 56 description [dɪskrípʃn]
- 57 promotional model, spokesmodel
- 58 flash [flǽʃ]
- 59 single-lens reflex camera
- 60 cameraperson [kǽmərəpɚːrsn]
- 61 reporter [rɪpɔ́ːrtɚr]
- 62 press corps
- 63 coverage [kʌ́vərɪdʒ]
- 64 mass media
- 65 broadcast [brɔ́ːdkæst]
- 66 personality [pɚ̀ːrsənǽləti]
- 67 apology [əpɑ́lədʒi]
- 68 scandal [skǽndl]
- 69 article [ɑ́ːrtɪkl]
- 70 issue [íʃuː]

55	host （テレビ番組などの）司会者	56	description 説明	57	promotional model, spokesmodel キャンペーンガール	58	flash フラッシュ
59	single-lens reflex camera 一眼レフカメラ	60	cameraperson カメラマン	61	reporter 記者	62	press corps 記者団
63	coverage 取材	64	mass media マスコミ，マスメディア	65	broadcast 放送	66	personality 著名人，タレント
67	apology 謝罪	68	scandal 不祥事	69	article 記事	70	issue 刊行物

Section 2　例文で覚える！

71. attract [ətrǽkt]
他 を引きつける
派 attractive「魅力的な」
反 distract「を紛らす」

The **copywriter**'s job is to write ads that **attract** people's attention.
コピーライターの仕事は人々の注意を引きつける宣伝を書くことだ。

72. eagerly [íːɡərli]
副 熱心に
関 enthusiastic「熱心な」

We **eagerly** launched a new **public relations** campaign.
我々は熱心に新しいPRキャンペーンを始めた。

73. reduce [ridjúːs]
他 を減少させる
自 減少する，下がる
派 reduction「削減，縮小」

The **reduced visibility** of the company resulted in lower sales.
その企業は注目度の低下により，売り上げが落ちてしまった。

74. classified [klǽsəfàid]
形 ①案内広告の
　 ②分類された

The paper carries a lot of **classified advertising** every day.
その新聞は毎日多くの案内広告を掲載している。

75. unveil [ʌnvéil]
他 を公にする
類 reveal

The **new item** was **unveiled** at the beginning of this month.
その新商品は今月の初めに発表された。

10. 宣伝・広報

76 top-selling [tápsèliŋ]
形 売れ行き第1位の
関 best-selling「ベストセラーの」

This has been a **top-selling** brand for many years.
こちらは長年にわたり売れ行き第1位のブランドです。

77 media [míːdiə]
名 マスコミ機関
関 the press「報道機関」

More **media** exposure is necessary.
マスコミ機関にもっと取り上げられることが必要だ。

78 modern [mádərn]
形 現代風の, 現代の
反 old-fashioned「旧式の, 流行遅れの」

We chose this furniture because of its **modern** design.
私たちは現代的なデザインなので，この家具を選んだ。

79 aim [éim]
他 を目指す
名 目標
派 aimless「目的のない」

This **advertisement** is **aimed** at people aged 50 and older.
この広告は50歳以上の人に向けられている。

80 a member of
～の一員

I am **a member of** the public relations department.
私は広報部の一員です。

― 199 ―

81	**decorate** [dékərèit]	他 を飾る	類 embellish

Colorful **banners decorated** the front of the building.
色とりどりの横断幕が建物の正面を飾っていた。

82	**take place**	自 行われる, 開催される	関 hold「を開催する」

Some **demonstrations** are **taking place** on the 5th floor.
5階でいくつかの実演販売が行われている。

83	**intend** [inténd]	他 を意図する	類 plan

This **brochure** is **intended** for use by our sales force.
このパンフレットは当社の販売員向けです。

84	**accumulate** [əkjú:mjəlèit]	他 ①〈ポイントなど〉をためる ②を積み上げる	

I **accumulated** a lot of points with my **repeat customer card**.
ポイントカードでたくさんポイントをためた。

85	**broadcast** [brɔ́:dkæst]	他 を放映する	関 on the air「放送中で」

Broadcasting TV **commercials** is very expensive.
テレビコマーシャルを放映するのはとても金がかかる。

10. 宣伝・広報

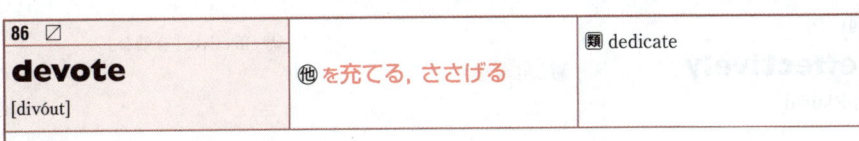

86 devote
[divóut]
他 を充てる, ささげる
類 dedicate

They'll **devote** the profit to spreading their brand.
彼らはブランドを広めるために利益**を充てる**予定だ。

87 finance
[fáinæns, finæns]
他 に融資する, 資金調達する

ABC borrowed money to **finance** a press **campaign**.
ABC 社はプレスキャンペーン**に調達する**金を借りた。

88 valid
[vælid]
形 有効な
反 invalid「無効な」

Your **coupon** will be **valid** till the end of the year.
あなたのクーポンは本年末まで**有効**です。

89 spread
[spréd]
自 広がる
他 を広げる
類 expand

Rumors about a new type of engine quickly **spread** by **word of mouth**.
新しいタイプのエンジンのうわさは口コミであっという間に**広まった**。

90 display
[displéi]
他 を表示する
類 exhibit

Our new products were **displayed** on the signboard.
当社の新製品が, 看板に**表示**されました。

91 effectively
[iféktivli]
副 効果的に
派 effective「有効な」

Artwork is used **effectively** in the book.
アートワークがその本の中で効果的に用いられている。

92 maintain
[meintéin]
他 を維持する
派 maintenance「メンテナンス，維持」

The staff tried to **maintain** high quality.
スタッフは高品質を維持しようと努めた。

93 available
[əvéiləbl]
形 入手できる，得られる
類 obtainable

This is a **special offer available** until tomorrow.
これは明日まで手に入れることができる，特別提供品です。

94 breathtakingly
[bréθtèikiŋli]
副 ①息をのむほど
　 ②はらはらするほど
派 breathtaking「息をのむような」

During your stay at the Star Hotel, you can enjoy the **breathtakingly** beautiful view from your room.
スターホテルに滞在中は，お部屋からの息をのむほど美しい眺めをお楽しみください。

95 distinctive
[distíŋktiv]
形 特徴的な
類 unique

The **logo** must be highly **distinctive**.
ロゴは極めて特徴的でなければならない。

10. 宣伝・広報

96. inexpensive [ìnikspénsiv]
形 手ごろな値段の
関 cheap「安い, 安っぽい, 質の悪い」

Next month, we will feature easy, quick and **inexpensive** recipes.
来月は，簡単で速くて，手ごろな値段でできるレシピを特集する予定です。

97. grab the headlines
大見出しで報じられる, 評判になる
類 hit [make, reach] the headlines

The topic **grabbed the headlines** in both papers this morning.
その話題は，今朝両紙の大見出しで報じられた。

98. impressive [imprésiv]
形 印象的な, 深い感動を与える
派 impress「に感銘を与える, 印象を与える」

TOS will launch an **impressive** line-up of new models for the Auto Expo.
TOSはオートエキスポに向けて，印象的な新型モデルのラインナップを出す。

99. rewrite [rì:ráit]
他 を書き直す

We should **rewrite** the **ad copy** once more.
我々は宣伝文句をもう一度書き直すべきだ。

100. fantastic [fæntǽstik]
形 ①とてもすばらしい ②けた外れの
派 fantasy「空想, 幻想」

Have fun sightseeing on this **fantastic** Tokyo tour!
このとてもすばらしい東京ツアーでの観光をお楽しみください。

101 flavorful
[fléivərfl]
形 風味のある、味のよい
派 flavor「(香りを伴った)味、香料」

Lemon Farm produces the safest and most **flavorful** fruits and vegetables in Wales.
レモンファームはウェールズで最も安全で味のよい青果を生産しています。

102 exhibit
[igzíbit]
他 を展示する
類 display

Old posters were **exhibited** at the museum.
古いポスターがその博物館に展示されていた。

103 full
[fúl]
形 富む、いっぱいの
類 abundant

This product comes with a **full** guarantee.
こちらの商品は完全保証付きです。

104 appear
[əpíər]
自 ①現れる、市場に出る ②のように思える、見える
反 disappear「姿を消す、見えなくなる」

As soon as the product **appeared** in the market, it aroused public interest.
その製品は市場に現れるとすぐに、人々の関心をかき立てた。

105 effective
[iféktiv]
形 ①効果的な ②(法律などが)実施されている
反 ineffective「効果のない」

I'll demonstrate some of our **effective** and inexpensive outdoor items.
当社の効果的で、手ごろなお値段のアウトドア商品をいくつか実演販売しましょう。

10. 宣伝・広報

106 compact
[kəmpǽkt, kámpækt]
形 ①小さくまとまった，小型の
②ぎっしりと詰まった
派 compactly「簡潔に，ぎっしりと」

The PC-MINI is extremely popular because it is **compact** and reasonably priced.
PC-MINI は，**コンパクト**で値段が手ごろなため，大変人気があります。

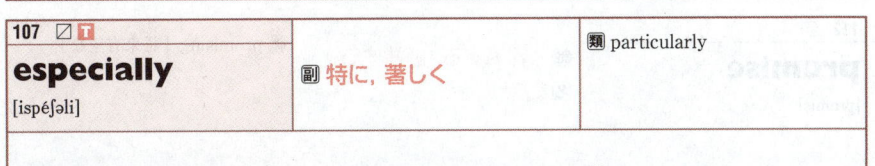

107 especially
[ispéʃəli]
副 特に，著しく
類 particularly

This type of ad is **especially** aimed at young people.
この種の宣伝は**特**に若者に向けられている。

108 eco-friendly
[ìːkoufréndli]
形 環境に優しい
類 earth-friendly

We offer you a truly **eco-friendly** alternative to conventional plastic bottles.
当社は従来のペットボトルに代わる，正真正銘**環境に優しい**商品を提供いたします。

109 await
[əwéit]
他 を待つ，待ち受ける
自 待つ
類 wait for

The company announced it would release a new cell phone, which has been long **awaited**.
その会社は，長らく**待た**れている新型の携帯電話を発売すると発表した。

110 cost-effective
[kɔ́(ː)stiféktiv]
形 費用効果の高い，経済的な
類 economical

The Internet is a **cost-effective** advertising medium.
インターネットは**費用効果の高い**宣伝媒体だ。

— 205 —

111 reasonable
[ríːznəbl]

形 ① (値段が) 手ごろな, 妥当な
② 理にかなった

関 low-priced「安価な」

You can purchase famous-brand PC accessories at **reasonable** prices.
有名ブランドのコンピュータ小物類を**お手ごろ**価格で買うことができます。

112 promise
[prámis]

他 を約束する, 断言する
名 約束

派 promising「将来有望な」

We **promise** you will be amazed at the quality and value of our products.
お客さまは当社の製品の質の高さと価値に驚くでしょう〔驚くこと**を約束します**〕。

113 positive
[pázitiv]

形 ① 肯定的な
② 積極的な

反 negative「否定的な」

Ms. Brown's latest novel received overwhelmingly **positive** reviews in London.
ブラウンさんの最新の小説は，ロンドンで大変**肯定的な**批評を受けました。

114 economical
[ìːkənámikl, èkə-]

形 経済的な, 倹約する

派 economically「無駄なく」

The WH-251 is our most **economical**, high-quality wheel.
WH-251 は，当社の最も**経済的**で高品質の車輪です。

115 worth
[wə́ːrθ]

形 〜の価値がある
名 価値, 値打ち

関 valuable「金銭的価値のある」

These LED light bulbs are truly something **worth** purchasing.
これらの LED 電球は本当に買う**価値のある**ものです。

— 206 —

10. 宣伝・広報

116 **completely** [kəmplíːtli]
副 完全に, 徹底的に
反 incompletely「不完全に」

Making good products and marketing them are **completely** different matters.
よい製品を作ることとそれを市場で売ることは**まったく**別の事柄だ。

117 **aggressive** [əgrésiv]
形 積極的な, 攻撃的な
類 vigorous

Every summer the company conducts an **aggressive** advertising campaign.
毎夏, その会社は**積極的な**宣伝キャンペーンを行う。

118 **emphasize** [émfəsàiz]
他 を強調する, 力説する
類 stress

He **emphasized** the importance of a TV commercial.
彼はテレビコマーシャルの重要性**を強調した**。

119 **marvelous** [máːrvələs]
形 ①驚くべき ②優秀な
類 wonderful

The S-Mobile's **marvelous** design is sure to attract lots of attention.
S-Mobileの**すばらしい**デザインは, きっと多くの人々の注目を集めることでしょう。

120 **reliably** [riláiəbli]
副 ①頼もしく ②信頼できる筋から
関 credible「信用できる」

Bob's Diner has won several awards for its **reliably** good food and service.
ボブズダイナーは, **確実に**よい食事とサービスでいくつかの賞を獲得した。

121 reflect
[riflékt]

他 ① を反映する
② を映す

派 reflection「反映」

The advertising campaign appropriately **reflects** the brand image of the company.
その広告キャンペーンは，会社のブランドイメージを適切に反映している。

122 station
[stéiʃn]

他 を配置する

派 stationary「動かない，増減[変動]のない」

Several **reporters** are **stationed** at the site.
数人の記者が，現場に配置されている。

123 break
[bréik]

自 生じる，起こる
他 を壊す

関 arise「(問題・困難などが)起こる」

An insider-trading **scandal broke** in March this year.
今年の3月に，インサイダー取引に関わるスキャンダルが起きた。

124 due
[djúː]

形 提出期限が来た

関 due to「〜のために」

The summary of your **article** is **due** today.
あなたの記事の要約の提出期限は今日です。

125 publish
[pʌ́bliʃ]

他 を出版する

類 issue

His thesis will be **published** in the next **issue**.
彼の論文は次の号で出版されます。

10. 宣伝・広報

126 fit [fít]
他 に一致する, 適合する
類 suit

It doesn't **fit** your **description**.
それはあなたの説明と一致しません。

127 reveal [rivíːl]
他 を明らかにする, 暴露する
類 disclose

The CEO **revealed** that he would have to take a temporary leave due to his illness.
CEO は, 病気のため臨時休暇を取らなければならないことを明らかにした。

128 consequently [kánsikwèntli]
副 その結果, したがって
類 as a result

Consequently, stock prices began to go up.
結果として, 株価は上がり始めた。

129 prohibit [prouhíbit, prə-]
他 を禁止する
類 forbid

Flash photography is **prohibited** in this museum.
フラッシュ撮影はこの博物館では禁じられています。

130 live [láiv]
形 実況の, 生の

Channel 4 will carry **live coverage** of the scene.
4 チャンネルは, その現場を実況で取材する予定だ。

— 209 —

Section 3　実際の文書で確認！

chap10_sec3

S&C is looking for a new logo!

Our present logo has been familiar to people throughout the country since S & C was established 25 years ago.
It has played a significant role in establishing our **brand equity** and **awareness**.
Now, in accordance with our focus on younger customers,
we will be offering an entire line of **new items** at highly **affordable prices**.
To gain **visibility** among the young,
we wish to change the image of our logo from
"solid and reliable" into "soft and friendly".
So, we are extending this invitation to
anyone who wishes to submit his or her idea for our new logo.
Your **design** should incorporate the following three ideas.

#1 It should be **impressive** and memorable.
#2 It should **reflect** the fashionable design of our products.
#3 It should project a "soft and friendly" image.

NOTE

★ The closing date: April 3rd 2011
★ Please send your **artwork** only through the format found on **our website**: http://www.S_and_C.com/
★ The result of the competition will be announced on our website on November 3rd, 2011.
★ The prizes
The winner of this competition will receive $10,000!
The winner of the second prize will receive a $1,000 travel **coupon**.
The third prize will be a coupon for our products **worth** $100.
And all participants will be awarded special giveaways.

We look forward to your participation in this **campaign**
and to your great idea for our new logo!

We **promise** to provide you with **high-quality** goods as ever.

http://www.S_and_C.com/

10. 宣伝・広報

和訳

S＆Cは新しいロゴを募集しています！

現在のロゴは当社の設立以来25年間,
全国で皆さまに親しまれてきました.
それは我々のブランド資産と認知度を築くのに大きな役割を果たしてきました.
今般,焦点を若いお客さまに合わせることに伴い,
大変お求めやすいお値段の新製品を商品に加えていこうと我々は考えています.
若い方からの認知度を得るために,
ロゴのイメージを「堅実さと信頼性」から
「心地よさと親しみやすさ」へ変更したいと考えています.
そこで,我々は新しいロゴのアイデアを皆さまから募集いたします.
以下の3つの発想をデザインに盛り込んでください.

1　印象的で記憶に残るもの.
2　当社の製品のおしゃれなデザインを思い起こさせるもの.
3　「心地よさと親しみやすさ」のイメージがあるもの.

記

★締め切り：2011年4月3日
★ウェブサイトのフォーマットからのみ作品をお送りください：http://www.S_and_C.com/

★コンクールの結果はウェブ上で2011年11月3日に発表されます.

★賞
　コンクール優勝者には10,000ドル！
　2位は1,000ドルの旅行クーポン券
　3位は100ドル分の当社製品のクーポン券
　さらにすべての参加者に粗品を差し上げます.

このキャンペーンへのあなたのご参加をお待ちしております！
当社の新しいロゴにすばらしいアイデアをお寄せください.

当社は高品質の製品をこれからもご提供することをお約束いたします.
http://www.S_and_C.com/

✳**Review Words**✳

☐ logo ➡ Sec.1-46	☐ brand equity ➡ Sec.1-18	☐ brand awareness ➡ Sec.1-17
☐ new item ➡ Sec.1-1	☐ affordable price ➡ Sec.1-48	☐ visibility ➡ Sec.1-15
☐ design ➡ Sec.1-5	☐ impressive ➡ Sec.2-98	☐ reflect ➡ Sec.2-121
☐ artwork ➡ Sec.1-43	☐ coupon ➡ Sec.1-34	☐ worth ➡ Sec.2-115
☐ campaign ➡ Sec.1-23	☐ promise ➡ Sec.2-112	☐ high quality ➡ Sec.1-47

第11章
営　業

英語で何と言うでしょうか？

```
S&C Inc.

  sales department  general manager
       Yamada Ichiro

  Waseda 1 chome    Phone: (81)3-456-7890
  Shinjuku-ku Tokyo  Fax: (81)3-345-6789
  123-4567 Japan    http://www.S_and_C.com
```

☞ 答えは P.214

Section 1 イラストで覚える！

✴ Sales representative[rep]「営業担当」✴

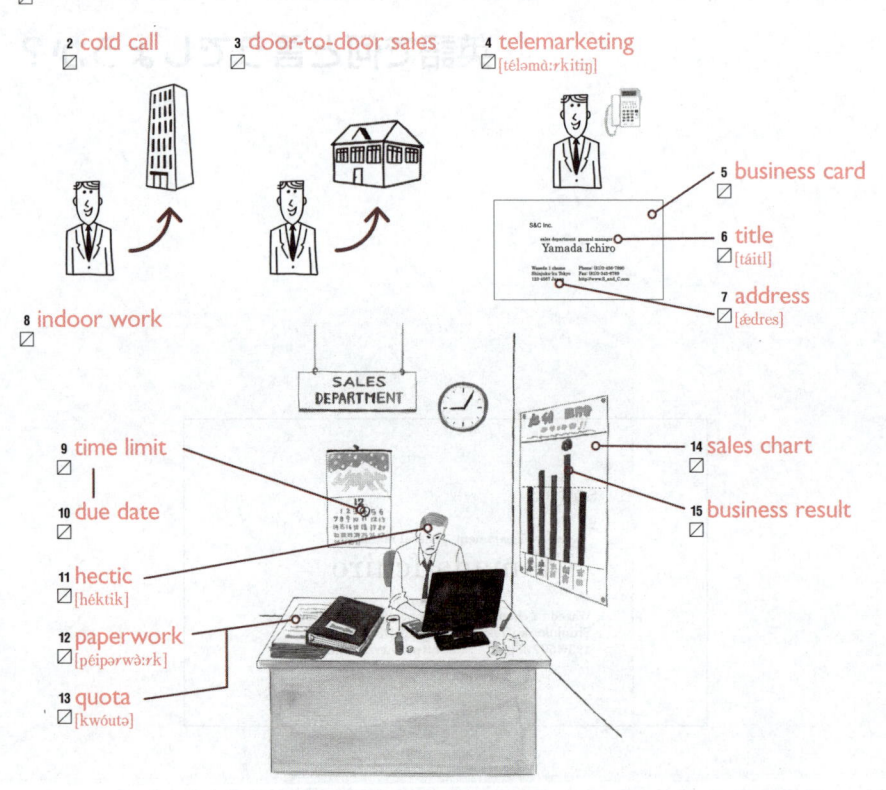

1. outside work
2. cold call
3. door-to-door sales
4. telemarketing [téləmàːrkitiŋ]
5. business card
6. title [táitl]
7. address [ǽdres]
8. indoor work
9. time limit
10. due date
11. hectic [héktik]
12. paperwork [péipərwɜ̀ːrk]
13. quota [kwóutə]
14. sales chart
15. business result

1	outside work 外回り	2	cold call 飛び込み営業	3	door-to-door sales 訪問販売	4	telemarketing 電話セールス
5	business card 名刺	6	title 肩書き	7	address 住所、アドレス	8	indoor work 内勤
9	time limit 時間制限	10	due date 期限日	11	hectic 大忙しの	12	paperwork 事務仕事
13	quota ノルマ	14	sales chart 売上表	15	business result 業務成績		

11. 営業

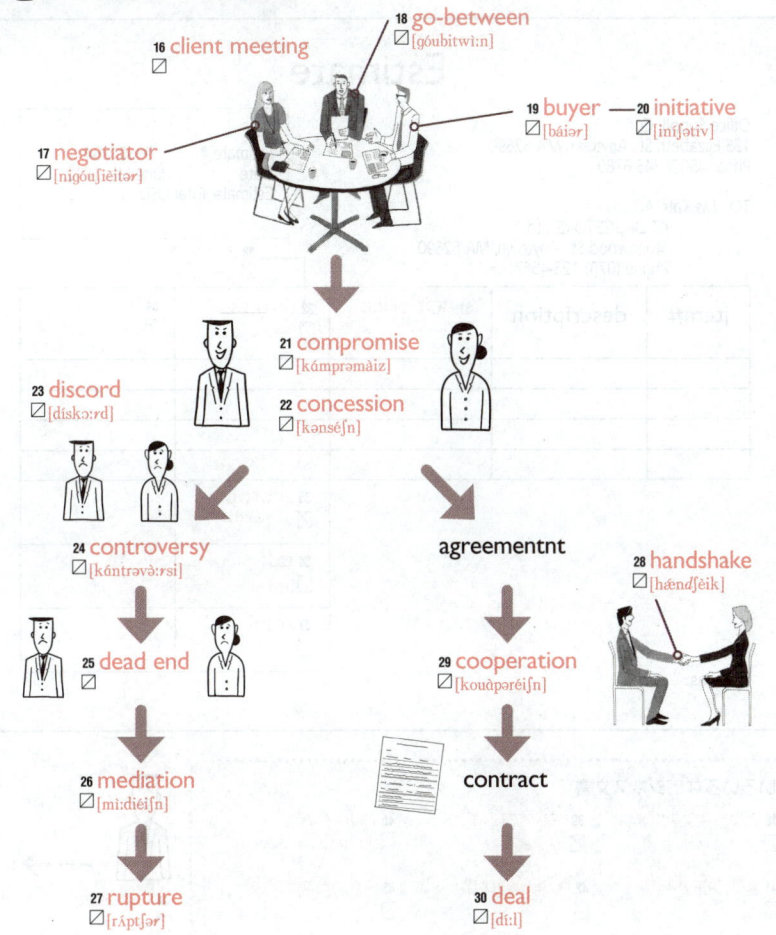

※Negotiation「交渉」

16 client meeting
17 negotiator [nigóuʃièitər]
18 go-between [góubitwìːn]
19 buyer [báiər]
20 initiative [iníʃətiv]
21 compromise [kámprəmàiz]
22 concession [kənséʃn]
23 discord [dískɔːrd]
24 controversy [kántrəvə̀ːrsi]
25 dead end
26 mediation [mìːdiéiʃn]
27 rupture [rʌ́ptʃər]
28 handshake [hǽndʃèik]
29 cooperation [kouàpəréiʃn]
30 deal [díːl]

agreementnt
contract

16 client meeting 依頼人との会合	17 negotiator 交渉者	18 go-between 仲介者	19 buyer 買い手、バイヤー
20 initiative 主導権	21 compromise 妥協	22 concession 譲歩	23 discord 意見の不一致
24 controversy 論争	25 dead end 行き詰まり	26 mediation 調停、仲裁	27 rupture 決裂
28 handshake 握手	29 cooperation 協力	30 deal 取引、契約	

— 215 —

✴Estimate, Quote 「見積もり」✴

Estimate

Office Supply Co.
135 Elizabeth St., Anytown MA 52690
Phone (507) 345-6789

TO Ms Kate Adams
    KT DRUGSTORE, Ltd.
    Stonewood St., Anytown, MA 52690
    Phone (078) 123-4567

Estimate #   00001234
Date   June 5th, 2012
Estimate Total USD $

33 amount
[əmáunt]

item#	description	**31 unit price** [ ]	**32 quantity** [kwántəti]	**34 price** [práis]
			35 subtotal [sʌ́btòutl]	
			36 tax [tæks]	
			37 total [tóutl]	

notes:

いろいろなビジネス文書

38 purchase order
39 statement of delivery
40 invoice [ínvɔis]
41 sign-off sheet
42 request form
43 written apology
44 submission, provision [səbmíʃn], [prəvíʒn]

31	unit price 単価	32	quantity 数量	33	amount 量	34	price 値段
35	subtotal 小計	36	tax 税	37	total 合計	38	purchase order 注文書
39	statement of delivery 納品書	40	invoice 送り状, 請求書	41	sign-off sheet 稟議書	42	request form 申請書
43	written apology 始末書	44	submission, provision 提出				

11. 営業

✳ Contract, Agreement 「契約」 ✳

いろいろな契約

- 45 sales contract
- 46 license agreement
- 47 joint venture agreement
- 48 lease contract

契約書でよく使われる定型表現

- 49 witnesseth [wítnəsiθ]
- 50 whereas [hwèəræz]
- 51 herein [hìərín]
- 52 in witness whereof

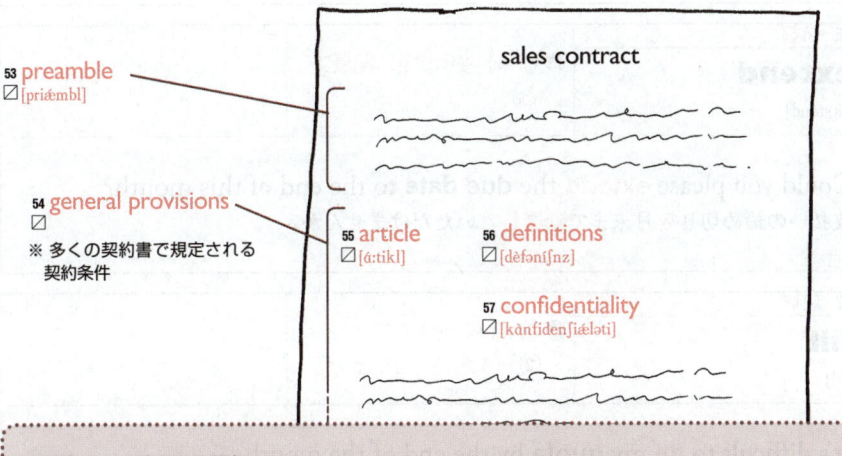

- 53 preamble [príæmbl]
- 54 general provisions
  ※ 多くの契約書で規定される契約条件
- 55 article [ɑ́:tikl]
- 56 definitions [dèfəníʃnz]
- 57 confidentiality [kɑ̀nfidenʃiǽləti]

sales contract

契約書でよく使われる語句

- 58 terms [tə́:rmz]
- 59 termination [tə̀:rmənéiʃn]
- 60 effect after termination
- 61 force majeure
- 62 waiver [wéivər]
- 63 amendment [əméndmənt]
- 64 obligation [ɑ̀bligéiʃn]

45	sales contract 売買契約	46	license agreement ライセンス契約	47	joint venture agreement 合併事業契約	48	lease contract リース契約
49	witnesseth 以下を証する	50	whereas であるのに対して	51	herein この文書に	52	in witness whereof 以上の証として
53	preamble 前文	54	general provisions 一般条項	55	article 条項	56	definitions 定義
57	confidentiality 秘密保持	58	terms 条件	59	termination 解除	60	effect after termination 契約解除の効果
61	force majeure 不可抗力	62	waiver 権利放棄	63	amendment 変更	64	obligation 義務, 責任

— 217 —

Section 2　例文で覚える！

65 succeed [səksíːd]
- 自 成功する
- 他 のあとを継ぐ
- 派 success「成功」

This chart shows whether each project **succeeded** or not.
この図でそれぞれの計画が**成功した**のかそうでなかったのかがわかる。

66 extend [iksténd]
- 他〈期間〉を延ばす，延長する

Could you please **extend** the **due date** to the end of this month?
支払いの締め切り**を**月末まで**延ばして**いただけませんか。

67 fill [fíl]
- 他 ①〈要求〉を満たす
- ②をいっぱいにする

It's difficult to **fill** my **quota** by the end of the month.
月末までにノルマ**を達成する**のは難しい。

68 modest [mάdist]
- 形 控えめな，謙そんした
- 派 modesty「謙虚さ」
- 反 boastful「自画自賛の」

They reported a **modest** sales increase for the product.
彼らはその製品の**わずかな**売り上げ上昇を報告した。

69 involve [inválv]
- 他 ①[be involved in/with で]と関係する，に参加する
- ②を巻き込む
- 派 involvement「巻き込まれること，参加」

He has been **involved** in creating a new incentive program.
彼は新しい奨励プログラムを作ることに**関わっている**。

— 218 —

11. 営業

70 accomplish [əkʌ́mpliʃ] — 他 を成し遂げる, 実現する — 類 achieve

He **accomplished** his main objectives as sales manager.
彼は営業部長としての主たる目標を成し遂げた。

71 take on — 他〈仕事など〉を引き受ける — 類 undertake

Nobody was willing to **take on** such a difficult task.
誰もそんな難しい仕事を引き受けようとはしなかった。

72 routine [ruːtíːn] — 形 決まりきった, 日常の — 類 regular

I spend most of my day doing **routine** paperwork.
私は1日の大部分をお決まりの事務作業をして過ごす。

73 maximize [mǽksəmàiz] — 他 を最大にする — 反 minimize「を最小限にする」

This system is designed to **maximize** energy efficiency.
このシステムはエネルギー効率を最大化するように設計されている。

74 enforce [infɔ́ːrs] — 他〈法律・規則など〉を守らせる, 実施する — 派 enforcement「(法律などの)施行」

Each talk will be 10 minutes, with the **time limit** strictly **enforced**.
各自の話の持ち時間は10分で, 時間制限は厳守です。

— 219 —

chap11 sec2_03

75 acceptable
[əkséptəbl]

形 受諾しうる，満足できる

類 passable

Your sales target for next year is not **acceptable**.
君の来年の売上目標は受諾できない。

76 accurate
[ǽkjərit]

形 正確な，間違いのない

類 precise

The net-income figure for our department was not **accurate**.
我々の部の純利益の数値は正確なものではなかった。

77 calculate
[kǽlkjəlèit]

他 を計算する，算出する

派 calculation「計算」

We **calculated** a rough estimate of the shipping charges.
我々は運送費の概算を算出した。

78 deposit
[dipázit]

他 〈金〉を(銀行に)預ける
名 預金

反 withdraw「を引き出す」

She **deposited** 5,000 dollars in the bank account.
彼女は銀行の口座に 5000 ドル預けた。

79 direct
[dirékt, dai-]

形 直接の

反 indirect「間接的な」

The government is considering putting a **direct** tax on carbon.
政府は炭素に直接税をかけることを検討している。

— 220 —

11. 営業

80 reject [rídʒékt]
- 他〈提案など〉を拒否する, 断る
- 反 accept「を受け入れる」

Our bid on the old painting was **rejected**.
その古い絵に対する我々の入札は却下された。

81 supply [səpláɪ]
- 他 を供給する
- 名 供給
- 反 demand「需要」

The factory **supplies** 1,000 units of its products to ABC Corp. every month.
その工場はABC社に毎月1000ユニットの製品を供給している。

82 estimate [éstəmèit]
- 他〈金額・数量など〉を見積もる, 概算する

He **estimated** the **amount** of time the task would take to complete.
彼はその仕事を終わらせるのにかかる時間を見積もった。

83 Thank you for ~.
〜をありがとうございます。

Thank you for your **cooperation** in meeting the deadlines.
締め切りに間に合うようご協力いただき，どうもありがとうございます。

84 concede [kənsíːd]
- 他 を（正しいとしぶしぶ）認める
- 自 譲歩する
- 反 deny「を否定する」

The president **conceded** that this month's sales are declining.
今月の売り上げは悪化していると社長はしぶしぶ認めた。

— 221 —

| 85 □ **cooperate** [kouápərèit] | 自 協力する, 共同する | 派 cooperation「協力」 |

They have to **cooperate** with each other in order to meet the deadline.
締め切りに間に合うように彼らはお互い協力しなければならない。

| 86 □ **tough** [tÁf] | 形 ①(性格が) 頑固な, 手ごわい
②(問題などが) やっかいな | |

She is well known as a **tough** negotiator.
彼女は手ごわい交渉相手としてよく知られている。

| 87 □ **prospective** [prəspéktiv] | 形 見込みのある, 期待される | 派 prospectively「将来を見越して」 |

The TV commercial successfully attracted the interest of **prospective buyers**.
そのテレビコマーシャルは買い手になる見込みのある人たちの関心を引くことに成功した。

| 88 □ **agree on** | 他 について合意する | |

We made a **compromise** and **agreed on** the price.
私たちは妥協して価格について合意した。

| 89 □ **reconcile** [rékənsàil] | 他 を和解させる | 類 settle |

The differing opinions of the managers were finally **reconciled**.
部長たちの異なる意見はようやく一致を見た。

11. 営業

90 **arise** [əráiz]
(自) 起こる, 生じる
(類) occur

A **controversy arose** over the renewal of the contract.
契約の更新に関してひともんちゃく**起きた**。

91 **offer** [ɔ́:fər]
(他) を提供する, 申し出る
(名) 申し出, 提案

We can **offer** another type of package tour.
別のタイプのパック旅行をご**提供**できます。

92 **sponsorship** [spánsərʃip]
(名) スポンサーであること

The soccer team signed a **sponsorship deal** with a major bank.
そのサッカーチームは大手銀行と**スポンサー**契約を結んだ。

93 **convince** [kənvíns]
(他) を納得させる, 説得する
(類) persuade

He tried to **convince** his client of the reliance of his company's service.
彼は会社のサービスの信頼性を得意先**に納得させ**ようと試みた。

94 **mutual** [mjú:tʃuəl]
(形) 相互の, お互いの
(派) mutuality「相互関係」

They finally reached an agreement through **mutual concessions**.
彼らは**互いに**譲歩してついに合意に達した。

95 persuade
[pərswéid]

他 を説得する

類 convince

It took a few months to **persuade** the board.
委員会を説得するのに数カ月かかった。

96 insist
[insíst]

他 ①だと主張する
②と要求する

派 insistence「主張，強調」

Our boss **insisted** that we should work on the plan as soon as possible.
できるだけ早くその企画に取り組むべきだと我々の上司は主張した。

97 seize
[síːz]

他 を握る，つかむ

類 grab

He **seized** the **initiative** in that negotiation and won the contract.
彼はその交渉において主導権を握り，契約を獲得した。

98 put together

他 をまとめる，組み立てる

We have to **put together** the budget proposal by tomorrow.
我々は明日までに予算案をまとめなければならない。

99 edit
[édit]

他 〈本・映画など〉を編集する

派 editor「編集者」

He was left to **edit** the annual report of the executive board.
彼は取締役会の年次報告書の編集を任された。

11. 営業

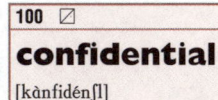

100 confidential
[kànfidénʃl]

形 極秘の，親展の

The entire contents of this file are **confidential**.
このファイルのすべての内容は極秘です。

101 outstanding
[àutstǽndiŋ]

形 ①未払いの
②目立った，傑出した

類 unpaid

Please pay the **outstanding invoice** by the due date.
期日までに未払い請求書のお支払いをお願いします。

102 finish up

他 を完成する

類 complete

She **finished up** her financial report in advance of the deadline.
彼女は締め切り前に会計報告書を完成させた。

103 quote
[kwóut]

名 引用文，引用語句
他 を引用する

類 citation

The slogan is a **quote** from a phrase in the Bible.
そのスローガンは聖書の一節からの引用だ。

104 online
[ánláin]

副 オンラインで
形 オンラインの

You can also fill out the application form **online**.
申請書はオンライン上で記入することもできます。

— 225 —

105 report
[ripɔ́:rt]
動 を報告する

Researchers **reported** that elderly customers were more impressed by the advertisement than younger ones.
調査者の報告によると，高齢の消費者の方が若い消費者よりもその広告に感銘を受けたということだ。

106 staple
[stéipl]
他 をホチキスで留める
名 ホチキスの針

派 stapler「ホチキス」

Print out this document and **staple** it to your expense report.
この文書を出力して，経費報告書にホチキスで留めてください。

107 add
[ǽd]
他 を加える

反 deduct「を差し引く」

Several **amendments** were **added** to the contract.
契約書にいくつか変更が加えられた。

108 protect
[prətékt]
他 を守る

派 protection「保護」

To **protect** your privacy, we will not disclose your personal information without your consent.
お客さまのプライバシーを守るため，お客さまの同意なしに個人情報を開示することはしません。

109 grant
[grǽnt]
他 を認める

類 admit

The management decided to **grant** a one-year contract extension.
経営陣は契約の1年延長を認めることにした。

11. 営業

110 near
[níər]
他 に近づく
類 approach

Final contract negotiations are **nearing** completion.
最後の契約交渉も終わりに近づきつつある。

111 conclude
[kənklúːd]
他 ①を締結する
②を終える，成し遂げる
派 conclusion「締結」

We **concluded** a contract with the trading company.
我々はその貿易会社と契約を結んだ。

112 indefinite
[indéfənit]
形 無期限の

According to the **terms** of the contract, all of the workers are employed for an **indefinite** period.
契約条件によると，従業員は全員雇用期間に期限はない。

113 liable for
に責任がある
類 responsible for

The court found that the company was **liable for** negligence.
法廷は，その会社に過失責任があるとした。

114 bid
[bíd]
自 (競売・入札で) 値を付ける
名 付け値

Our company **bid** on the construction of the bridge.
当社はその橋の建設に入札した。

― 227 ―

115 terminate
[tə́ːrmənèit]

他 を終わらせる
自 終わる

派 termination「終了，（契約などの）満了」

The contract can be **terminated** at any time if both parties agree.
両者が同意すれば，契約はいつでも解消することができる。

116 affix
[əfíks]

他 を添付する，書き添える

類 attach

Make sure to **affix** your signature to the contract.
契約書には必ず署名を書き添えるように。

117 material
[mətíəriəl]

形 ①重要な，本質的な
②物質の

類 important

Such failure will be regarded as a **material** breach of contract.
そのような不履行は契約の重大な違反と見なされます。

118 tentative
[téntətiv]

形 試験的な，仮の

類 temporary

They made a **tentative** agreement on the retail price.
彼らは小売値について仮の合意に達した。

119 dissolve
[dizálv]

他 を解消する，〈固体〉を溶かす
自 （団体・議会などが）解散する

派 dissolution「解約」

The contract did not expire, but was **dissolved**.
その契約は満了したのではなく，解消されたのだ。

11. 営業

120 include [inklú:d]
他 を含む
派 inclusion「算入，含有物」

This contract **includes** lengthy clauses on royalty payments.
この契約書はロイヤルティの支払いに関する長たらしい条項**を含んでいる**。

121 comply [kəmplái]
自 従う，応じる
類 obey

We cannot **comply** with your request.
我々はあなたの要求に**応じる**ことはできません。

122 take effect
自 効果を生じる，有効になる

At the end of this month, the deal will **take effect**.
今月末に，その契約は**有効になる**。

123 law [lɔ́:]
名 法律
派 lawyer「弁護士，法律家」

Compliance with the **law** is expected of all the workers.
すべての労働者に対して**法**の順守が求められている。

124 therefore [ðéərfɔ̀:r]
副 その結果
類 so

Therefore we signed an agreement to continue the construction.
その結果，我々は建設を続ける契約にサインをした。

Section 3　実際の文書で確認！

LICENSE AGREEMENT

This Agreement ("Agreement") is made by and between SoftStore Inc., a Japanese corporation ("SS"), and Global Systems Corporation, a corporation of the United States of America ("GSC"). The Agreement shall be effective as of the 1st day of September, 2010 ("Effective Date"), and the License Agreement, dated April 15, 2005, shall be terminated on the Effective Date of this Agreement.

WHEREAS, SS is in the business of developing advanced 3D computer graphics software and related products; and

WHEREAS, GSC desires to purchase licenses to certain SS software products in order to develop, manufacture, and market computing products incorporating such SS software and technology. SS agrees to grant such licenses to GSC in accordance with the terms and conditions set forth below; and

NOW, THEREFORE, in consideration of the mutual covenants and obligations stated herein, SS and GSC agree as follows:

⋮

— 230 —

和訳

ライセンス契約

この契約（以下「契約」）は，日本法人であるソフトストアー株式会社（「SS」）と米国法人であるグローバル・システムズ・コーポレーション（「GSC」）の間で締結される。契約は 2010 年 9 月 1 日（「発効日」）に発効し，2005 年 4 月 15 日付けのライセンス契約は本契約の発効日に終了する。

よって，SS は先端的な 3D コンピュータグラフィックスのソフトウエアと関連製品を開発する業務を行っており，

よって，GSC は SS の特定のソフトウエア製品のライセンスを購入することで，そのような SS のソフトウエアと技術を組み込んだコンピュータ製品を開発，製造，販売することを望んでいる。SS は，以下に述べられた条項と条件に従い GSC にライセンスを与えることに異存はなく，

従って，ここに述べられた相互の誓約と義務を考慮し，SS と GSC は以下の通り合意する。

⋮

✳Review Words✳

☐ license agreement ➡ Sec.1-46	☐ terminate ➡ Sec.2-115	☐ whereas ➡ Sec.1-50
☐ grant ➡ Sec.2-109	☐ terms ➡ Sec.1-58	☐ therefore ➡ Sec.2-124
☐ mutual ➡ Sec.2-94	☐ obligation ➡ Sec.1-64	☐ herein ➡ Sec.1-51

第 12 章
販　売

英語で何と言うでしょうか？

☞ 答えは P.234

Section 1 イラストで覚える！

♪ *Sales floor* 「売り場」

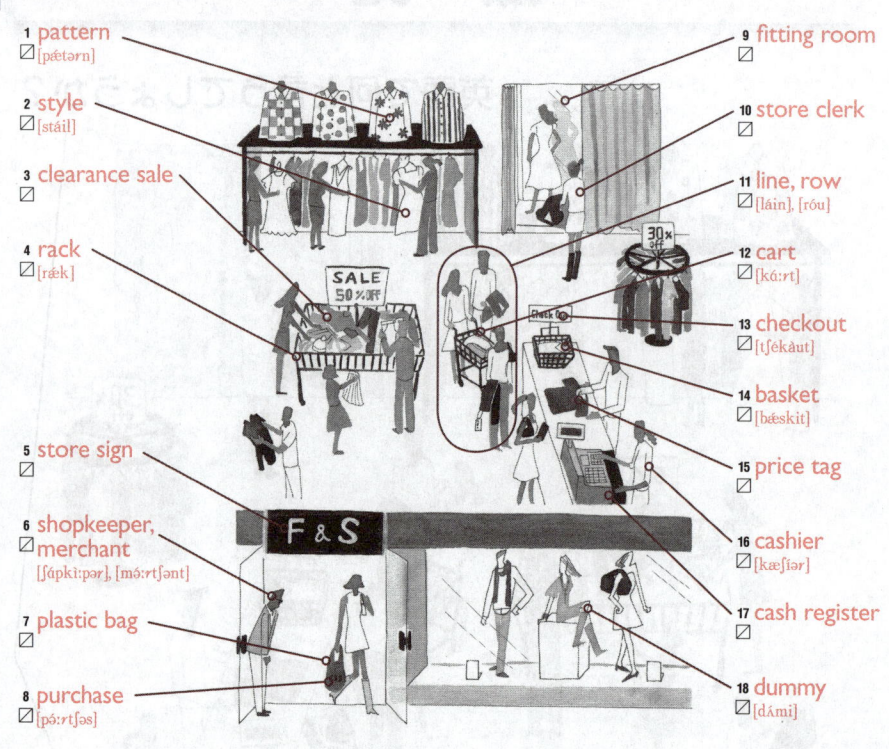

chap12_sec1_1

1. pattern [pǽtərn]
2. style [stáil]
3. clearance sale
4. rack [rǽk]
5. store sign
6. shopkeeper, merchant [ʃúpkìːpər], [mɔ́ːrtʃənt]
7. plastic bag
8. purchase [pə́ːrtʃəs]
9. fitting room
10. store clerk
11. line, row [láin], [róu]
12. cart [kάːrt]
13. checkout [tʃékàut]
14. basket [bǽskit]
15. price tag
16. cashier [kæʃíər]
17. cash register
18. dummy [dʌ́mi]

1	pattern 柄, 模様	2	style 様式, 型, スタイル	3	clearance sale 在庫一掃セール	4	rack 〜入れ, ラック
5	store sign 看板	6	shopkeeper, merchant 小売店主	7	plastic bag ビニール袋, レジ袋	8	purchase 購入品
9	fitting room 試着室	10	store clerk 店員	11	line, row 列	12	cart ショッピングカート
13	checkout 精算	14	basket かご	15	price tag 値札	16	cashier レジ係
17	cash register レジ	18	dummy マネキン				

― 234 ―

12. 販売

✻Complaint「苦情, クレーム」✻

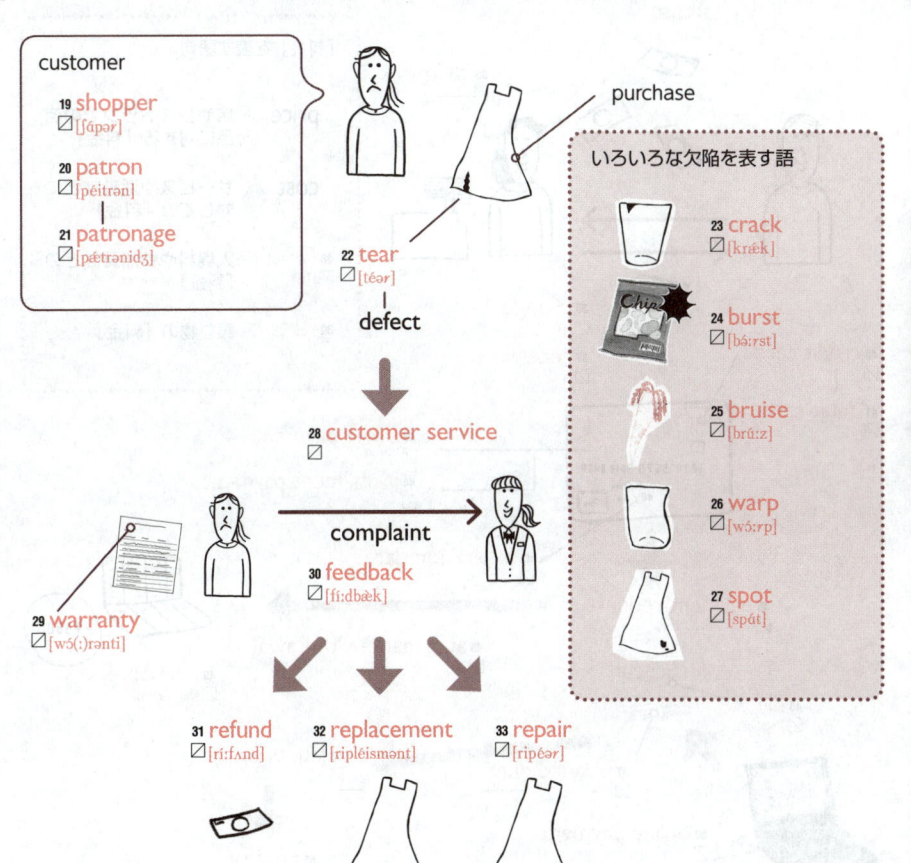

customer
- 19 **shopper** [ʃɑ́pər]
- 20 **patron** [péitrən]
- 21 **patronage** [pǽtrənidʒ]

purchase

22 **tear** [téər]

↓ defect

28 **customer service**

→ complaint

30 **feedback** [fíːdbæk]

29 **warranty** [wɔ́(ː)rənti]

いろいろな欠陥を表す語
- 23 **crack** [krǽk]
- 24 **burst** [báːrst]
- 25 **bruise** [brúːz]
- 26 **warp** [wɔ́ːrp]
- 27 **spot** [spɑ́t]

- 31 **refund** [ríːfʌnd]
- 32 **replacement** [ripléismənt]
- 33 **repair** [ripéər]

19	shopper 買い物客	20	patron お客様	21	patronage 愛顧	22	tear 破れ
23	crack ひび	24	burst 破裂	25	bruise (野菜・果物の)傷み	26	warp 歪み
27	spot しみ	28	customer service カスタマーサービス	29	warranty 保証(書)	30	feedback フィードバック, 消費者の反応
31	refund 払い戻し	32	replacement 取り換え	33	repair 修理		

— 235 —

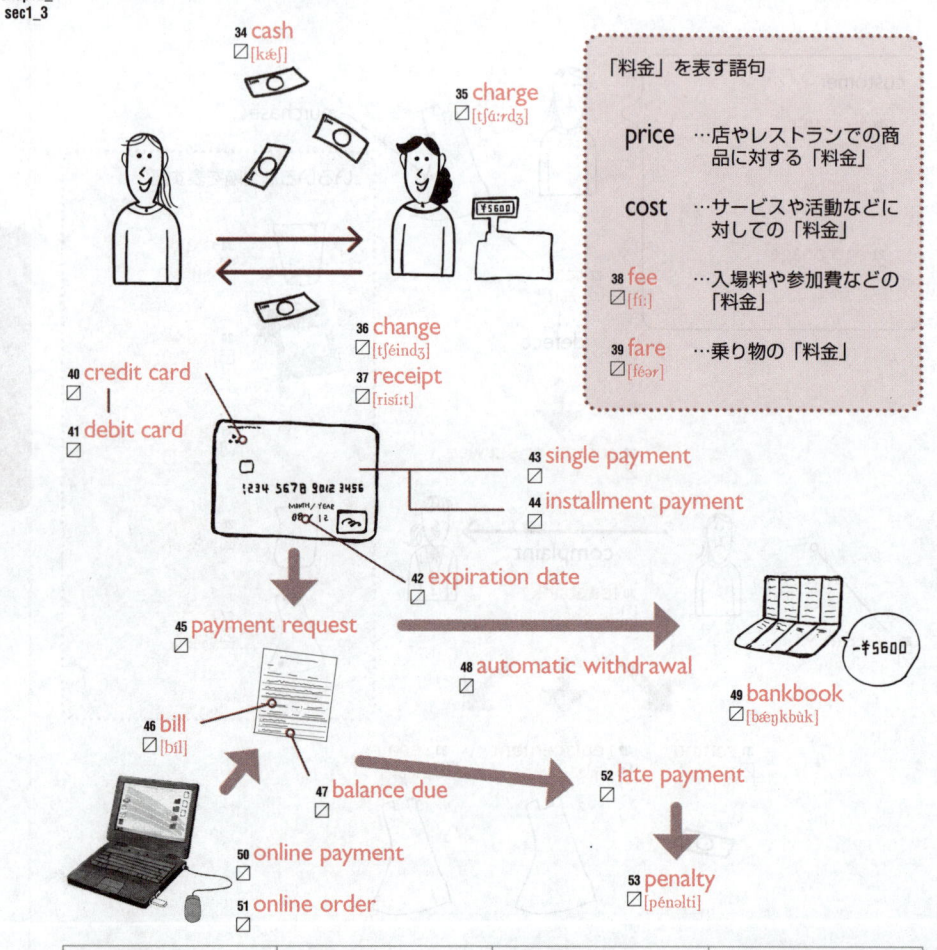

Payment「支払い」

「料金」を表す語句

price	…店やレストランでの商品に対する「料金」
cost	…サービスや活動などに対しての「料金」
38 fee [fíː]	…入場料や参加費などの「料金」
39 fare [féər]	…乗り物の「料金」

- 34 cash [kǽʃ]
- 35 charge [tʃáːrdʒ]
- 36 change [tʃéindʒ]
- 37 receipt [risíːt]
- 40 credit card
- 41 debit card
- 42 expiration date
- 43 single payment
- 44 installment payment
- 45 payment request
- 46 bill [bíl]
- 47 balance due
- 48 automatic withdrawal
- 49 bankbook [bǽŋkbùk]
- 50 online payment
- 51 online order
- 52 late payment
- 53 penalty [pénəlti]

34	cash 現金	35	charge 料金	36	change つり銭	37	receipt 領収書
38	fee 料金	39	fare 乗車料金, 運賃	40	credit card クレジットカード	41	debit card デビットカード
42	expiration date 有効期限	43	single payment 一括払い	44	installment payment 分割払い	45	payment request 支払請求
46	bill 請求書	47	balance due 不足額	48	automatic withdrawal 自動引き落とし	49	bankbook 預金通帳
50	online payment オンラインでの支払い	51	online order オンライン注文	52	late payment 支払遅延	53	penalty ペナルティ

12. 販売

✴Inventory management「在庫管理」✴

store, shop

54 storehouse, warehouse
[stɔ́ːrhàus], [wéərhàus]

55 inventory
[ínvəntɔ̀ːri]

56 in stock

57 out of stock

58 order
[ɔ́ːrdər]

59 order form

60 item
[áitəm]

61 catalog
[kǽtəlɔ̀ːg]

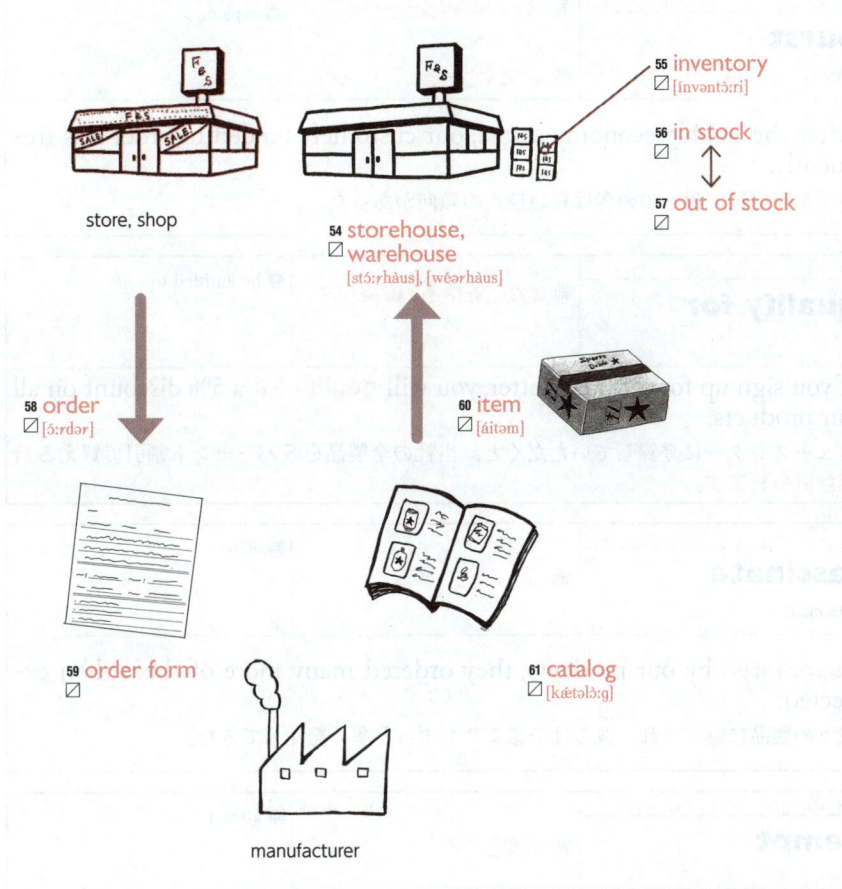

manufacturer

54	storehouse, warehouse 倉庫	55	inventory 在庫品, 品ぞろえ	56	in stock 在庫がある	57	out of stock 在庫切れで
58	order 注文	59	order form 注文伝票	60	item 商品	61	catalog カタログ

— 237 —

Section 2 例文で覚える！

62 burst [bə́ːrst]
- 圓 (管・風船などが) 破裂する
- 他 を破裂させる
- 類 explode

After the bubble economy **burst**, our customers tended to order less frequently.
バブル崩壊後, 我々の顧客は買い控えの傾向があった。

63 qualify for
- 他 の資格を得る, 資格がある
- 類 be entitled to

If you sign up for our newsletter, you will **qualify for** a 5% discount on all our products.
ニュースレターに登録していただくと, 当社の全製品を5パーセント割引で買える資格が得られます。

64 fascinate [fǽsənèit]
- 他 〈人〉を魅惑する
- 類 allure

Fascinated by our products, they ordered many more of them than expected.
我々の製品に魅了され, 彼らは予想よりもずっと多く発注してきた。

65 tempt [témpt]
- 他 を誘惑する
- 類 attract

Retailers are trying every possible means to **tempt shoppers** to spend more.
買い物客をもっとお金を使う気にさせようと, 小売店はあの手この手を試している。

66 loyal [lɔ́iəl]
- 形 忠実な
- 派 loyalty「忠実, 忠誠」

We appreciate your **loyal patronage** and look forward to serving you in the future.
お客さまの忠実なご愛顧に感謝するとともに, これからもお仕えしていく所存です。

— 238 —

12. 販売

67 non-returnable
[nànritə́ːrnəbl]
形 返品できない

Please note that special-order items are **non-returnable**.
特注品は返品不可となっておりますのでご注意ください。

68 formal
[fɔ́ːrml]
形 フォーマルな，正式な

反 informal「略式の，くだけた」

This **style** of shirt can be worn on casual as well as **formal** occasions.
このスタイルのシャツでしたら，フォーマルでもカジュアルでも着ていただけます。

69 launch
[lɔ́ːntʃ, lɑ́ːntʃ]
他 を始める
名 開始

類 embark

The company announced it will **launch** a new line of LED products.
その会社は，LED 製品の新しいラインナップを発売すると発表した。

70 high-tech
[háiték]
形 ハイテクの

We are a **high-tech** company producing a wide range of electronic goods.
当社は幅広い電気製品を製造するハイテク企業です。

71 track
[trǽk]
他 を追跡する，たどる
名 (人・動物などが通った) 跡，足跡

Log in to **track** your shipment or view your **purchase** history.
発送品を追跡するか購入履歴を見るにはログインしてください。

― 239 ―

72	**a variety of**	さまざまな〜	

Our handmade rugs come in **a variety of** sizes, colors, and **patterns**.
当店の手作りのじゅうたんは，サイズ，色，柄を各種取りそろえています。

73	**line up**	自 1列に並ぶ	

The **shopkeeper** asked the people waiting to **line up**.
店主は待っている人たちに，列を作るよう頼んだ。

74	**fade** [féid]	自（色などが）あせる	

The letters on the **store sign** have **faded** and the paint is coming off.
店の看板の文字はあせていて，塗料がはがれてきている。

75	**empty** [émpti]	形 空の 他 を空にする	類 vacant

There was no **empty** basket available in the supermarket.
スーパーには空のかごがなかった。

76	**load** [lóud]	他〈荷物〉を積む	反 unload「〈荷物〉を降ろす」

The store was full of women pushing **carts loaded** with food.
店内は食料品を積んだカートを押して歩く女性でいっぱいだった。

12. 販売

77 courteous
[kə́ːrtiəs]
形 礼儀正しい, 丁寧な
類 polite

The sales manager gave me a **courteous** bow at the entrance.
販売部長は入り口で私に丁寧なお辞儀をした。

78 motivate
[móutəvèit]
他 〈人〉に動機を与える, を刺激する
派 motivation「動機」

This will **motivate** the customers to buy our new product.
このことは我が社の新製品の顧客の購買意欲を刺激するだろう。

79 add up
他 を合計する
類 sum up

The **cashier added up** prices with a calculator.
レジ係は電卓で値段を合計した。

80 attempt
[ətémpt]
他 を試みる
名 試み
類 try

He **attempted** to keep calm despite the customer's rude behavior.
彼はその客の無礼な態度にもかかわらず, 冷静でいようと試みた。

81 abolish
[əbáliʃ]
他 を廃止する
類 do away with

Abolishing free **plastic bags** will help reduce plastic waste.
無料のレジ袋をやめればプラスチックごみの減量に役立つ。

82 store
[stɔ́:r]

他 を貯蔵する
名 店

類 keep

Thirty bottles of wine can be **stored** in this **rack**.
このラックはワインボトルを 30 本貯蔵することができる。

83 recommend
[rèkəménd]

他 を勧める

派 recommendation「推薦」

We **recommend** that you purchase both software programs.
両方のソフトウエアプログラムを購入されることをお勧めします。

84 reimburse
[rì:imbə́:rs]

他〈人〉に返済する，弁償する

派 reimbursement「返済」

We would **reimburse** you for any damages incurred.
私どもはお客さまが被られたあらゆる損失を弁償致します。

85 automotive
[ɔ̀:təmóutiv]

形 自動車の

We deal in all kinds of **automotive repair** tools.
当店はあらゆる自動車修理用工具を扱っています。

86 advise
[ədváiz]

他 ①に忠告する，勧める
　②を通知する

派 advice「忠告」

We would **advise** you to clean the filter once a month.
月に一度，フィルターを掃除することをお勧めします。

12. 販売

87 undertake [ʌ̀ndərtéik]
他 に着手する, を行う
類 start

The company **undertook** an extensive customer survey, involving over 100,000 customers.
その会社は, 10万人以上を対象とする大規模な顧客調査を実施した。

88 support [səpɔ́ːrt]
名 支持
他 を支持する
派 supporter「支持者」

The company won customer **support** by extending its product **warranty** to three years.
その会社は製品保証を3年に延長して顧客の支持を獲得した。

89 claim [kléim]
他 ①を主張する
②を要求する, 請求する

He **claimed** the repair should be done at no cost to him.
彼は無料で修理がなされるべきだと主張した。

90 excessive [iksésiv]
形 度を超えた, 法外な
派 excessively「過度に」

She was totally upset about the customer's **excessive** demands.
彼女はその客の度を超えた要求に完全にうろたえた。

91 resolve [rizálv]
他〈問題・困難など〉を解決する
名 決心
類 solve

Our maintenance staff will quickly **resolve** any problem with the equipment.
当社のメンテナンススタッフがその装置のどんな問題も早急に解決致します。

92 follow up
他 に続いて行う

I **followed up** my apology call with a visit.
私はおわびの電話をし，それ**に続いて**訪問をした。

93 expose
[ikspóuz]

他 ①を（日光・風雨などに）さらす
②を暴露する

反 hide「を隠す」

The insurance is invalid if the device is **exposed** to the sun.
その機器を日光に**さらした**場合，保証は無効です。

94 24 hours a day
1日24時間

You can call our customer service **24 hours a day**.
当社のカスタマーサービスは24時間無休で電話を受け付けています。

95 in need of
〜が必要で

Your tires are almost worn out and **in need of** immediate **replacement**.
タイヤがほとんど擦り切れていますから，すぐに交換**が必要**です。

96 purchase
[pə́ːrtʃəs]

他 を購入する
名 購入

類 buy

Thanks for **purchasing** a subscription to our paper.
私どもの新聞を**購読**くださりありがとうございます。

12. 販売

97 withstand
[wiθstǽnd, wið-]
⑩ に耐える

The product isn't designed to **withstand** extremely low temperatures.
その製品は極端な低温に耐えるようには設計されていません。

98 be flooded with
〜が殺到している
関 crowded「込み合った」

The company **is flooded with** complaints about their defective product.
欠陥品に関する苦情がその会社に殺到している。

99 ensure
[inʃúər]
⑩ ①を確保する
②を保証する、確実にする
類 assure

To **ensure** safety, always store this product out of the reach of children.
安全を確保するため、この商品は常にお子さまの手の届かない場所に保管してください。

100 I regret to inform you that
残念ながら〜です
関 I'm afraid to say「残念ながら〜です」

I regret to inform you that the warranty period has expired.
保証期間は残念ながら過ぎています。

101 complain
[kəmpléin]
⑩ であると不満を言う、訴える
⾃ 不満を言う、訴える
派 complaint「クレーム」

He **complained** that our staff's service was poor.
彼は我々のスタッフのサービスが悪いと苦情を言った。

102 satisfy
[sǽtisfài]

他 ① を満足させる, 納得させる
② 〈義務など〉を履行する

派 satisfaction「満足」

I am sure our after-sale service will **satisfy** you.
私どものアフターサービスに満足していただけると確信致しております。

103 restore
[ristɔ́ːr]

他 を回復する

類 revive

We have to improve the quality of our services to **restore** customer satisfaction.
顧客の満足を回復するため, サービスの質を向上させなければならない。

104 cover
[kʌ́vər]

他 をまかなう, 補償する

関 compensate「(損失などを)償う」

This auto insurance policy also **covers** damage to rental cars.
この自動車保険はレンタカーの損害も補償する。

105 incur
[inkə́ːr]

他 〈損害など〉を被る

We will compensate you for any additional cost **incurred**.
あなたの負ったいかなる追加の費用も補償致します。

106 dent
[dént]

名 へこみ, 減少
他 をへこませる

関 make a dent in「に影響を与える」

Several small **dents** were found on the surface.
表面に数カ所の小さなへこみが認められた。

— 246 —

12. 販売

107 favorable [féivərəbl]
形 好意的な
反 unfavorable「好意的でない」

Customer **feedback** on our new product has been **favorable** so far.
我が社の新製品に対する顧客の反応はこれまでのところ好意的だ。

108 deal with
他 を扱う, 処理する
類 handle「を扱う」

We need more hands to **deal with** customer requests more quickly.
顧客の要望をもっと迅速に処理するためにはもっと人手が必要だ。

109 in advance
副 前もって, あらかじめ
類 beforehand

Please register for the convention at least three days **in advance**.
少なくとも3日前までに大会に登録してください。

110 credit [krédit]
名 掛け, クレジット
派 creditable「称賛に値する」

A debit card has nothing to do with **credit**; you can't spend more than you have in your account.
デビットカードはクレジットとは関係ない。口座にある以上のお金を使うことはできない。

111 authentic [ɔːθéntik]
形 本物の, 信頼できる
派 authenticity「信頼性」
反 fake「偽物の」

He examined whether the signature was **authentic** or not.
彼はそのサインが本物であるかどうか調べた。

— 247 —

112 demand [dimǽnd]

他 を要求する
名 要求, 請求

類 request

The company **demanded** advance payment for the material.
その会社は材料の前払い**を要求した**。

113 pass [pǽs]

他 を過ぎる

You can't use these gift certificates. They have **passed** their **expiration date**.
この商品券は使えません。有効期限**を過ぎ**ています。

114 waive [wéiv]

他 〈権利など〉を放棄する

類 renounce

We will **waive** setup **fees** until the end of the month.
今月末までセットアップ料金**はいただきません**。

115 expire [ikspáiər]

自 期限切れになる, 失効する

派 expiration「(期限・任期などの)満了」

We will send you a new **credit card** before your old one **expires**.
古いクレジットカードが**期限切れになる**前に新しいカードをお送りします。

116 consume [kəns(j)úːm]

他 を消費する, 使い果たす
自 消費される, 尽きる

派 consumption「消費」

This new procedure will allow customers to **consume** less time placing **orders**.
この新しい方法によって, 客はより短時間で注文できるようになるだろう〔より短い時間**を**注文に**消費する**だろう〕。

12. 販売

117 likely
[láikli]

- 形 ありそうな, 起こりそうな
- 副 たぶん, おそらく
- 反 unlikely「ありそうもない」

I guess this model is the most **likely** to become popular.
この型が最も人気が出そうだと推測する。

118 total
[tóutl]

- 形 全部の, 完全な
- 他 総計して(ある数)になる
- 類 sum

The **total** number of items ordered is 100 more than we expected.
注文総数は予想していたより100多い。

119 combine
[kəmbáin]

- 他 を同時に行う, 結合する
- 自 結合する
- 派 combination「結合」

We can reduce the cost of delivery by **combining** orders.
注文を同時に行うことで, 我々は配送料を削減できる。

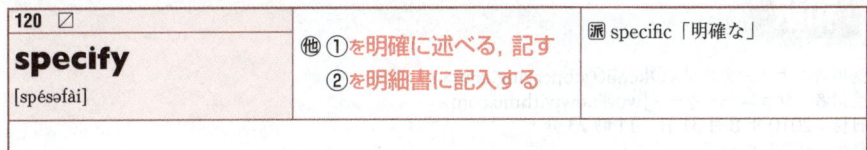

120 specify
[spésəfài]

- 他 ①を明確に述べる, 記す
  ②を明細書に記入する
- 派 specific「明確な」

Those items are **specified** in the document we sent.
それらの品目は弊社がお送りした資料に明記されております。

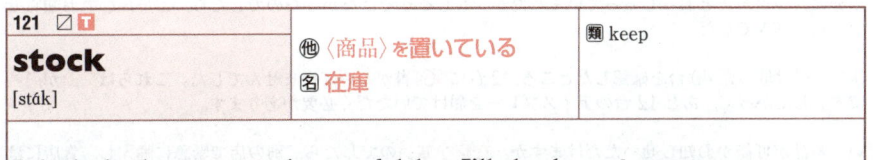

121 stock
[sták]

- 他 〈商品〉を置いている
- 名 在庫
- 類 keep

I don't think we **stock** that model, but I'll check our **inventory**.
その機種は当店に置いていないと思いますが, 在庫を当たってみます。

– 249 –

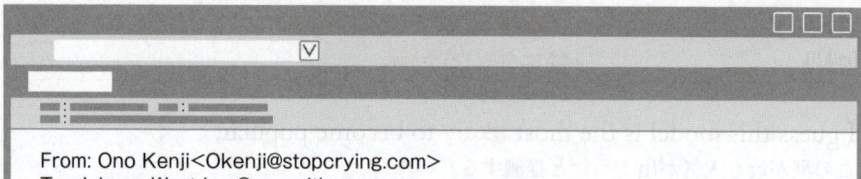

Section 3 実際のメールで確認！

From: Ono Kenji<Okenji@stopcrying.com>
To: Johnny Wu<Jwu@nowwithme.com>
Date: August 31, 2010 11:23
Subject: About Our Order

Dear Mr. Wu
I am writing to inform you that the goods we ordered from your store have not been supplied correctly. First, as for the quantity, we placed an order for 50 LED displays. The consignment arrived today, and we received only 40. You had told me that you had enough in stock, but if that was not the case, you should have let me know in advance.

Secondly, we checked the 40 units we received and found two of them didn't come with a warranty card. They are in need of replacement. Consequently, you'll need to deliver us a total of 12 more displays.

Could you let me know when you'll be able to supply them? If you are out of stock, we'll have to make an emergency purchase at another store and demand a refund from you. I hope you'll resolve the matter as quickly as possible.

Sincerely,
Ono Kenji

和訳

送信者：オノ・ケンジ <Okenji@stopcrying.com>
受信者：ジョニー・ウー <Jwu@nowwithme.com>
日付：2010年8月31日　11時23分
件名：注文について

ウー様
貴店に注文した商品が正しく納品されなかったことをお知らせします。まず，数量についてですが，こちらの注文はLEDディスプレー50台でした。今日荷物が届きましたが，受け取ったのは40台だけです。十分に在庫があるとおっしゃっていましたが，もしそうではなかったのでしたら，あらかじめお知らせいただくべきでした。

次に，受け取った40台を確認したところ，2台に保証書がついていませんでした。これらは交換が必要です。したがって，あと12台のディスプレーを届けていただく必要があります。

いつ納品が可能かお知らせいただけますか。在庫がないのでしたら，別の店で緊急に購入し，貴店には払い戻しを要求しなければなりません。できるだけ早く問題を解決していただきたいと思います。

敬具
オノ・ケンジ

12. 販売

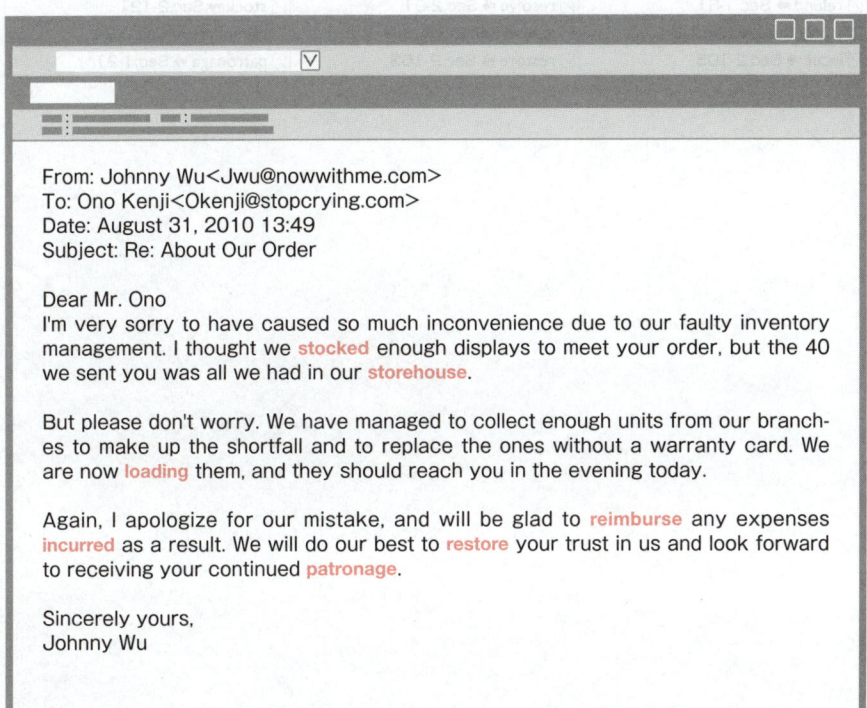

From: Johnny Wu <Jwu@nowwithme.com>
To: Ono Kenji <Okenji@stopcrying.com>
Date: August 31, 2010 13:49
Subject: Re: About Our Order

Dear Mr. Ono

I'm very sorry to have caused so much inconvenience due to our faulty inventory management. I thought we stocked enough displays to meet your order, but the 40 we sent you was all we had in our storehouse.

But please don't worry. We have managed to collect enough units from our branches to make up the shortfall and to replace the ones without a warranty card. We are now loading them, and they should reach you in the evening today.

Again, I apologize for our mistake, and will be glad to reimburse any expenses incurred as a result. We will do our best to restore your trust in us and look forward to receiving your continued patronage.

Sincerely yours,
Johnny Wu

和訳

送信者：ジョニー・ウー <Jwu@nowwithme.com>
受信者：オノ・ケンジ <Okenji@stopcrying.com>
日付：2010年8月31日　13時49分
件名：Re：注文について

オノ様

当店の在庫管理の不備のため御社に多大なご迷惑をおかけし、まことに申し訳ありません。ご注文に応じるだけのディスプレーの在庫があると思っていたのですが、お送りした40台が倉庫にある全部でした。

しかし、ご心配はなさらないでください。不足分を補い保証書のないものと交換できるだけの台数を支店から何とか集めることができました。今積み込んでいるところですので、今日の夕方にはそちらにお届けできると思います。

不手際を再度おわびいたします。そして、この結果生じた費用はすべて弁償させていただきます。お客さまの信頼を回復するために最善を尽くしますので、引き続きご愛顧いただけるようお願いいたします。

敬具
ジョニー・ウー

✴Review Words✴

☐ order ➡ Sec.1-58	☐ in stock ➡ Sec.1-56	☐ in advance ➡ Sec.2-109
☐ warranty ➡ Sec.1-29	☐ in need of ➡ Sec.2-95	☐ replacement ➡ Sec.1-32
☐ out of stock ➡ Sec.1-57	☐ purchase ➡ Sec.2-96	☐ demand ➡ Sec.2-112
☐ refund ➡ Sec.1-31	☐ resolve ➡ Sec.2-91	☐ stock ➡ Sec.2-121
☐ storehouse ➡ Sec.1-54	☐ load ➡ Sec.2-76	☐ reimburse ➡ Sec.2-84
☐ incur ➡ Sec.2-105	☐ restore ➡ Sec.2-103	☐ patronage ➡ Sec.1-21

第13章
流　通

英語で何と言うでしょうか？

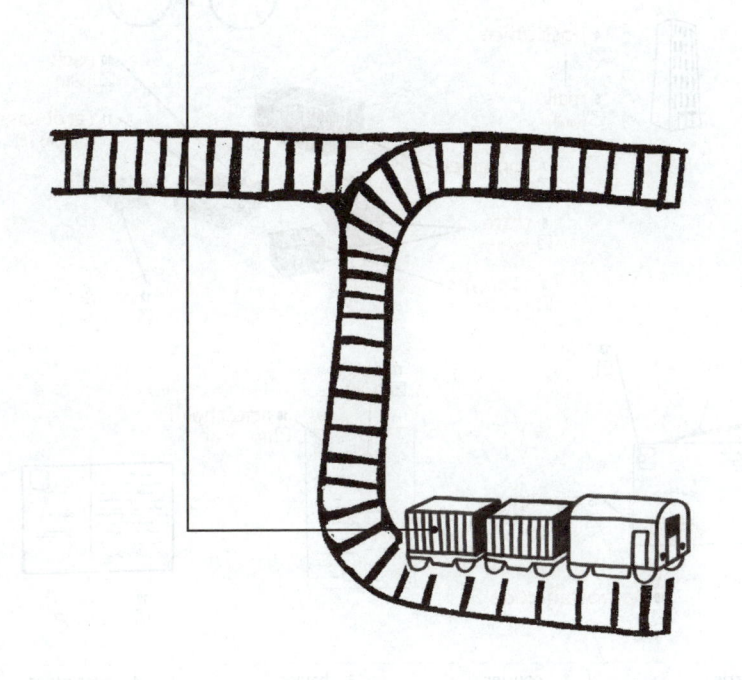

☞ 答えは P.255

Section 1　イラストで覚える！

✴Delivery service「配達サービス」✴

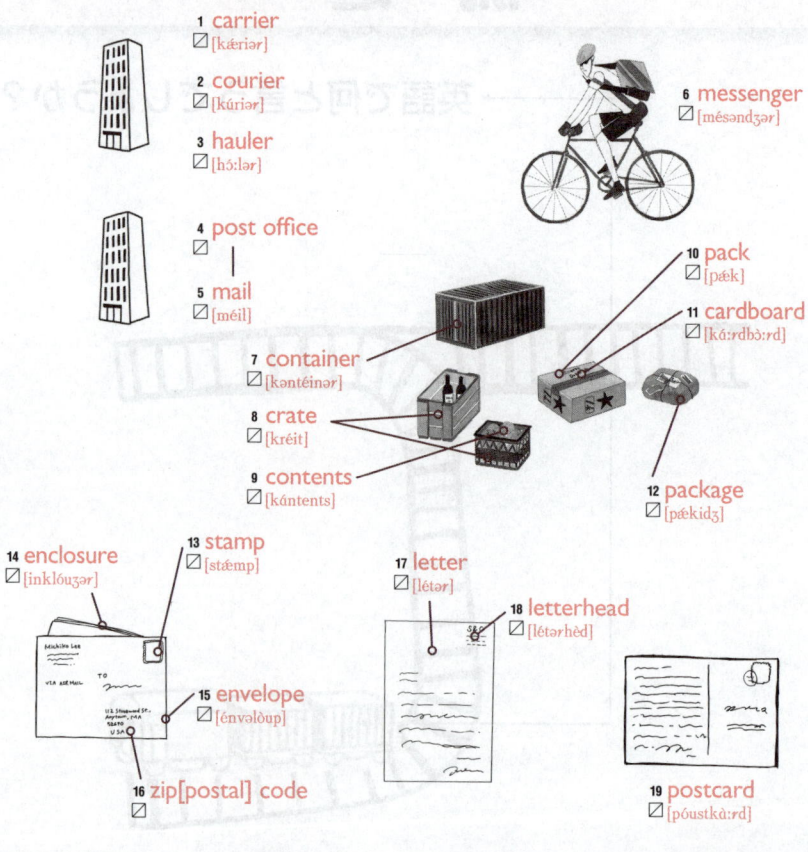

1. carrier [kǽriər]
2. courier [kúriər]
3. hauler [hɔ́:lər]
4. post office
5. mail [méil]
6. messenger [mésəndʒər]
7. container [kəntéinər]
8. crate [kréit]
9. contents [kántents]
10. pack [pǽk]
11. cardboard [kɑ́:rdbɔ̀:rd]
12. package [pǽkidʒ]
13. stamp [stǽmp]
14. enclosure [inklóuʒər]
15. envelope [énvəlòup]
16. zip[postal] code
17. letter [létər]
18. letterhead [létərhèd]
19. postcard [póustkɑ̀:rd]

1 carrier 運送会社	2 courier 宅配業者	3 hauler 運送会社	4 post office 郵便局
5 mail 郵便（物）	6 messenger 配達人	7 container 入れ物, 容器, コンテナ	8 crate 梱包用の箱
9 contents 内容, 中身	10 pack 一箱, 一包み	11 cardboard ダンボール	12 package 小包
13 stamp 切手	14 enclosure 同封（物）	15 envelope 封筒	16 zip[postal] code 郵便番号
17 letter 手紙, 文字	18 letterhead レターヘッド	19 postcard はがき	

13. 流通

✳ Transportation 「輸送」

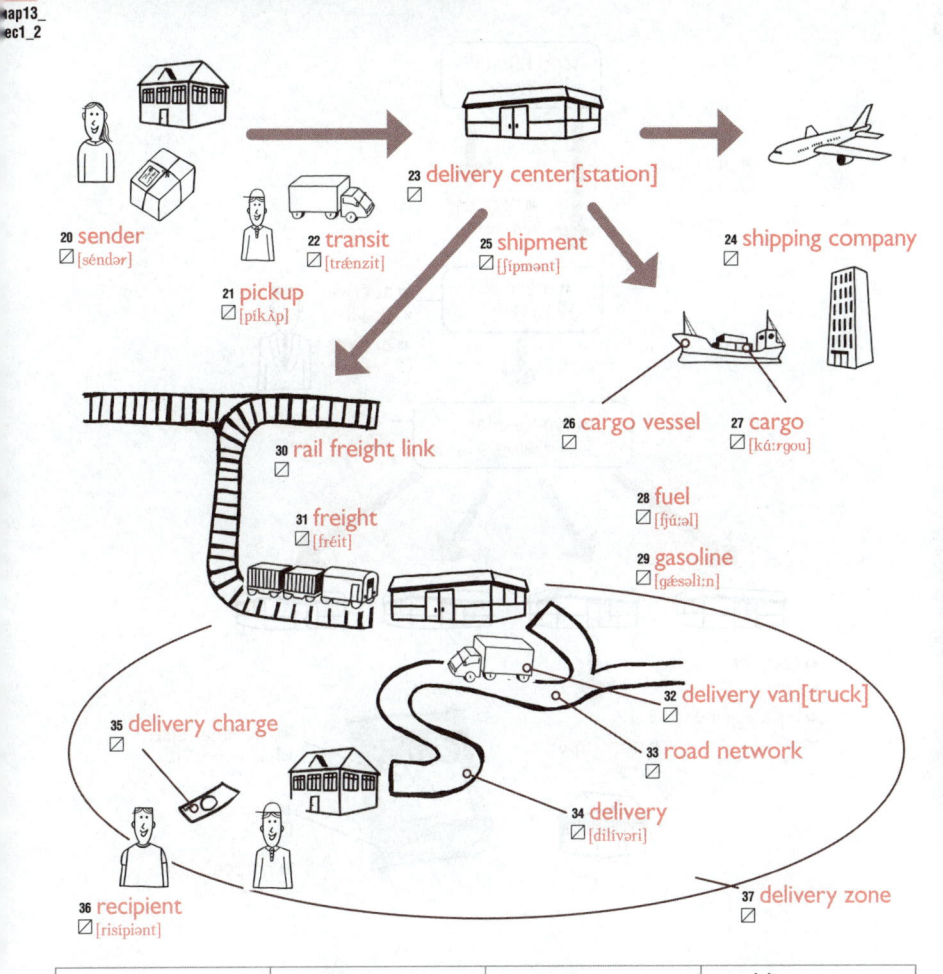

20 sender [séndər]
21 pickup [píkʌp]
22 transit [trænzit]
23 delivery center[station]
24 shipping company
25 shipment [ʃípmənt]
26 cargo vessel
27 cargo [káːrgou]
28 fuel [fjúːəl]
29 gasoline [gǽsəliːn]
30 rail freight link
31 freight [fréit]
32 delivery van[truck]
33 road network
34 delivery [dilívəri]
35 delivery charge
36 recipient [risípiənt]
37 delivery zone

20	sender 送り主	21	pickup 集荷	22	transit 運送，輸送	23	delivery center[station] 配送センター
24	shipping company 船舶会社，海運会社	25	shipment 発送，出荷	26	cargo vessel 貨物船	27	cargo （船・飛行機などの）積み荷
28	fuel 燃料	29	gasoline ガソリン	30	rail freight link 鉄道貨物網	31	freight （貨物の）積み荷，貨物便
32	delivery van[truck] 配送車	33	road network 道路網	34	delivery 配達	35	delivery charge 配送料
36	recipient 受取人	37	delivery zone 配達地域				

Distribution 「流通」

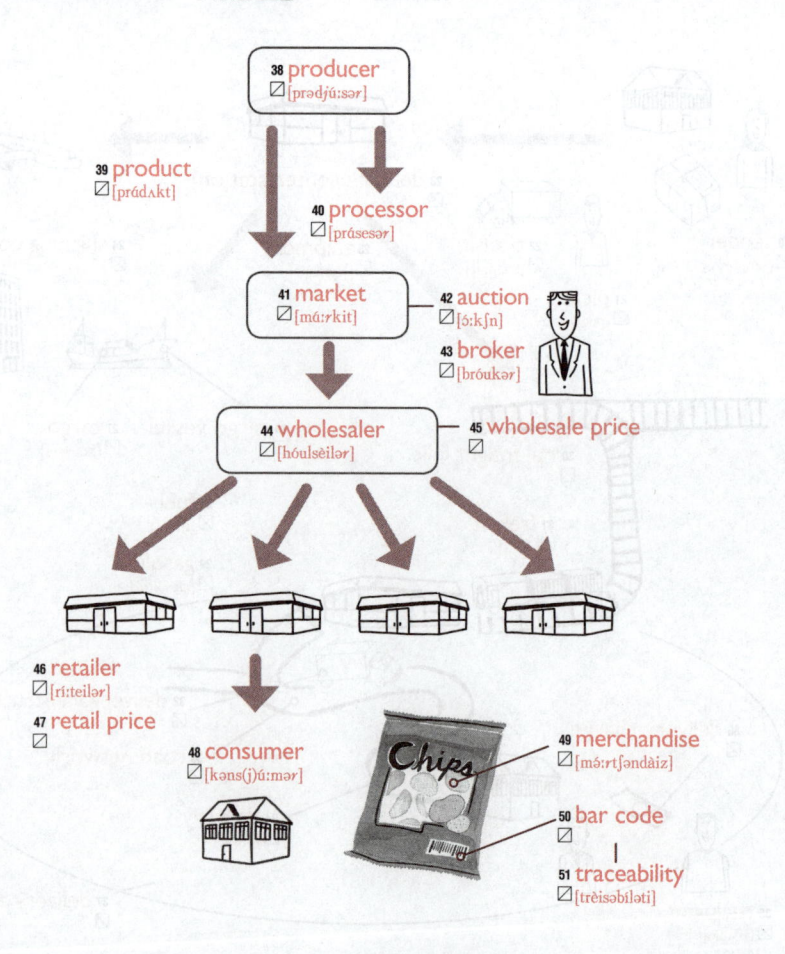

- 38 producer [prədjúːsər]
- 39 product [prádʌkt]
- 40 processor [prásesər]
- 41 market [máːrkit]
- 42 auction [ɔ́ːkʃn]
- 43 broker [bróukər]
- 44 wholesaler [hóulsèilər]
- 45 wholesale price
- 46 retailer [ríːteilər]
- 47 retail price
- 48 consumer [kənsjúːmər]
- 49 merchandise [mɔ́ːrtʃəndàiz]
- 50 bar code
- 51 traceability [trèisəbíləti]

38	producer 生産者	39	product 製品	40	processor 加工業者	41	market 市場
42	auction せり	43	broker 仲買人	44	wholesaler 卸売業者, 問屋	45	wholesale price 卸売値
46	retailer 小売業者	47	retail price 小売値	48	consumer 消費者	49	merchandise 商品
50	bar code バーコード	51	traceability 追跡可能				

13. 流通

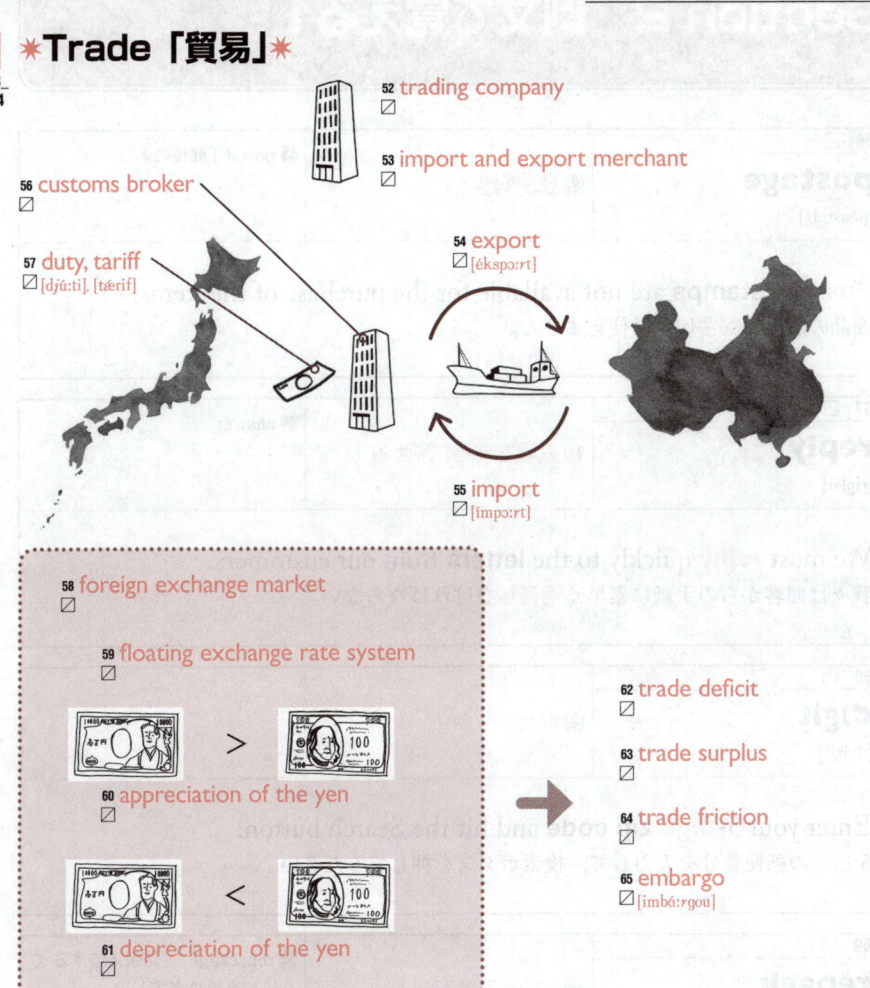

✳ Trade 「貿易」 ✳

- 52 trading company
- 53 import and export merchant
- 56 customs broker
- 57 duty, tariff [djúːti], [tǽrif]
- 54 export [ékspɔːrt]
- 55 import [ímpɔːrt]
- 58 foreign exchange market
- 59 floating exchange rate system
- 60 appreciation of the yen
- 61 depreciation of the yen
- 62 trade deficit
- 63 trade surplus
- 64 trade friction
- 65 embargo [imbáːrgou]

52	trading company 貿易会社	53	import and export merchant 輸出入業者	54	export 輸出	55	import 輸入
56	customs broker 通関業者	57	duty, tariff 関税	58	foreign exchange market 外国為替市場	59	floating exchange rate system 変動為替相場制
60	appreciation of the yen 円高	61	depreciation of the yen 円安	62	trade deficit 貿易赤字	63	trade surplus 貿易黒字
64	trade friction 貿易摩擦	65	embargo 通商禁止				

— 257 —

Section 2　例文で覚える！

66 postage [póustidʒ]　名 郵便料金　関 postal「郵便の」

Postage stamps are not available for the purchase of the items.
商品の購入に郵便切手は使えません。

67 reply [riplái]　自 返事をする，答える　類 answer

We must reply quickly to the letters from our customers.
我々は顧客からの手紙に素早く返答しなければならない。

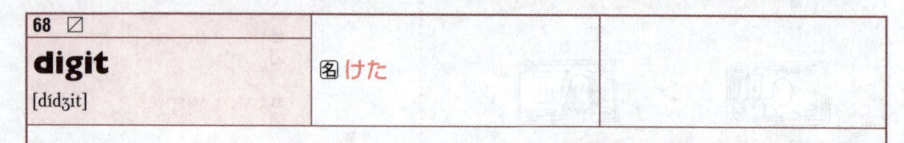

68 digit [dídʒit]　名 けた

Enter your 5-digit zip code and hit the Search button.
5けたの郵便番号を入力して，検索ボタンを押してください。

69 repack [rì:pǽk]　他 を詰め直す　関 repackage「(見栄えのするように) を詰め直す」

It would be better to repack these bottles into another crate.
これらのびんを別の箱に詰め直した方がよい。

70 waterproof [wɔ́:tərprù:f]　形 防水の　関 fireproof「防火の」

This waterproof container is not only useful but also eco-friendly.
この防水容器は役に立つだけでなく環境にも優しい。

— 258 —

13. 流通

71. public [pʌ́blik]
- 形 公共の
- 名 一般の人々
- 反 private「個人の」

Boats are widely used as **public** transportation on this island.
この島では船が公共の輸送手段として広く用いられている。

72. mail [méil]
- 他 を郵送する
- 名 郵便(物)
- 類 post

Please fill out and **mail** the enclosed **postcard** by July 10.
7月10日までに同封のはがきに記入して郵送してください。

73. nationwide [néiʃnwáid]
- 副 全国的に
- 形 全国的な
- 関 worldwide「世界的な」

In recent years this **carrier** has expanded its branch offices **nationwide**.
近年、この運送会社は全国的に支店を拡大してきた。

74. sort [sɔ́ːrt]
- 他 を分類する
- 名 種類
- 類 classify

They **sorted** the **mail** according to the addresses.
彼らは住所ごとに郵便物を分類した。

75. integrate [íntigrèit]
- 他 をまとめる
- 類 gather

When an order contains multiple items, they are **integrated** into one package at the **delivery center**.
注文が複数の品を含む場合、それらは配送センターで1つの箱にまとめられる。

| 76 | unleaded [ʌ̀nlédid] | 形 (ガソリンなどが)無鉛の | 反 leaded「鉛を含んだ」 |

It is expected that **unleaded fuels** will become more popular.
無鉛燃料がもっと普及することが期待されている。

| 77 | fixed [fíkst] | 形 一定の，固定された | 派 fix「を修理する，固定する」 |

Our **delivery charge** is **fixed** and is the same all over Japan.
当社の配送料は日本全国，同一価格で**固定され**ています。

| 78 | guzzle [gʌ́zl] | 他 〈燃料〉を大量に消費する | 類 waste |

This traditional car **guzzles gasoline**.
この旧式の自動車はガソリン**を食う**。

| 79 | up to | | ～まで，～に達して | |

We can deliver **up to** 10 truckloads per day.
1日にトラック10台分**まで**配送できます。

| 80 | during [djúəriŋ] | 前 ～の間に | 類 through |

We will not be held responsible for damage that occurs **during transit**.
運送**中**に生じた破損について，当社は責任を負わないものとします。

13. 流通

81. unload [ʌnlóud]
- 他 〈荷物など〉を降ろす
- 反 load「〈荷物など〉を積む」

The workers **unloaded** the **cargo**.
作業員は積荷を降ろした。

82. express [iksprés]
- 形 速達便の
- 他 〈思想・感情など〉を表現する

We'll send the item you ordered by **express delivery** tomorrow.
ご注文の商品は明日，速達で送付致します。

83. unknown [ʌnnóun]
- 形 不明の

If you receive a package from an **unknown sender**, don't open it.
送り主不明の荷物を受け取ったら，開けてはいけません。

84. widespread [wáidspréd]
- 形 広範囲に及ぶ
- 類 extensive

This country has a fairly **widespread road network**.
この国にはかなり広範囲に及ぶ道路網がある。

85. drop off
- 他 を(車などから)降ろす，(車などで)届ける

Will you **drop off** this parcel at their office on your way?
行きがけにこの荷物を彼らの事務所に届けてください。

86 suppose
[səpóuz]

他 ①[be supposed to *do* で]…することになっている
②だと思う

派 suppposing「もし～ならば」

The samples are **supposed** to be delivered to us by August 25.
見本は8月25日までに当社に届けられる**ことになっている**。

87 waste
[wéist]

名 浪費, 無駄にすること
他 を浪費する, 無駄に使う

派 wasteful「不経済な, 無駄な」

We should reduce the **waste** of packaging materials.
梱包材の**無駄**を減らすべきだ。

88 respectively
[rispéktivli]

副 それぞれ, めいめいに

Shipment to Hokkaido and Okinawa requires an extra charge of 3 and 5 percent **respectively**.
北海道および沖縄への配送は**それぞれ**3パーセントと5パーセントの追加料金が必要です。

89 entail
[intéil]

他 を必要とする, 伴う

Delivery to customers outside Japan **entails** considerable paperwork.
日本国外の顧客への配送はかなりの量の事務処理**を必要とする**。

90 transport
[trænspɔ́ːrt] 動, [trǽnspɔːrt] 名

他 を運ぶ, 輸送する
名 輸送, 輸送手段

派 transportation「輸送」

The building materials were **transported** by truck.
その建材はトラックで**輸送**された。

13. 流通

91 exceptional
[iksépʃənl]
形 ① 例外的な
② 優秀な
反 unexceptional「通例の」

The recent delay in shipment was an **exceptional** case.
最近の発送の遅れは例外的なケースだった。

92 ship
[ʃíp]
他 ①〈商品〉を出荷する，発送する
② を輸送する
派 shipment「発送，積荷」

Your order will be **shipped** within five days.
お客さまのご注文は，5日以内に発送されます。

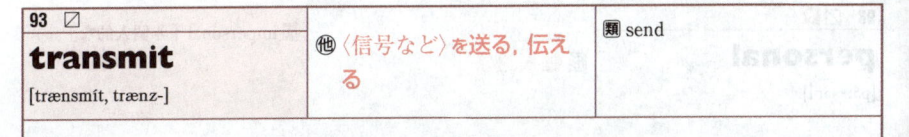

93 transmit
[trænsmít, trænz-]
他〈信号など〉を送る，伝える
類 send

I **transmitted** the order to the manufacturer by e-mail.
私はメールでその製造業者に注文を送った。

94 prepay
[prì:péi]
他 を先払いする
派 prepaid[PPD]「前払いの，前納の」

If your purchases exceed $1,000, you will be required to **prepay** a deposit.
お客さまの購入品が1000ドルを超える場合は，手付金を前払いすることが必要です。

95 currently
[kə́:rəntli]
副 現在は，今のところは
類 presently

We **currently** do not ship orders outside of Japan.
当社は現在，日本国外への注文の発送を行っておりません。

96 charter
[tʃɑ́ːrtər]

他 〈船・飛行機など〉を借り切る, チャーターする
名 契約使用
類 hire

They **chartered** three ships to transport those goods.
彼らはそれらの商品を運ぶために船を3隻チャーターした。

97 handle
[hǽndl]

他 ①〈仕事〉を管理する, 〈商品〉を扱う
②をうまく扱う
類 manage

This port **handles** more than 80 percent of the maritime containers in the area.
その地域の海上コンテナの80パーセント以上が, この港で扱われている。

98 personal
[pə́ːrsənl]

形 個人的な
反 impersonal「非個人的な」

You cannot cancel the order for a **personal** reason after it is confirmed.
ご注文が確定した後は, 個人的な理由でキャンセルすることはできません。

99 internal
[intə́ːrnl]

形 ①内部の
②体内の

Our **internal** investigation showed that your order was shipped yesterday.
社内で調査をしたところ, お客さまのご注文は昨日発送されたことがわかりました。

100 excluding
[iksklúːdiŋ]

前 を除いて
派 exclude「を除外する, 締め出す」

Delivery is available Monday through Saturday, **excluding** national holidays.
配達は祝日を除いて, 月曜日から土曜日まで利用できます。

13. 流通

101 standard [stǽndərd]
形 標準の, 普通の
類 regular

Overnight delivery is 1,000 yen in addition to the **standard** delivery charge.
翌日便は標準の配送料に加えて千円かかります。

102 emit [imít]
他 ①〈ガスなど〉を排出する ②〈光・熱など〉を放出する
派 emission「排出, 放出」

Natural gas trucks **emit** less CO_2 than diesel trucks.
天然ガストラックはディーゼルトラックよりも二酸化炭素の排出が少ない。

103 insure [inʃúər]
他 に保険をかける
派 insurance「保険」

We recommend that you **insure** the package.
その小包に保険をかけることをお勧めします。

104 immediate [imíːdiət]
形 ①即時の, 目前の ②直接の
派 immdediately「即座に, 直接に」

All our products are available for **immediate** delivery.
当社のすべての製品は, すぐに配達できます。

105 process [práses]
他 〈食品〉を加工する, 〈データなど〉を処理する
名 過程, 製法
関 be in process「進行中である」

The fish are transported to this facility and **processed** into fish sausages.
魚はこの施設に運ばれて, 魚肉ソーセージに加工される。

— 265 —

106 domestic
[dəméstik]

形 ①国内の
②家庭用の，家庭の

反 foreign「海外の」

Domestic beef **producers** are threatened by cheap beef from foreign countries.
国内の牛肉生産者は，外国からの安い牛肉に脅かされている。

107 scan
[skǽn]

他 をスキャンする
名 精査

関 scanner「スキャナ」

Just **scanning** the **bar code** enables you to get various kinds of information.
バーコードをスキャンするだけでさまざまな種類の情報が得られる。

108 monopolize
[mənápəlàiz]

他 を独占する

関 monopolization「独占」

A large company has **monopolized** the **market** for several years.
ある大企業が数年にわたり市場を独占している。

109 major
[méidʒər]

形 主要な
名 （大学での）専攻科目

反 minor「重要でない」

Major retailers will ship the ordered items within the day.
主な小売業者は注文品をその日のうちに発送する。

110 produce
[prədjúːs]

他 を製造する

反 consume「を消費する」

Our products are **produced** mainly in Southeast Asia.
当社の製品は主に東南アジアで製造されている。

13. 流通

111 put up
他 を(売りに)出す, (せりに)かける

A giant tuna weighing over 300 kilograms was **put up** for **auction**.
300キロを超える巨大マグロがせりにかけられた。

112 prevent [privént]
他 を防ぐ
類 stop

We should **prevent** future **trade friction** with the United States.
米国との今後の貿易摩擦を防がなければならない。

113 expand [ikspǽnd]
他 を拡大する
自 膨張する
反 reduce「を縮小する」

The strong dollar has **expanded** the country's **trade deficit**.
ドル高はその国の貿易赤字を拡大させた。

114 intervene [ìntərvíːn]
自 介入する
類 interfere

The Bank of Japan decided to **intervene** in the **foreign exchange market**.
日本銀行は,外国為替市場に介入することを決定した。

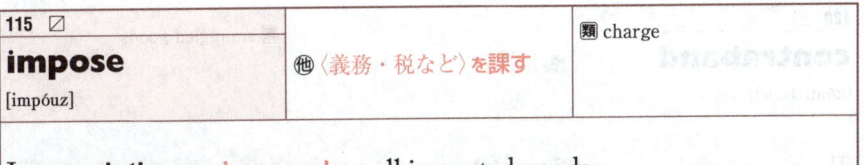

115 impose [impóuz]
他〈義務・税など〉を課す
類 charge

Import **duties** are **imposed** on all imported goods.
輸入税はすべての輸入品に課せられる。

― 267 ―

116 boost
[bú:st]

他 を増加する
名 上昇

類 increase

The government should take some measures immediately to boost imports.
政府は輸入を増やすために，早急に何らかの対策を講じなければならない。

117 ban
[bǽn]

他 を(法的に)禁止する
名 禁止

類 prohibit

Export of the animals shown below is strictly banned.
下に示された動物の輸出は厳しく禁止されている。

118 govern
[gʌ́vərn]

他 を管理する, 規制する

類 control

The new law governs the trade with that nation.
新法はその国との貿易を規制している。

119 post
[póust]

他 を計上する

China posted a larger trade surplus last month.
中国は先月，さらなる貿易黒字を計上した。

120 contraband
[kɑ́ntrəbænd]

名 密輸品

類 smuggled goods

The cargo was inspected for contraband.
その積み荷は密輸品がないか検査された。

13. 流通

121 regulate [régjəlèit]
- 他 ① を規制する, 取り締まる
- ② 〈機器など〉を調整する
- 派 regulation「規則, 調整」

The country strictly **regulates** the import and export of weapons.
その国は武器の輸出入を厳しく規制している。

122 widen [wáidn]
- 他 を広くする
- 自 広くなる
- 反 narrow「を縮小する」

The team was organized to **widen** our delivery network.
配送ネットワークを広げるために, そのチームは編成された。

123 unbalanced [ʌnbǽlənst]
- 形 不均衡な
- 類 uneven

The cargo was poorly loaded and became **unbalanced**.
その積み荷は雑に積まれて, バランスを欠いてしまった。

124 lift [líft]
- 他 ① を解禁する
- ② を持ち上げる

The ban on import of the fruit will be **lifted** soon.
その果物の輸入規制はすぐに解除されるだろう。

125 numerous [njúːmərəs]
- 形 多数の, たくさんの

The company imports **numerous** items of clothing from Taiwan.
その会社はたくさんの衣料品を台湾から輸入している。

Section 3　実際のファックスで確認！

```
KT DRUGSTORE, Inc.
112 Stonewood St., Anytown, MA
52690
Phone (507)123-4567
Fax (507)234-5678
http://www.ktd.com

TO : Ms. Michiko Lee
Fax: (81)3-345-6789
FROM: Kate Adams
Phone (81)3-456-7890
Pages: 1 page
Regarding: About the products
DATE： Oct.1, 2010
```

Dear Ms. Lee:

I would like to inquire about the price of 10 packets of E-495, E-678 and J-912 **respectively**, and the total cost including shipping charges.
Can you deliver your **products** to us by October 11th?
I would appreciate your reply as soon as possible.

Sincerely,
Kate Adams
Owner, KT DRUGSTORE

和訳

```
KT ドラッグストア（株）
52690　マサチューセッツ州　エニイタウン
ストーンウッド通り　112
電話 (507)123-4567
ファックス (507)234-5678
http://www.ktd.com

宛先：ミチコ・リー様
ファックス：(81)3-345-6789
送信元：ケイト・アダムス
電話 (81)3-456-7890
ページ：1 ページ
件名：製品について
日付： 2010 年 10 月 1 日
```

リー様：

それぞれ 10 パケットの E-495、E-678、J-912 のお値段と，配送料を含めた総額をお知らせください。10 月 11 日までに**製品**を送っていただくことは可能でしょうか？
早急のお返事をお待ち致しております。

敬具

ケイト・アダムス
KT ドラッグストア　店主

Fax Transmission

FROM
S&C Inc.
Waseda 1 chome
Shinjuku-ku Tokyo 123-4567 Japan
Fax: (81)3-345-6789
Phone: (81)3-456-7890
http://www.S_and_C.com

TO
Ms. Kate Adams
KT DRUGSTORE, Inc.
112 Stonewood St., Anytown, MA
52690
Fax (507)234-5678
Pages: 1
Regarding: Your inquiry

Date: 10. 1. 2010

Dear Kate Adams:

Thank you for your inquiry. The information you requested is shown below.
NOTE: The delivery service we use is now offering a 5% discount on shipments made before November 11th, 2010; the discount is reflected in the amount shown. Shipping usually requires at least five days, so please place an immediate order so that we can ship the items to you by the date requested.

Product number	Quantity	Packet Price	Crate price	Total Price
E-495	10 packets	$15	$5(waterproof)	$155
E-678	10 packets	$12	$5(waterproof)	$125
J-912	10 packets	$10	$5(waterproof)	$105
Subtotal				$385
Delivery charge	Express Delivery			$15
			Total	$400

*All goods are insured during transportation.

If you have any questions, contact us by e-mail at milee@sc.com or call Michiko Lee directly at (81)3-456-7890.

Sincerely,
Michiko Lee
Sales Department

和訳

ファックス通信

送信元
S&C（株）
123-4567
日本国東京都新宿区早稲田1丁目
ファックス：(81)3-345-6789
電話：(81)3-456-7890
http://www.S_and_C.com

宛先
ケイト・アダムス様
KT ドラッグストア（株）
52690　マサチューセッツ州　エニイタウン
ストーンウッド通り　112
ファックス：(507)234-5678
ページ：1
件名：お問い合わせについて

2010年10月1日

ケイト・アダムス様：

お問い合わせありがとうございます。お尋ねになられました情報は以下でございます。
お知らせ：私どもの使用している配送サービスでは2010年11月11日までの発送に現在5%の割引を提供しております；提示した料金に割引は反映してあります。発送には通常最短で5日間を要しますので，ご要望の日に商品をお送りできるように，どうぞお早めの御注文をよろしくお願い致します。

商品番号	量	パケット代	箱代	総計
E-495	10パケット	15ドル	5ドル（防水）	155ドル
E-678	10パケット	12ドル	5ドル（防水）	125ドル
J-912	10パケット	10ドル	5ドル（防水）	105ドル
小計				385ドル
配送料	速達			15ドル
			総額	400ドル

＊すべての品には輸送の間保険がかけられます。

ご質問がありましたらEメール milee@sc.com または，お電話で直接ミチコ・リー (81)3-456-7890 までどうぞ。

敬具

ミチコ・リー
営業部

✻ Review Words ✻		
☐ respectively ➡ Sec.2-88	☐ product ➡ Sec.1-39	☐ immediate ➡ Sec.2-104
☐ ship ➡ Sec.2-92	☐ crate ➡ Sec.1-8	☐ waterproof ➡ Sec.2-70
☐ delivery charge ➡ Sec.1-35	☐ delivery ➡ Sec.1-34	☐ insure ➡ Sec.2-103
☐ during ➡ Sec.2-80		

第14章
出　張

英語で何と言うでしょうか？

☞ 答えは P.275

Section 1　イラストで覚える！

✻ Business trip 「出張」✻

1. application [æplikéiʃn]
2. itinerary [aitínərèri]
3. travel expenses
4. travel allowance
5. reservation, booking [rèzərvéiʃn], [búkiŋ]
6. tentative reservation[booking]
7. travel agency
8. travel advisory
9. airplane ticket
10. vacancy [véikənsi]
11. mileage [máilidʒ]
12. visa [víːzə]
13. accommodation [əkɑ̀mədéiʃn]
14. vaccination [væksənéiʃn]
15. travel, trip [trǽvl], [tríp]

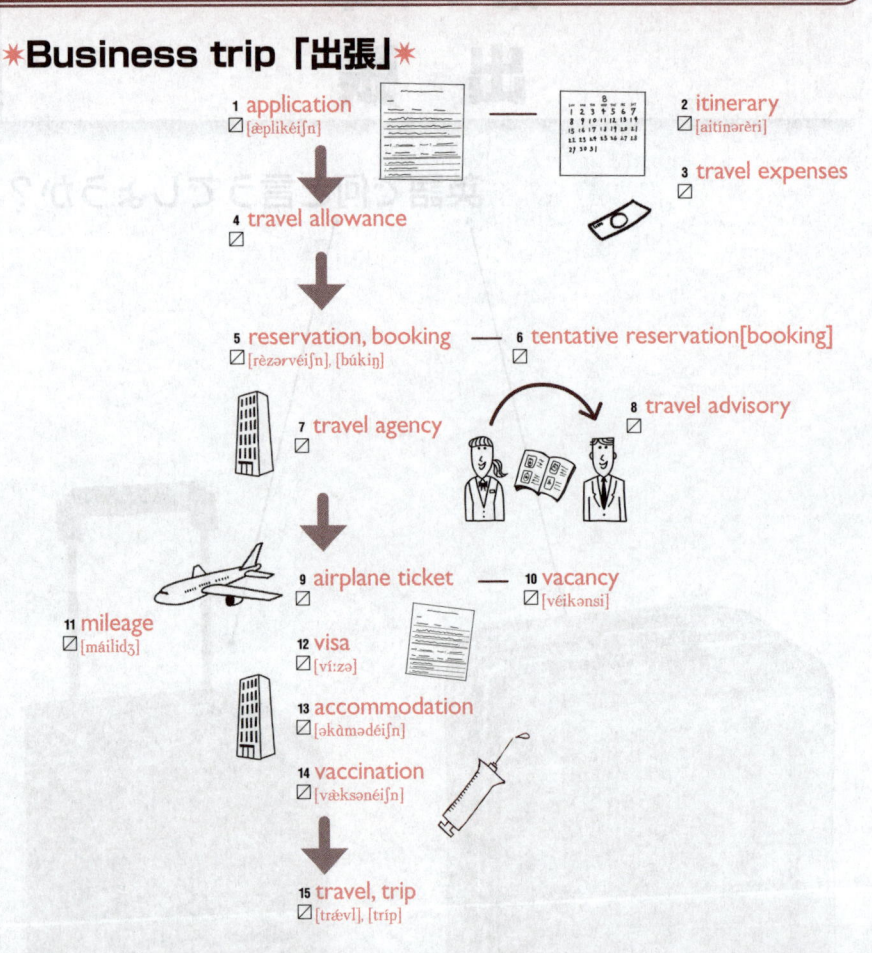

1 application 申請	2 itinerary 旅程	3 travel expenses 出張旅費	4 travel allowance 出張手当
5 reservation, booking 予約	6 tentative reservation [booking] 仮予約	7 travel agency 旅行代理店	8 travel advisory 渡航情報
9 airplane ticket 航空チケット	10 vacancy 空き	11 mileage マイレージ	12 visa ビザ
13 accommodation 宿泊施設	14 vaccination 予防接種	15 travel, trip 旅行	

14. 出張

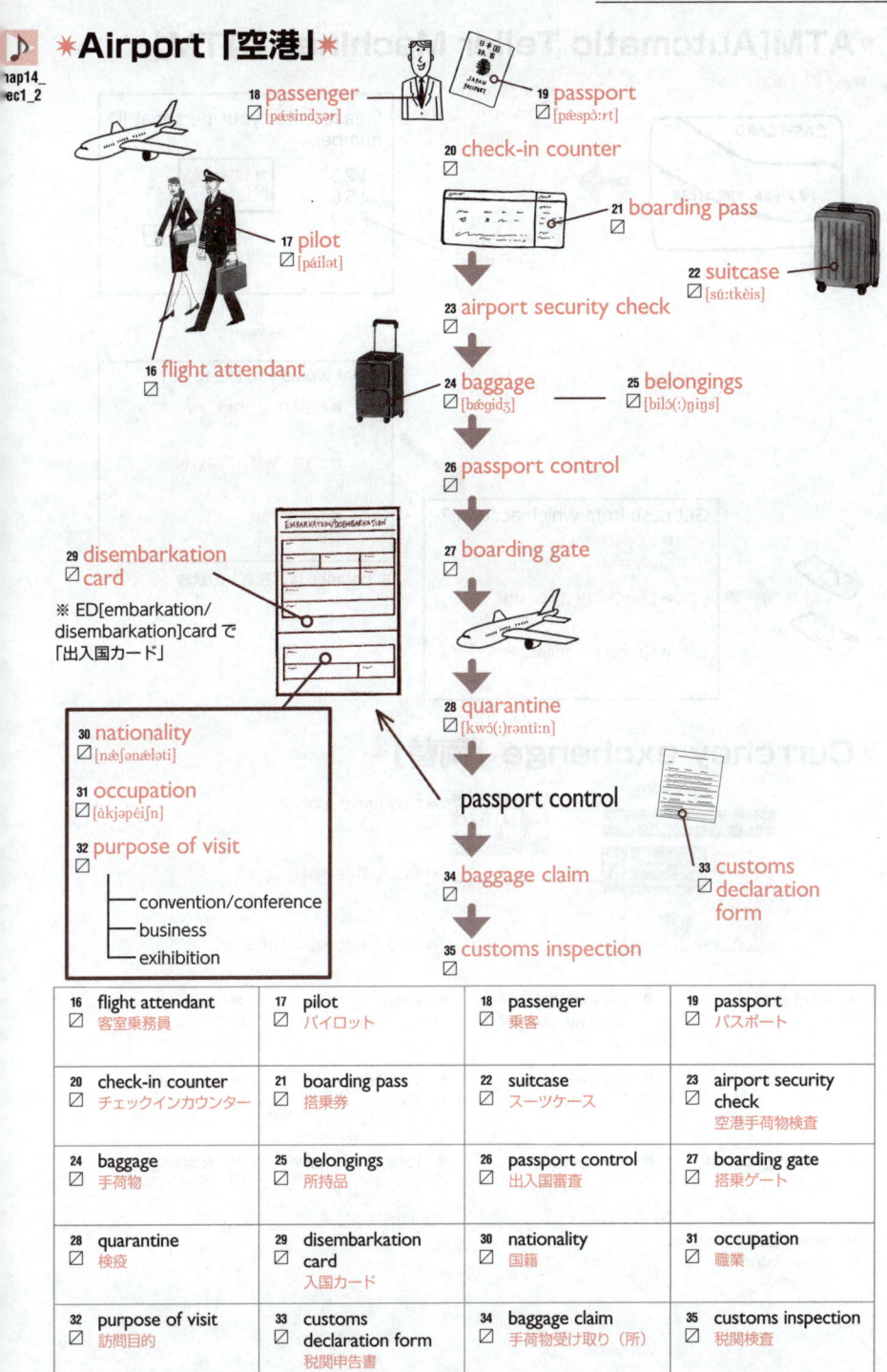

✱Airport「空港」✱

- 16 flight attendant
- 17 pilot [páilət]
- 18 passenger [pǽsindʒɚ]
- 19 passport [pǽspɔ̀ːrt]
- 20 check-in counter
- 21 boarding pass
- 22 suitcase [súːtkèis]
- 23 airport security check
- 24 baggage [bǽgidʒ]
- 25 belongings [bilɔ́(ː)ŋiŋs]
- 26 passport control
- 27 boarding gate
- 28 quarantine [kwɔ́(ː)rəntìːn]
- 29 disembarkation card
  ※ ED[embarkation/disembarkation]card で「出入国カード」
- 30 nationality [næ̀ʃənǽləti]
- 31 occupation [ɑ̀kjəpéiʃn]
- 32 purpose of visit
  - convention/conference
  - business
  - exihibition
- 33 customs declaration form
- 34 baggage claim
- 35 customs inspection

16 flight attendant 客室乗務員	17 pilot パイロット	18 passenger 乗客	19 passport パスポート
20 check-in counter チェックインカウンター	21 boarding pass 搭乗券	22 suitcase スーツケース	23 airport security check 空港手荷物検査
24 baggage 手荷物	25 belongings 所持品	26 passport control 出入国審査	27 boarding gate 搭乗ゲート
28 quarantine 検疫	29 disembarkation card 入国カード	30 nationality 国籍	31 occupation 職業
32 purpose of visit 訪問目的	33 customs declaration form 税関申告書	34 baggage claim 手荷物受け取り（所）	35 customs inspection 税関検査

— 275 —

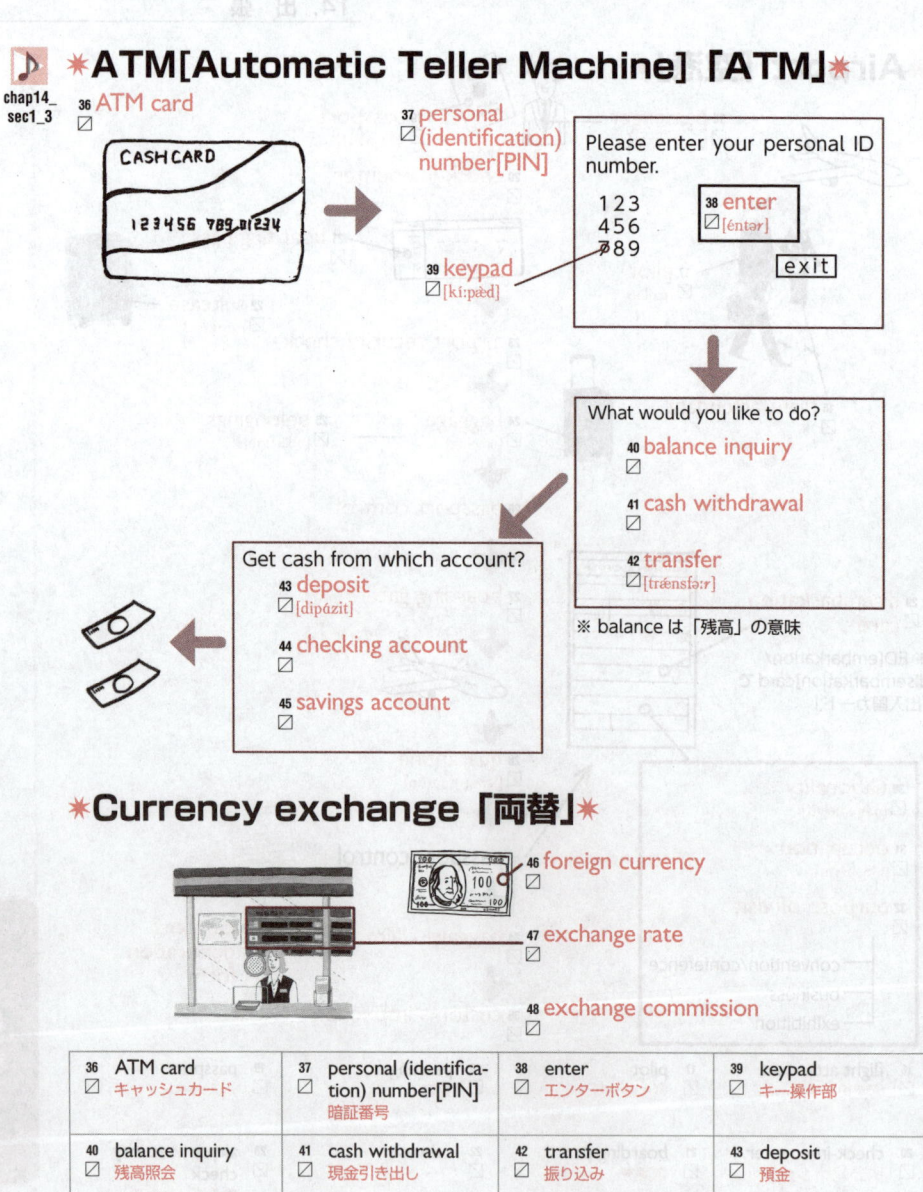

✱ATM[Automatic Teller Machine] 「ATM」✱

36 ATM card

37 personal (identification) number[PIN]

Please enter your personal ID number.
1 2 3
4 5 6
7 8 9

38 enter [éntər]

exit

39 keypad [kíːpæd]

What would you like to do?
40 balance inquiry
41 cash withdrawal
42 transfer [trǽnsfəːr]

※ balance は「残高」の意味

Get cash from which account?
43 deposit [dipázit]
44 checking account
45 savings account

✱Currency exchange 「両替」✱

46 foreign currency

47 exchange rate

48 exchange commission

36	ATM card キャッシュカード	37	personal (identification) number[PIN] 暗証番号	38	enter エンターボタン	39	keypad キー操作部
40	balance inquiry 残高照会	41	cash withdrawal 現金引き出し	42	transfer 振り込み	43	deposit 預金
44	checking account 当座預金	45	savings account 普通預金口座	46	foreign currency 外貨	47	exchange rate 為替レート
48	exchange commission 両替手数料						

— 276 —

14. 出張

✳Airport timetable「空港の時刻表」✳

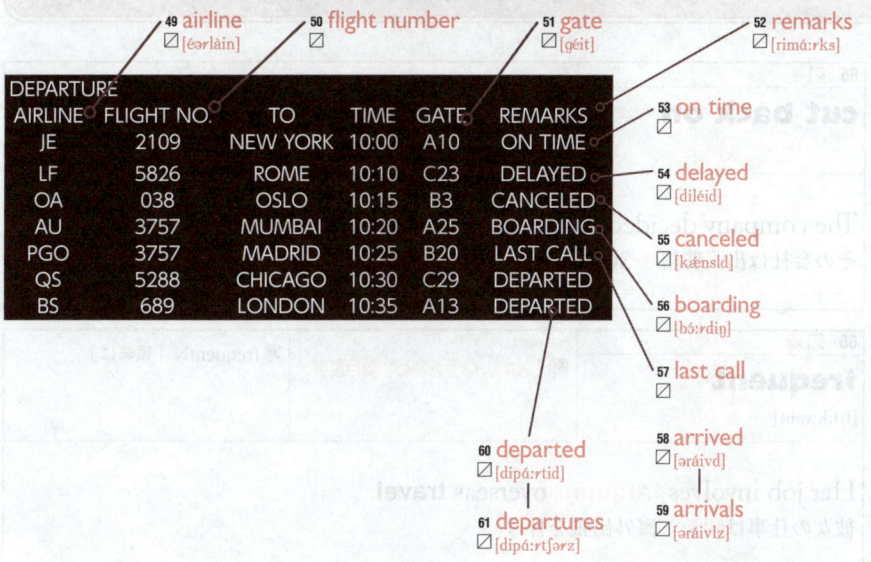

```
DEPARTURE
AIRLINE   FLIGHT NO.   TO         TIME    GATE   REMARKS
  JE        2109       NEW YORK   10:00   A10    ON TIME
  LF        5826       ROME       10:10   C23    DELAYED
  OA        038        OSLO       10:15   B3     CANCELED
  AU        3757       MUMBAI     10:20   A25    BOARDING
  PGO       3757       MADRID     10:25   B20    LAST CALL
  QS        5288       CHICAGO    10:30   C29    DEPARTED
  BS        689        LONDON     10:35   A13    DEPARTED
```

- 49 airline [éərlàin]
- 50 flight number
- 51 gate [géit]
- 52 remarks [rimáːrks]
- 53 on time
- 54 delayed [diléid]
- 55 canceled [kǽnsld]
- 56 boarding [bɔ́ːrdiŋ]
- 57 last call
- 58 arrived [əráivd]
- 59 arrivals [əráivlz]
- 60 departed [dipáːrtid]
- 61 departures [dipáːrtʃərz]

✳Boarding pass「搭乗券」✳

```
                    AIR UNITED
  ECONOMY CLASS
  Flight & Date    Gate      Seat          Seat
  AU 3757          A25       38 B          38 B

  From SYDNEY      To  MUMBAI              To MUMBAI
                                           Remarks
  Name
   Yamada Ichiro ,    00858
```

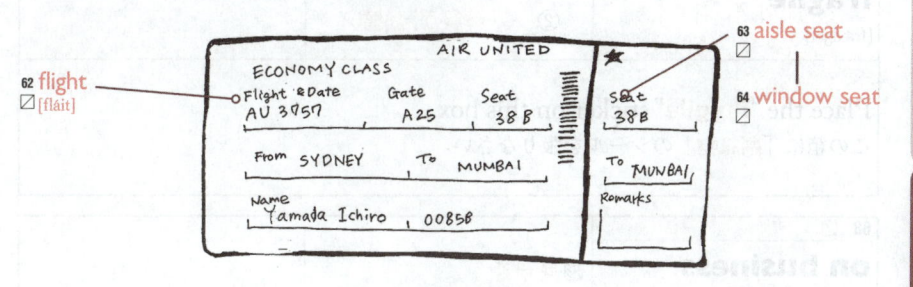

- 62 flight [fláit]
- 63 aisle seat
- 64 window seat

49	airline 航空会社，定期航空(路)	50	flight number 便名	51	gate ゲート	52	remarks 備考
53	on time 定刻に	54	delayed 遅延の	55	canceled 欠航の	56	boarding 搭乗中
57	last call 最終案内	58	arrived 到着済	59	arrivals 到着	60	departed 出発済
61	departures 出発	62	flight フライト，（航空機の）定期便	63	aisle seat 通路側の席	64	window seat 窓側の席

— 277 —

Section 2 例文で覚える！

65 cut back on
他〈経費など〉を削減する
類 cut down

The company decided to **cut back on** travel expenses by 30%.
その会社は出張費用を 30 パーセント削減することにした。

66 frequent [fríːkwənt]
形 しばしば起こる，頻発する
派 frequently「頻繁に」

Her job involves **frequent** overseas **travel**.
彼女の仕事は頻繁な海外出張を伴う。

67 fragile [frǽdʒəl]
形 ①壊れやすい
②（人・体質が）か弱い
類 delicate

Place the "**Fragile**" sticker on this box.
この箱に「割れ物」のシールを張りなさい。

68 on business
形 商用で

I was in Beijing **on business** last week.
先週は商用で北京に行っていました。

69 normal [nɔ́ːrml]
形 通常の，標準の
名 標準，常態
反 abnormal「異常な」

I visit my client companies only during their **normal** business hours.
私は取引先の企業をその企業の通常の勤務時間内にのみ訪問する。

― 278 ―

14. 出張

70. besides [bisáidz]
- 前 ～の他に, ～に加えて
- 副 その上, さらに
- 類 in addition to

Besides making sure we keep our regular customers, we should cultivate new ones.
得意先の確保の他に, 我々は新たな顧客を開拓しなければならない。

71. desire [dizáiər]
- 他 を強く望む
- 名 願望, 要望
- 類 wish

A transportation system that is more eco-friendly is **desired**.
もっと環境に優しい交通システムが望まれている。

72. use [júːz]
- 他 を使う
- 派 useful「役に立つ, 有益な」

I **used** my accumulated **mileage** to upgrade to business class.
たまったマイレージを使ってビジネスクラスにアップグレードしてもらった。

73. busy [bízi]
- 形 忙しい
- 類 occupied

This is a very **busy** itinerary, so we won't have time to do any sightseeing.
とても忙しい旅程なので, 観光をしている時間はまったくない。

74. ideal [aidíːəl]
- 形 理想的な, 申し分のない
- 名 理想
- 類 perfect

This hotel is an **ideal** choice of **accommodation** for business travelers.
このホテルは, 出張する人の宿泊施設としては理想的な選択肢だ。

75 secure
[sikjúər]

- 他 を確保する
- 形 確実な, 保証された

派 security「警備, セキュリティー」

We need to **secure** financial support for establishing a new laboratory.
新たな研究所の設立のためには, 経済的援助の確保が必要だ。

76 remain
[riméin]

- 自 残っている, とどまる
- 名 残り

During the off-peak season, even discounted **airplane tickets remain** unsold.
オフシーズンの間は, 値下げした飛行機のチケットですら売れ残る。

77 out of town

- 形 出張中で

関 go on a business trip「出張する」

I'll be **out of town** until Friday, so we'll talk about that next week.
金曜日まで出張で留守にするので, その件は来週話し合おう。

78 book
[búk]

- 他 を予約する
- 名 本

類 reserve

I **booked** a **trip** to Bangkok to meet a client.
クライアントと会うため, バンコクへの旅を予約した。

79 until further notice
追って通知があるまで

Because of the volcanic explosion, the airport is closed **until further notice**.
火山の噴火のため, 空港は追って通知があるまで閉鎖されている。

14. 出張

80 weigh [wéi]
- 自 重さが〜である
- 他 の重さを量る
- 派 weight「重さ」

I had to check my bag because it **weighed** more than 10 kilograms.
私のかばんは 10 キロ以上の重さがあったので，預けなければならなかった。

81 missing [mísiŋ]
- 形 行方不明の
- 類 lost

I found my bags **missing** at the **baggage claim**.
手荷物受取所で，私のかばんがなくなっていることに気づいた。

82 overbook [òuvərbúk]
- 他 に定員以上の予約をとる
- 関 double-book「を二重に予約する」

My **flight** was **overbooked**, so I volunteered to take a later flight.
私の乗る便がオーバーブッキングしていたので，後の便に乗ると自ら申し出た。

83 comfortable [kʌ́mfərtəbl]
- 形 心地よい，快適な
- 反 uncomfortable「心地よくない」

The airline provides **passengers** with **comfortable** seats and good food.
その航空会社は心地よい座席と良質の食事を乗客に提供する。

84 boast [bóust]
- 他 を達成する，実現する
- 自 自慢する

The **airline boasts** a high safety rating.
その航空会社は高い水準の安全性を達成している。

— 281 —

85 void
[vɔ́id]
- 形 無効な
- 他 を無効にする
- 類 invalid

I was late for my flight, and my ticket became **void**.
私は飛行機に乗り遅れ，チケットが無効になった。

86 see off
- 他 を見送る
- 反 meet「出迎える」

My colleagues **saw** me **off** at the airport.
同僚たちが私を空港で見送ってくれた。

87 rate
[réit]
- 名 (サービスなどの) 料金
- 他 を評価する，見積もる
- 類 price

That airline's tickets are sold at drastically reduced **rates**.
その航空会社のチケットは大幅に値下げした料金で売られている。

88 vary
[véəri]
- 自 異なる，変わる
- 他 を変える
- 類 differ

The flight time **varies** according to weather conditions.
飛行時間は気象条件によって変わる。

89 check in
- 自 搭乗手続きをする，宿泊手続きをする
- 反 check out「チェックアウトする」

Please proceed to the security check area after you **check in**.
搭乗手続きを済ませたら，保安検査場にお進みください。

— 282 —

14. 出張

90 aboard [əbɔ́:rd]
- 前 〜に乗って
- 副 乗船して, 搭乗して
- 関 board「に搭乗する」

Most of the passengers **aboard** the plane were suited businessmen.
飛行機に乗っていた乗客のほとんどは, スーツ姿のビジネスマンだった。

91 excess [ékses] 形, [iksés] 名
- 形 超過した, 余分の
- 名 超過, 過剰, 超過度
- 派 excessive「過度の」

I was charged 50 dollars for **excess** baggage.
超過手荷物料金50ドルを請求された。

92 cause [kɔ́:z]
- 他 を引き起こす
- 名 原因, 理由
- 類 give rise to

The delay of my flight **caused** me much trouble.
乗った便が遅れて, 私は大迷惑を被った〔私の乗った便の遅れは, 私に大迷惑をもたらした〕。

93 economy [ikánəmi]
- 形 安価な
- 名 経済
- 派 economical「安価な」

The **economy** seat was very narrow and terribly uncomfortable.
エコノミーの座席はとても狭く, ものすごく座り心地が悪かった。

94 limit [límit]
- 名 制限, 限度
- 他 を制限する
- 派 limitless「無制限の」

There is a **limit** of one carry-on bag per passenger.
乗客一人につき, 機内持ち込み荷物1個という制限がある。

95. in line
並んで

I had to wait **in line** for 30 minutes at the **check-in counter**.
チェックインカウンターで30分並んで待たなければならなかった。

96. exchange
[ikstʃéindʒ]

他 を交換する, 両替する
名 交換, 両替

類 barter

I **exchanged** my yen for yuan at the bank in the airport.
空港の銀行で手持ちの円を元に両替した。

97. via
[váiə, víːə]

前 〜経由で

類 by way of

She took a plane to Sydney **via** Singapore.
彼女はシンガポール経由のシドニー行きの飛行機に乗った。

98. except for
前 〜を除いて

関 aside from「〜は別として」

I usually take trains for business trips, **except for** trips to Hokkaido and Okinawa.
北海道と沖縄を除き, 出張にはだいたい列車を使う。

99. take off
自 離陸する

反 land「着陸する」

The incident happened shortly after the plane **took off** from the airport.
事件は飛行機が空港を離陸して間もなく起こった。

14. 出張

100 issue [íʃuː]
- 他 を発行する, 出版する
- 名 発行, 出版物
- 類 publish

My **passport** was **issued** three days before my business trip.
私のパスポートは出張の3日前に発行された。

101 detain [ditéin]
- 他 を引き留める, 拘留する
- 類 retain

He was **detained** at immigration and questioned for several hours.
彼は入国管理で拘束され, 数時間尋問された。

102 steal [stíːl]
- 他 を盗む
- 類 rob

I had all my **belongings stolen** while dozing in the lounge.
ロビーでうとうとしている間に, 所持品を全部盗まれた。

103 land [lænd]
- 他 を着陸させる, 上陸させる
- 自 着陸する, 着地する
- 反 take off「離陸する」

Under the heavy wind, the captain **landed** the plane safely.
強風の中, 機長は無事に飛行機を着陸させた。

104 screen [skríːn]
- 他 を検査する
- 名 画面, スクリーン
- 関 investigate「を調査する」

Carry-on bags are **screened** by X-ray devices at the **airport security check**.
機内持ち込みのかばんは, 空港の手荷物検査所でX線装置によって検査される。

105 get off

| 他〈乗り物〉から降りる | 反 get on「乗る」 |

I filled out my **customs declaration form** before **getting off** the plane.
飛行機を降りる前に税関申告書に記入した。

106 behind schedule

| 副 予定より遅れて | 反 ahead of schedule「予定より早く」 |

Our plane arrived in Shanghai two hours **behind schedule**.
私たちの乗った飛行機は2時間遅れで上海に到着した。

107 cost
[kɔ́ːst]

| 他（人に）〈費用など〉がかかる
名 値段, 代価 | 関 costly「損失の大きい, 高価な」 |

I took a taxi from the airport to the hotel, which **cost** me 40 dollars.
空港からホテルまでタクシーを利用したら, 40ドルかかった。

108 drag
[drǽg]

| 他 を引きずる | |

I **dragged** my heavy **suitcase** all the way to the airport.
私は重いスーツケースを空港までずっと引きずって運んだ。

109 currency
[kə́ːrənsi]

| 名 通貨 | 関 monetary「貨幣の, 金融の」 |

The customs officer asked me if I had any foreign **currency**.
税関の役人に, 外国の通貨を持っているかと聞かれた。

14. 出張

110 confiscate [kánfəskèit] — 他 を没収する — 派 confiscation「没収，押収」

I had some items **confiscated** by Customs.
税関でいくつか品物を没収された。

111 admit [ədmít] — 他 を認める — 派 admittance「入場許可」

I **admitted** failing to declare the souvenir.
私はそのお土産を申告し損ねたことを認めた。

112 dual [djúːəl] — 形 二重の，2つの部分から成る — 類 double

I found my boss has **dual** nationality.
私の上司は二重国籍を持っていることを知った。

113 garment bag — 名 スーツバッグ，衣装バッグ

I was asked to open my **garment bag** for inspection.
検査のため，スーツバッグを開けてほしいと言われた。

114 withdraw [wiðdrɔ́ː, wiθ-] — 他 ①〈預金〉を引き出す ②を引っ込める — 派 withdrawal「（預金の）引き出し」

It is risky to **withdraw** lots of money at once.
一度に大金を引き出すのは危険だ。

115 deny
[dinái]
他 を拒否する, 与えない
反 admit「を認める」

My credit card was **denied** at the restaurant.
そのレストランでは，私のクレジットカードは使えなかった。

116 authorize
[ɔ́:θəràiz]
他 に権限を与える
派 authorized「許可された」

I'm **authorized** to negotiate on behalf of my company.
私は会社を代表して交渉する権限を与えられている。

117 be subject to
〜に従属している

During the **customs inspection**, I was told several items **were subject to** taxation.
税関の検査の間に，いくつかの品が課税対象になると言われた。

118 reconfirm
[rì:kənfə́:rm]
他 を再確認する, リコンファームする
類 reaffirm

I'd like to **reconfirm** my flight. My **flight number** is 208.
フライトのリコンファームをしたいのですが。フライトの便名は 208 です。

119 board
[bɔ́:rd]
自 搭乗する
関 aboard「乗船して，搭乗して」

There was an announcement to **board** at Gate 13.
13 番ゲートから搭乗するようにというアナウンスがあった。

14. 出張

120 prefer [prifə́:r]
- 他 を好む
- 派 preference「好み, 選択」

I **prefer** window seats, but only **aisle seats** were available this time.
窓側の席の方が好きなのだが, 今回は通路側の席しか空いていなかった。

121 depart [dipɑ́:rt]
- 自 出発する
- 他 を出発する
- 派 departure「出発」

My plane **departed** from Haneda **on time**.
私の飛行機は定刻通りに羽田を出発した。

122 delay [diléi]
- 他 を遅れさせる, 延期する
- 類 put off

My flight **departure** was **delayed** because of heavy snow.
私の乗る便の出発は, 大雪のため遅れた。

123 arrive [əráiv]
- 自 着く, 到着する
- 派 arrival「到着」

The plane **arrived** at its destination safely.
飛行機は無事, 目的地に到着した。

124 fly [flái]
- 他〈航空会社〉を利用する
- 自 飛ぶ

I always **fly** this airline, because it offers the cheapest fares.
料金が一番安いので, 私はいつもこの航空会社を利用している。

— 289 —

Section 3　実際の会話で確認！

1

- **M**: I'd like to check in.
- **W**: Sure. Oh, your flight is departing on time and has just started boarding. You must hurry.
- **M**: I chatted too long with my friends who saw me off.
- **W**: Do you have any baggage to check?
- **M**: No. I have only this bag to carry on.
- **W**: Fine. Do you see those gates over there?
- **M**: Yes, but a lot of people are waiting in line.
- **W**: Tell the officer your flight number and that it's taking off in 20 minutes, and he'll let you go through the gate first.
- **M**: What if they open my bag for inspection?
- **W**: Do you have an item that is prohibited on the plane?
- **M**: Yes. A large plastic bottle of water.
- **W**: Hand it to them before they confiscate it. That will make things faster.
- **M**: I see.
- **W**: Now hurry up, or you'll be late for the plane.
- **M**: Thank you very much.
- **W**: Have a nice trip!

2

- **M**: Excuse me. I'm afraid my baggage is missing.
- **W**: What does it look like?
- **M**: It's a large, green suitcase.
- **W**: What flight were you on? May I see your boarding pass?
- **M**: Here it is.
- **W**: So you arrived here on a connecting flight.
- **M**: Right.
- **W**: It is most likely that your baggage wasn't transferred to your plane at the connecting airport. It probably went to the wrong destination.
- **M**: What should I do? Most of my belongings are in the suitcase.
- **W**: Where are you going to stay tonight?
- **M**: I have a reservation at the Riverside Hotel.
- **W**: We're very sorry to have caused you so much trouble, but could you wait at the hotel until we call you?
- **M**: I can't wait forever. I'm here on business and have a very busy itinerary.
- **W**: We'll make every effort to find your baggage.

14. 出張

和訳

1

M: 搭乗手続きをしたいのですが。
W: はい。ああ，お客さまの便は定刻に出発するので，ちょうど搭乗し始めたところです。お急ぎください。
M: 見送りをしてくれた友人たちとおしゃべりしすぎました。
W: お預けになるお荷物はありますか。
M: いいえ。このバッグを持ち込むだけです。
W: 結構です。あちらにあるゲートが見えますか。
M: ええ，でも大勢の人が並んで待っています。
W: 係員にフライト番号と，あと20分で離陸すると言えば，先に通してもらえますよ。
M: 検査のためにバッグを開けられたらどうしましょう。
W: 機内への持ち込みが禁止されているものを何かお持ちですか。
M: ええ。水の大きなペットボトルなんですが。
W: 没収される前に渡してください。その方が早く済みますから。
M: わかりました。
W: さあ急いで。飛行機に遅れますよ。
M: どうもありがとう。
W: よい旅を。

2

M: すみません，荷物が行方不明になったようなんですが。
W: どんな荷物ですか。
M: 大きな緑色のスーツケースです。
W: どの便にご搭乗でしたか。搭乗券を見せていただけますか。
M: どうぞ。
W: 乗り継ぎ便でここに到着されたわけですね。
M: そうです。
W: お荷物は，乗り継ぎの空港でお客さまの飛行機に乗せ替えられなかった可能性が高いですね。おそらく間違った目的地に行ってしまったのだと思います。
M: どうすればいいんですか。所持品はほとんどスーツケースに入っているんですよ。
W: 今夜はどこにお泊まりですか。
M: リバーサイドホテルに予約を取ってあります。
W: ご迷惑をおかけしてまことに申し訳ないのですが，ホテルでこちらからの電話をお待ちいただけないでしょうか。
M: いつまでも待つわけにはいかないですよ。ここには商用で来ていて，とても忙しい旅程なんです。
W: お荷物を見つけるために全力を尽くします。

✳ Review Words ✳

☐ check in ➡ Sec.2-89	☐ flight ➡ Sec.1-62	☐ depart ➡ Sec.2-121
☐ on time ➡ Sec.1-53	☐ board ➡ Sec.2-119	☐ see off ➡ Sec.2-86
☐ baggage ➡ Sec.1-24	☐ gate ➡ Sec.1-51	☐ in line ➡ Sec.2-95
☐ flight number ➡ Sec.1-50	☐ take off ➡ Sec.2-99	☐ confiscate ➡ Sec.2-110
☐ trip ➡ Sec.1-15	☐ missing ➡ Sec.2-81	☐ suitcase ➡ Sec.1-22
☐ boarding pass ➡ Sec.1-21	☐ arrive ➡ Sec.2-123	☐ belongings ➡ Sec.1-25
☐ reservation ➡ Sec.1-5	☐ cause ➡ Sec.2-92	☐ on business ➡ Sec.2-68
☐ busy ➡ Sec.2-73	☐ itinerary ➡ Sec.1-2	

第15章
ビジネスプラン・財務

英語で何と言うでしょうか？

☞答えは P.294

Section 1 イラストで覚える！

♪ ✲Business expansion strategy「事業拡大戦略」✲

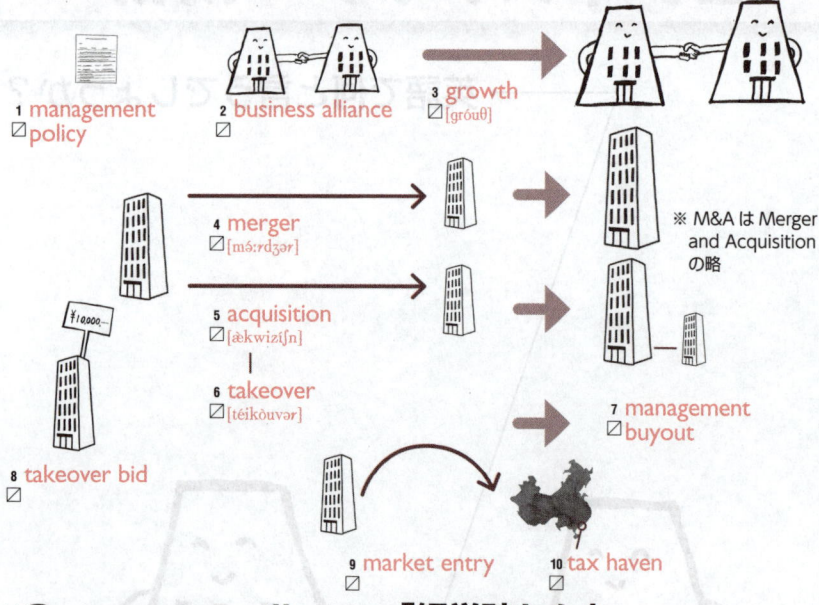

1. management policy
2. business alliance
3. growth [gróuθ]
4. merger [mə́ːrdʒər]
5. acquisition [ækwizíʃn]
6. takeover [téikòuvər]
7. management buyout
8. takeover bid
9. market entry
10. tax haven

※ M&A は Merger and Acquisition の略

✲Corporate collapse「経営破たん」✲

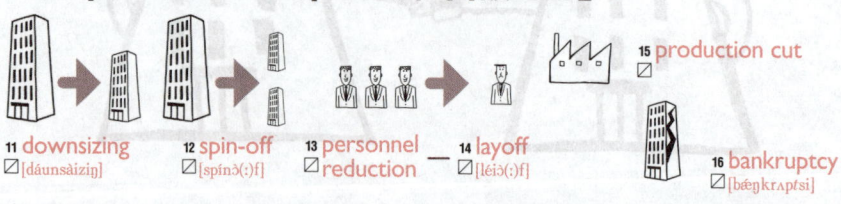

11. downsizing [dáunsàiziŋ]
12. spin-off [spínɔ(ː)f]
13. personnel reduction
14. layoff [léiɔ(ː)f]
15. production cut
16. bankruptcy [bǽŋkrʌptsi]

1 management policy 経営方針	2 business alliance 業務提携	3 growth 成長	4 merger 合併
5 acquisition 買収	6 takeover 乗っ取り、買収	7 management buyout 経営陣による自社株買い取り	8 takeover bid 企業の公開買い付け
9 market entry 市場参入	10 tax haven 税金避難地、租税回避地	11 downsizing 事業縮小	12 spin-off 会社分割
13 personnel reduction 人員削減	14 layoff 一時解雇	15 production cut 減産	16 bankruptcy 倒産

15. ビジネスプラン・財務

✽Marketing「マーケティング」✽

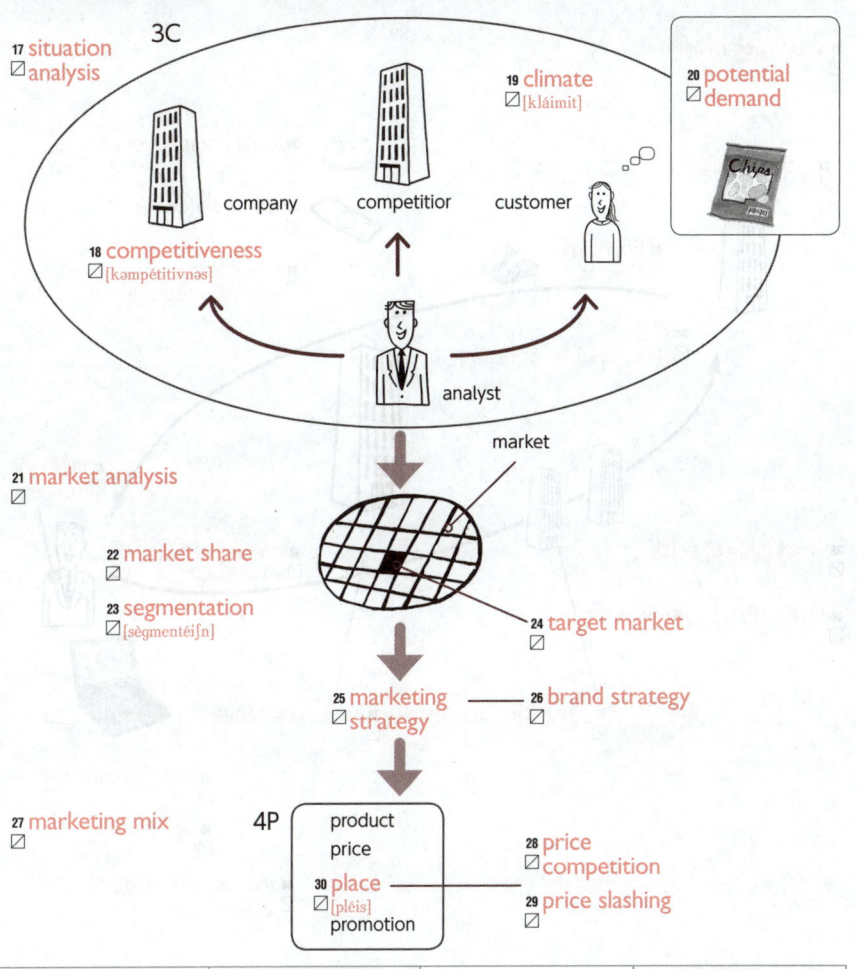

3C
- company
- competitior
- customer
- analyst

17 situation analysis
18 competitiveness [kəmpétitivnəs]
19 climate [kláimit]
20 potential demand

market

21 market analysis
22 market share
23 segmentation [sègmentéiʃn]
24 target market

25 marketing strategy
26 brand strategy

27 marketing mix

4P
- product
- price
- place [pléis]
- promotion

28 price competition
29 price slashing
30 place

17	situation analysis 状況分析	18	competitiveness 競争力	19	climate 環境	20	potential demand 潜在需要
21	market analysis 市場分析	22	market share 市場占有率	23	segmentation 細分化	24	target market 目標市場
25	marketing strategy マーケティング戦略	26	brand strategy ブランド戦略	27	marketing mix マーケティングミックス	28	price competition 価格競争
29	price slashing 価格破壊	30	place 流通					

営業 / 販売 / 流通 / 出張 / ビジネスプラン・財務

– 295 –

✳ Share, Stock 「株」 ✳

chap15_sec1_3

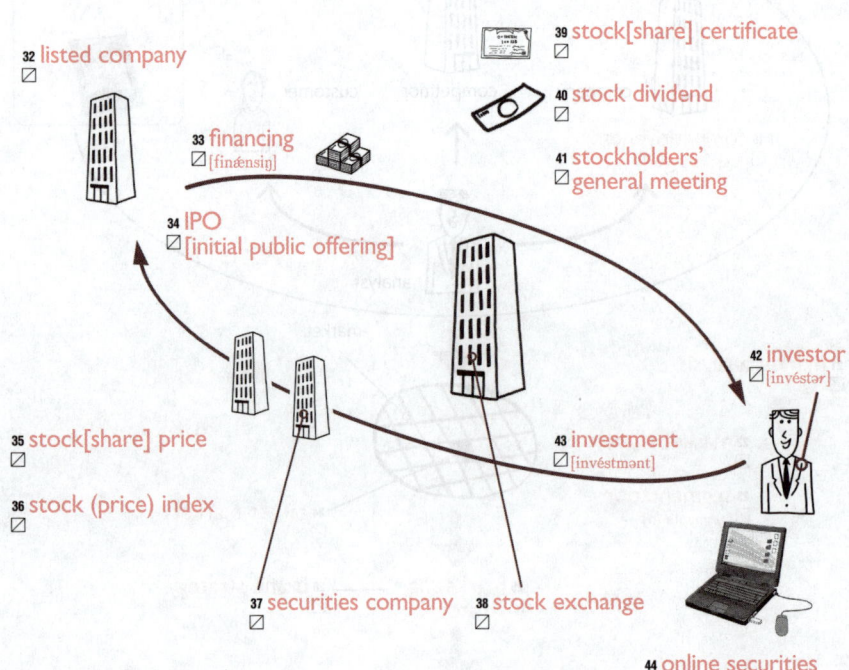

31 securities market
32 listed company
33 financing [fɪnǽnsɪŋ]
34 IPO [initial public offering]
35 stock[share] price
36 stock (price) index
37 securities company
38 stock exchange
39 stock[share] certificate
40 stock dividend
41 stockholders' general meeting
42 investor [ɪnvéstər]
43 investment [ɪnvéstmənt]
44 online securities
45 net banking
46 shareholder, stockholder [ʃéərhòuldər], [stʌ́khòuldər]

31	securities market 証券市場	32	listed company 上場企業	33	financing 資金調達	34	IPO[initial public offering] 株式公開
35	stock[share] price 株価	36	stock (price) index 株価指数	37	securities company 証券会社	38	stock exchange 証券取引所
39	stock[share] certificate 株券	40	stock dividend 株式配当金	41	stockholders' general meeting 株主総会	42	investor 投資家
43	investment 投資	44	online securities オンライン証券	45	net banking ネットバンキング	46	shareholder, stockholder 株主

Financial statements 「財務諸表」

- 47 income statement
- 48 balance sheet
- 49 cash flow statement

```
Income Statement
For the period ending December 31, 2012

  50 revenue
     [révənjùː]
  51 gross profit
  52 expense
     [ikspéns]
  53 operating profit
  54 net income/(loss)
```

```
S&C Co.
Balance Sheet
December 31, 2012

  55 asset
     [æset]
  56 liability
     [làiəbíləti]
  57 stockholder's equity
```

47 income statement 損益計算書	48 balance sheet 貸借対照表	49 cash flow statement キャッシュフロー計算書	50 revenue 歳入
51 gross profit 売上総利益	52 expense 支出	53 operating profit 営業利益	54 net income/(loss) 純損益
55 asset 資産	56 liability 負債	57 stockholder's equity 株主持分	

Section 2　例文で覚える！

58　strategic [strətí:dʒik]
形 戦略の
派 strategy「戦略」

The company's **strategic** acquisition shocked us.
その企業の戦略的買収は我々に衝撃を与えた。

59　incorporate [inkɔ́:rpərèit]
他 を法人化する
派 incorporation「法人団体, 結合」

It took three years to **incorporate** our business in Thailand.
タイで我々の商売を法人化するのに3年を要した。

60　survive [sərváiv]
他 を切り抜けて生き残る
自 生き残る, なんとかやっていく
派 survival「生存, 生き残ること」

Only the strongest companies **survived** the depression.
体力のある企業だけがその不況を切り抜けた。

61　bankrupt [bǽŋkrʌpt]
形 倒産した, 支払い能力のない
名 破産者
派 bankruptcy「破産」

Our team worked out a solid plan to avoid going **bankrupt**.
我がチームは倒産を逃れるためのしっかりした策をひねり出した。

62　ailing [éiliŋ]
形 業績の振るわない, 落ち込んでいる
派 ailment「（軽い）病気」

It is clear that the steel industry is **ailing**.
鉄鋼業が今不振だということは明らかだ。

15. ビジネスプラン・財務

63 multinational [mʌltinǽʃnəl]
形 多国籍の
類 international

This is one of the biggest **multinational** corporations in the field.
この会社はその分野で最も大きな多国籍企業の1つだ。

64 impending [impéndiŋ]
形 今にも起こりそうな, 差し迫った
類 approaching

All the employees are talking about the **impending** spin-off.
社員は皆, 差し迫った会社分割の話をしている。

65 according to
前 ～によると

According to management policy, travel expenses will be reimbursed.
経営方針によれば出張費は返金される。

66 partner [pɑ́ːrtnər]
名 仲間, 共同経営者
類 associate

It seems risky to make that new company our business **partner**.
その新しい会社をビジネスパートナーとするのは危険そうだ。

67 reform [rifɔ́ːrm]
名 改革, 改善
他 を改革する, 改善する
類 improvement

The plan for financial **reform** needs further discussion.
その財政改革計画はさらなる議論が必要だ。

68 moderate
[mάdərit] 形, [mάdərèit] 動

形 緩やかな, 適度な
他 を加減する, 和らげる

派 moderation「節度」

Our business experienced **moderate** growth last month.
我々の商況は先月緩やかな成長を見せた。

69 extremely
[ikstrí:mli]

副 大変, 極端に

類 excessively

Raising the necessary funds was **extremely** hard for the foundation.
その財団にとって必要な資金を調達するのは非常に難しかった。

70 skeptical
[sképtikl]

形 懐疑的な, 疑い深い

類 doubtful

The board of directors remain **skeptical** about our business plans.
役員会は我々のビジネス計画に依然懐疑的である。

71 block
[blάk]

他〈計画など〉を妨害する
名 区画

類 obstruct

The two giant IT companies' **merger** was **blocked**.
その巨大IT企業2社の合併は阻止された。

72 donate
[dóuneit, −́−]

他 を寄付する, 寄贈する

派 donation「寄付」

The company **donated** some of its profit to a local charity.
その会社は地元の慈善団体に利益の一部を寄付した。

15. ビジネスプラン・財務

73 steady [stédi]
形 安定した，着実な
派 steadily「着実に」

Even in this depression, my company enjoys **steady** growth.
この不況下にもかかわらず，私の会社は**安定した**成長を享受している。

74 slash [slǽʃ]
他〈人員・予算など〉を削減する
名 削減，切り下げ
類 reduce

His company is being forced to **slash** the workforce.
彼の会社は人員**削減**を余儀なくされている。

75 mass [mǽs]
名 多量，集団
派 massive「大規模な，大量の」

Mass layoffs are not rare in this country.
この国では**大量**一時解雇は珍しくない。

76 plot [plάt]
他 をたくらむ
名 構想，プロット
類 scheme

They **plotted** a takeover of a Japanese company.
彼らはある日本企業の乗っ取り**を企てた**。

77 collaborate [kəlǽbərèit]
自 協力する，合作する
派 collaboration「コラボ，共同制作」

We need to **collaborate** closely with our business partners.
我々は提携先と緊密に**協力する**必要がある。

78 on the verge of

| | 前 〜の寸前で | 類 on the brink of |

His company is **on the verge of** bankruptcy.
彼の会社は倒産**寸前**だ。

79 forge
[fɔ́ːrdʒ]

| | 他 ①〈関係〉を築く
　②〈計画など〉を案出する | |

The company **forged** a business alliance with its rival company.
その会社はライバル会社と業務提携**を築いた**。

80 municipal
[mjuːnísəpl]

| | 形 市の, 町の | 派 municipality「地方自治体」 |

They will bid on the construction of the **municipal** housing.
彼らは**市営**住宅の建設に入札する予定だ。

81 lead to

| | 他 に至る, をもたらす | 関 bring in「〈利益など〉をもたらす」 |

This policy could **lead to** another corporate collapse.
この方針はさらなる経営破たん**をもたらし**かねない。

82 prosperous
[prɑ́spərəs]

| | 形 繁栄している, 成功した | 類 successful |

Agribusiness is a **prosperous** industry.
農業関連産業は**繁栄している**産業だ。

15. ビジネスプラン・財務

83 **transact** [trænsǽkt, trænz-]
他〈取引など〉を行う
類 carry out

Mr. Lee **transacts** business with that trading company.
リー氏はその貿易会社と事業取引をしている。

84 **backlash** [bǽklæʃ]
名 反発, 抵抗
関 kickback「(強い)反動, 割戻金」

The euro **backlash** will hit our company hard.
ユーロの反発は我が社にひどく打撃を与えるだろう。

85 **allegedly** [əlédʒidli]
副 伝えられるところでは
派 allege「を申し立てる」

The company is **allegedly** going to start an agriculture business.
伝えられるところでは, その会社は農業ビジネスを始めるらしい。

86 **alert** [ələ́ːrt]
形 油断のない, 敏感な
名 警戒態勢
類 sharp

He is always **alert** to changes in the price of oil.
彼はいつも石油価格の動きに油断がない。

87 **strengthen** [stréŋkθən]
他 を強化する
類 reinforce

Each company tries to **strengthen** its **competitiveness**.
それぞれの会社が競争力を高めようと努めている。

88 consecutive
[kənsékjətiv]
形 連続した
類 successive

The cell phone market experienced three quarters of **consecutive** declines.
携帯電話市場は三四半期連続で下落を見た。

89 economic
[ìːkənámik, èkə-]
形 経済の, 経済学の
派 economical「経済的な」

We must adjust our plans according to the **economic** climate.
我々は経済情勢に応じてプランを調整すべきだ。

90 quantify
[kwántəfài]
他 の量を定める, を量で示す
関 quantity「質」

Our team **quantified** the **potential demand** for electric cars.
我々のチームは電気自動車の潜在需要を数量化した。

91 systematic
[sìstəmǽtik]
形 組織的な, 体系的な
類 methodical

We should carry out more **systematic market analysis**.
我々はもっと系統立った市場分析を行わなければならない。

92 adequate
[ǽdikwit]
形 適した, ちょうどの
類 enough, sufficient

Without **adequate price competition**, prices will rise.
適正な価格競争がないと,価格は上がるだろう。

93 eventually
[ivéntʃuəli]

副 ①ゆくゆくは、いずれ
②結局は、ついに

類 finally

Eventually the bond market will improve.
債券市場は**いずれ**回復するだろう。

94 niche
[níːʃ, nítʃ]

名 市場のすき間、ニッチ

They did some **niche** marketing of natural foods.
彼らは自然食品の**ニッチ**マーケティングを行った。

95 advance
[ədvǽns]

自 (率などが) 上がる
名 前進、進出

類 rise

The **stock index advanced** to an eight-month high yesterday.
株価指数は昨日、ここ8ヵ月での最高値に**上がった**。

96 utilize
[júːtəlàiz]

他 を利用する、役立たせる

類 use

Our company **utilizes** online banking to cut the service charge.
我が社はサービス料を削減するためにネットバンキング**を利用している**。

97 gain
[géin]

他 を得る

類 obtain

The product **gained** a significant **market share** through heavy advertising.
その製品は大々的な宣伝を通じて、かなりの市場シェア**を得た**。

| 98 **own** [óun] | 他 を所有する
形 自身の | 類 have |

Does the company **own** intellectual property created by employees?
従業員が生み出した知的財産は会社が**所有する**のだろうか。

| 99 **significant** [signífikənt] | 形 ①（数量が）かなりの，相当の
②重要な，重大な | |

He made a **significant** investment in bonds.
彼は債券に**かなりの**投資をした。

| 100 **huge** [hjúːdʒ] | 形 巨大な，膨大な | 反 tiny「小さな」 |

We raised a **huge** amount of money to invest in stocks.
我々は株に投資するため，**巨**額の資金を調達した。

| 101 **forecast** [fɔ́ːrkæst] | 名 予測，予報
他 を予想する，予測する | 類 prediction |

The government's economic **forecast** will be released tomorrow.
政府の景気**予測**は明日発表される。

| 102 **advice** [ədváis] | 名 助言，アドバイス | 派 advise「にアドバイスする」 |

Some **investors** find it useful to get professional **advice**.
一部の投資家たちはプロの**アドバイス**をもらうことは有用だと気づいている。

15. ビジネスプラン・財務

103 trade [tréid]
- 他 を取引する
- 名 貿易, 通商
- 派 trader「貿易業者」

Is your company's stock being **traded** on the **stock exchange**?
御社の株は証券取引所で取引されているのですか。

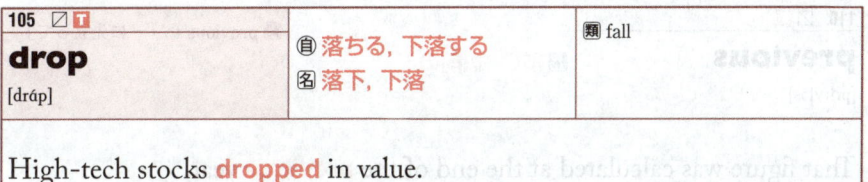

104 cover up
- 他〈悪事など〉を隠す
- 類 suppress

The CEO tried to **cover up** the insider trading.
その CEO はインサイダー取引を隠そうとした。

105 drop [dráp]
- 自 落ちる, 下落する
- 名 落下, 下落
- 類 fall

High-tech stocks **dropped** in value.
ハイテク株の価格は下がった。

106 authorized [ɔ́ːθəràizd]
- 形 権限を与えられた, 公認された
- 派 authorize「に権限を与える」

The amount of **authorized** spending on the project was beyond my expectation.
そのプロジェクトに許可された経費は私の予想を超えていた。

107 roughly [rʌ́fli]
- 副 ①おおよそ ②乱暴に
- 類 nearly

Monthly production of this item has dropped by **roughly** 3 percent.
この製品の月間生産量はおおよそ3パーセント落ち込んだ。

– 307 –

108 consolidated
[kənsálidèitid]
形 統合された，連結方式の
派 consolidate「〈会社など〉を統合する」

He prepared a **consolidated** financial statement for review by management.
彼は経営陣が再検討するための連結財務表を用意した。

109 optimistic
[ὰptəmístik]
形 楽観的な，過大評価の
反 pessimistic「悲観的な」

The company's financial forecast was too **optimistic**.
その会社の財務予測はあまりにも楽観的だった。

110 previous
[príːviəs]
形 前の，以前の
関 previous to「〜に先立って」

That figure was calculated at the end of the **previous** year.
その数字は前年の終わりに計算されたものだ。

111 inflate
[infléit]
他 を膨張させる，誇張する
自 インフレになる
派 inflation「インフレ」

The cost estimate was improperly **inflated**.
その経費見積もりは不適正に水増しされていた。

112 generate
[dʒénərèit]
他 を生み出す，発生させる
類 produce

The sale of stock **generated** a large amount of capital for the company.
株の売却は会社に巨額の資産を生み出した。

15. ビジネスプラン・財務

113
yield [jíːld]
- 他〈利益など〉を生じる
- 自 屈する, 負ける

類 bear

ABC Company's product sales **yielded** sufficient operating income this year.
ABC 社の製品売り上げは今年, 十分な営業利益を生み出した。

114
fall [fɔ́ːl]
- 自 落ちる, 落下する
- 名 下落, 落下

類 drop

My company saw its ordinary profit **fall** by $1 million.
我が社は経常利益が 100 万ドル下落した。

115
invest [invést]
- 他 を投資する

派 investment「投資」

I **invested** my cash **assets** in the stock market.
私は現金資産を株式市場に投資した。

116
suffer [sʌ́fər]
- 他〈損害など〉を被る, 受ける
- 自 痛手を被る, あおりを受ける

反 benefit「利益を得る」

The company **suffered** a great loss in the last fiscal year.
その会社は前年度, 多大な損失を被った。

117
jump [dʒʌ́mp]
- 自 急騰する, 急増する
- 他〈価格など〉を急騰させる

類 skyrocket

3A Technologies' net profit **jumped** over 20 percent.
3A テクノロジーの純利益は 20 パーセント以上急上昇した。

— 309 —

Section 3　実際の記事で確認！

Pharmaceutical Companies Merger

Rolling Pharmaceuticals Inc. announced that it signed a merger agreement with Stones Inc., a global pharmaceutical company. Stones has agreed to acquire Rolling for $3.45 per share, or roughly $13 billion in total. Rolling's stock price jumped to $4.20 per share yesterday, its highest since 2001. The combined assets of the two companies exceed $100 billion.

The two companies have been strengthening their relationship since 2003, when Rolling was on the verge of bankruptcy and Stones helped the ailing company with a business alliance. According to a Stones executive, they have been considering a merger for two years and have just overcome the biggest obstacles: disagreement over management policy and backlash from the unions.

The merger is part of a business expansion strategy for Stones, which aims to gain a larger market share by acquiring a number of Rolling's popular over-the-counter drugs. Stones also hopes to restore shareholder trust that was lost because of the company's recent insider trading scandal.

This new chapter will be of benefit to merger partner Rolling as well. The company's poor risk management led to the 2003 crisis, and it has been losing competitiveness since then. In addition, its old-fashioned management style has blocked needed corporate governance reform at the company. "We will enter a new era of growth," says a Rolling board member. "We're very optimistic about our future."

However, some experts are skeptical about the merger. An economic analyst says, "This merger is a strategic error for Rolling. The company should reorganize the management and try to turn things around on its own. If they conduct thorough market analysis and develop an effective brand strategy, it is very likely that they would survive. Why should they be swallowed up by a larger company and give up their brand-name drugs, which continue to yield huge profits?"

和訳

製薬会社の合併

　ローリング製薬株式会社は，世界的な製薬会社であるストーンズ株式会社との合併契約にサインしたと発表した。ストーンズは1株当たり3.45ドル，総額およそ130億ドルでローリングを買収することに合意した。昨日ローリングの株価は，2001年以来の最高値である1株当たり4.20ドルに急騰した。2社を合わせた資産は1,000億ドルを超える。

　ローリングが破産寸前になりストーンズがこの業績の振るわない会社を業務提携で救った2003年以来，両社は関係を強化してきた。ストーンズの重役によると，両社は2年前から合併を検討していたが，経営方針をめぐる不一致と組合からの反発という最大の障害を乗り越えたとのことである。

　ストーンズにとって合併は事業拡大戦略の一部であり，ローリングの多くの市販大衆薬を獲得することによりさらに大きな市場占有率を得ることをねらっている。ストーンズはまた，同社の最近のインサイダー取引事件により失われた株主の信頼を回復したいと考えている。

　この新たな1章は，合併のパートナーであるローリングにとっても利益になる。まずい危機管理が2003年の危機をもたらし，それ以来ローリングは競争力を失ってきている。加えて，古風な経営スタイルは同社が必要とするコーポレートガバナンスの改革を妨げてきた。「新しい成長の時代に入るのです」とローリングの役員は言う。「私たちは将来について非常に楽観的です」。

　しかし，合併に懐疑的な専門家もいる。ある経済アナリストはこう言う。「この合併はローリングにとっては戦略的な誤りです。ローリングは経営陣を再編し，自力で状況を好転させるべきです。徹底した市場分析を行い効果的なブランド戦略を開発すれば，ローリングが生き残る可能性はとても高いです。なぜ大企業に飲み込まれて，巨大な利益を生み続けている自社ブランドの薬を手放さなければならないのでしょうか」。

☀Review Words☀

☐ merger ➡ Sec.1-4	☐ roughly ➡ Sec.2-107	☐ stock price ➡ Sec.1-35
☐ jump ➡ Sec.2-117	☐ asset ➡ Sec.1-55	☐ strengthen ➡ Sec.2-87
☐ on the verge of ➡ Sec.2-78	☐ bankruptcy ➡ Sec.1-16	☐ ailing ➡ Sec.2-62
☐ business alliance ➡ Sec.1-2	☐ according to ➡ Sec.2-65	☐ management policy ➡ Sec.1-1
☐ backlash ➡ Sec.2-84	☐ gain ➡ Sec.2-97	☐ market share ➡ Sec.1-22
☐ shareholder ➡ Sec.1-46	☐ partner ➡ Sec.2-66	☐ lead to ➡ Sec.2-81
☐ competitiveness ➡ Sec.1-18	☐ block ➡ Sec.2-71	☐ reform ➡ Sec.2-67
☐ growth ➡ Sec.1-3	☐ optimistic ➡ Sec.2-109	☐ skeptical ➡ Sec.2-70
☐ economic ➡ Sec.2-89	☐ strategic ➡ Sec.2-58	☐ market analysis ➡ Sec.1-21
☐ brand strategy ➡ Sec.1-26	☐ survive ➡ Sec.2-60	☐ yield ➡ Sec.2-113
☐ huge ➡ Sec.2-100		

INDEX

- 見出し語（番号付きの語）を掲載しています。参考語（類義語，関連語，派生語，反意語）は掲載していません。
- 数字は掲載ページを表します。細字の数字は Section 3 の掲載ページを表しています。

A

- a member of 199
- a pair of 29
- a variety of 240
- abandon 163
- abide by 128
- ability 95
- aboard 283
- abolish 241
- above 64
- above-mentioned 169
- abundant 180
- accept 98
- acceptable 220
- access 41, 50
- accommodate 64
- accommodation 274
- accompany 22
- accomplish 219
- accomplishment 95
- according to 299, 310
- accountant 76
- accounting department 77, 90
- accumulate 200
- accurate 220
- achieve 105
- achievement 95
- acquisition 294
- activate 47
- actual 126
- actually 22
- ad copy 196
- add 226
- add up 241
- additionally 103
- address 214
- adequate 304
- adhere to 124
- adjourn 144
- adjust 138
- admit 287
- adopt 121
- advance 305
- advertise 38
- advertisement 194
- advertising 194
- advertising agency 194
- advice 306
- advise 242
- affect 25
- affiliated company 75
- affix 228
- afford 118
- affordable price 196, 210
- after tax 119
- agency 75
- agenda 135
- aggressive 207
- agree 22
- agree on 222
- agreement 94
- agricultural products 176
- ahead of the times 184
- ailing 298, 310
- aim 199
- air shower booth 175, 190
- airline 277
- airplane ticket 274
- airport security check 275
- aisle seat 277
- alert 303
- allegedly 303
- allot 162
- allow 21
- alphabetically 168
- alteration 141
- alternate 159
- alternative 140
- amendment 217
- amount 216
- analysis 154, 170
- analyst 155
- analytical 108
- analyze 166
- announce 129
- annual 127
- annual conference 134
- annual leave 115
- annual salary 115
- answering machine 66
- anticipate 163
- antiseptic solution 175, 190
- apartment house 34
- apologize 139, 150
- apology 197
- appear 204
- appearance 94
- appendix 157
- applicant 94
- application 94, 274
- application form 94
- apply 29
- apply for 99
- appoint 82
- appointment 134
- appointment book 16
- appreciate 108
- appreciation of the yen 257
- approach 25

― 314 ―

INDEX

- ☐ appropriate 161
- ☐ approval 135
- ☐ approve 80
- ☐ approximately 126
- ☐ area code 56
- ☐ arise 223
- ☐ arrange 144
- ☐ arrangement 134
- ☐ arrivals 277
- ☐ arrive 289, 290
- ☐ arrived 277
- ☐ article 197, 217
- ☐ artificial 187
- ☐ artwork 196, 210
- ☐ as soon as possible 63, 70
- ☐ ascend 49
- ☐ ascertain 82
- ☐ assemble 185
- ☐ assembly 134
- ☐ assess 183
- ☐ asset 297, 310
- ☐ assign 84, 145
- ☐ assignment 14
- ☐ assist 82
- ☐ assistant manager 76
- ☐ assume 82
- ☐ assure 88
- ☐ at random 167
- ☐ ATM card 276
- ☐ attach 60
- ☐ attempt 241
- ☐ attend 20, 30
- ☐ attendance 135
- ☐ attendee 135
- ☐ attract 198
- ☐ attribute 83
- ☐ auction 256
- ☐ audience 136
- ☐ audit committee 77

- ☐ auditor 76
- ☐ authentic 247
- ☐ authorize 288
- ☐ authorized 307
- ☐ automatic ticket gate 15
- ☐ automatic withdrawal 236
- ☐ automotive 242
- ☐ available 202
- ☐ avenue 34
- ☐ average 149
- ☐ avoid 27
- ☐ await 205
- ☐ award 96, 110
- ☐ award ceremony 96
- ☐ aware 19

B

- ☐ background 157
- ☐ backlash 303, 310
- ☐ baggage 275, 290
- ☐ baggage claim 275
- ☐ balance due 236
- ☐ balance inquiry 276
- ☐ balance sheet 297
- ☐ ban 268
- ☐ bankbook 236
- ☐ bankrupt 298
- ☐ bankruptcy 294, 310
- ☐ banner 194, 195
- ☐ bar chart 137
- ☐ bar code 256
- ☐ bar graph 137
- ☐ base 39
- ☐ basket 234
- ☐ BCC 56
- ☐ be concerned 187
- ☐ be entitled to 122

- ☐ be flooded with 245
- ☐ be known for 184
- ☐ be stuck in 39
- ☐ be stuffed with 28
- ☐ be subject to 288
- ☐ beaker 156
- ☐ because of 185
- ☐ beep 56
- ☐ behavior 94
- ☐ behind schedule 286
- ☐ believe 100
- ☐ belong to 44
- ☐ belongings 275, 290
- ☐ below 67
- ☐ belt 16
- ☐ beneficiary 89
- ☐ benefit 116
- ☐ besides 279
- ☐ bestow 105
- ☐ bid 227
- ☐ bill 236
- ☐ billboard 34
- ☐ black & white copy 57
- ☐ blind carbon copy 56
- ☐ block 300, 310
- ☐ blog 55
- ☐ blusher 17
- ☐ board 288, 290
- ☐ board of directors 76
- ☐ boarding 277
- ☐ boarding gate 275
- ☐ boarding pass 275, 290
- ☐ boast 281
- ☐ body 196
- ☐ bonus 96
- ☐ book 280
- ☐ booking 274
- ☐ bookshelf 36, 50
- ☐ boost 268

– 315 –

☐boots	175	☐buyer	215	☐challenging	18
☐borrow	43			☐change	
☐boss	96				134, 142, 150, 236
☐bother	63	**C**		☐characterize	158
☐bouffant cap	175	☐cable	55	☐charge	80, 236
☐bound for	26	☐cafeteria	37, 50	☐chart	136
☐branch office	76, 90	☐calculate	220	☐charter	264
☐brand	194	☐calculator	35	☐check	26
☐brand awareness		☐caliber	87	☐check in	282, 290
	194, 210	☐call for	120	☐check-in counter	275
☐brand equity	194, 210	☐cameraperson	197	☐checking account	276
☐brand strategy		☐campaign	195, 210	☐checking e-mail	14
	295, 310	☐cancel	148	☐checkout	234
☐break	14, 208	☐canceled	277	☐checkup	116
☐break down	181	☐capable	88	☐chef	97
☐breathtakingly	202	☐carbon copy	56	☐chemical products	176
☐brew	46	☐cardboard	254	☐chemistry apparatus	
☐brief	146	☐cardigan	17		156
☐briefcase	16	☐career	95	☐chief executive officer	
☐broadcast	197, 200	☐careful	163		76
☐brochure	195	☐cargo	255	☐chief operating officer	
☐broken line	137	☐cargo vessel	255		76
☐broker	256	☐carrier	254	☐childcare leave	115
☐browse	58	☐carry out	158	☐choose	42, 50
☐bruise	235	☐cart	234	☐claim	243
☐brush	17	☐carton	175	☐clarify	143
☐budget	157	☐cash	236	☐classified	198
☐build	41	☐cash flow statement		☐classified ads	195
☐bulletin board	36, 50		297	☐clear	42, 50
☐burst	235, 238	☐cash register	234	☐clearance sale	234
☐bus	15	☐cash withdrawal	276	☐clerical work [duties]	
☐business alliance		☐cashier	234		14
	294, 310	☐catalog	237	☐clerk	97
☐business card	214	☐cause	283, 290	☐click	61
☐business conference		☐CC	56	☐client	14, 30, 54
	134	☐celebrate	107	☐client meeting	215
☐business meeting	134	☐cell phone	16	☐climate	295
☐business result	214	☐CEO	76	☐clip	35, 44
☐busy	279, 290	☐certain	101	☐Co.	75
☐button	28	☐chairperson	135	☐coffee machine	36

INDEX

- ☑coincide 182
- ☑cold call 214
- ☑collaborate 301
- ☑collapse 126
- ☑collar 16
- ☑colleague 96
- ☑collect 168
- ☑colorful 196
- ☑column 137
- ☑combine 249
- ☑comfortable 281
- ☑comment 143
- ☑commercial 195
- ☑commercial district 34
- ☑commercial jingle 195
- ☑commit 83
- ☑communicate 18
- ☑communications industry 74
- ☑commute 26
- ☑commuter pass 15, 30
- ☑commuter rush hour 15
- ☑commuter train 15
- ☑compact 205
- ☑company 75
- ☑company management 76
- ☑company pension 116
- ☑company('s) regulations [rules] 114, 130
- ☑compare 165
- ☑compatible 63
- ☑compensate 127
- ☑competent 106
- ☑competitive 163
- ☑competitiveness 295, 310
- ☑competitor 75

- ☑compile 148
- ☑complain 245
- ☑complete 22
- ☑completely 207
- ☑complex 34
- ☑complicated 149
- ☑comply 229
- ☑components 177
- ☑comprehensive 123
- ☑compromise 122, 215
- ☑computer screen 55, 70
- ☑computer virus 54, 70
- ☑concede 221
- ☑concentrate 43
- ☑concession 215
- ☑conclude 227
- ☑conclusion 157
- ☑concrete 139
- ☑conduct 160
- ☑conference 134
- ☑conference room 37, 50
- ☑confident 141
- ☑confidential 225
- ☑confidentiality 217
- ☑confirm 141
- ☑confiscate 287, 290
- ☑conform 122
- ☑confuse 58
- ☑congratulate 105
- ☑connect 61
- ☑consecutive 304
- ☑consent 135
- ☑consequently 209
- ☑consider 23
- ☑consist of 85
- ☑consolidated 308
- ☑construct 59
- ☑construction industry 74

- ☑constructive 138
- ☑consult 127
- ☑consultant 97
- ☑consume 248
- ☑consumer 256
- ☑contact 68, 70
- ☑contain 45
- ☑container 254
- ☑contents 254
- ☑continue 167
- ☑contraband 268
- ☑contract 14, 30
- ☑contract employee 115
- ☑contribute 105
- ☑contribution 96, 110
- ☑control 80
- ☑control panel 57
- ☑controversial 142
- ☑controversy 215
- ☑convenient 140
- ☑convention 134
- ☑conveyor 175, 190
- ☑convince 223
- ☑COO 76
- ☑cooperate 222
- ☑cooperation 215
- ☑coordinator 134
- ☑copy 57
- ☑copy machine 57, 70
- ☑copy quantity 57
- ☑copywriter 194
- ☑corporation 75
- ☑correction tape 35
- ☑cosmetic products 176
- ☑cost 157, 286
- ☑cost-cutting 123
- ☑cost-effective 205
- ☑counseling 116
- ☑counselor 116
- ☑coupon 195, 210

− 317 −

☐courier 254
☐courteous 241
☐cover 157, 246
☐cover up 307
☐coverage 197
☐coworker 96
☐crack 235
☐crate 254, 271
☐create 88
☐credit 247
☐credit card 236
☐critical 85
☐cross 24
☐crossing 15
☐crucial 188
☐cubicle 35
☐cuff 16
☐currency 286
☐current 99
☐currently 263
☐customer 154, 170
☐customer satisfaction survey 155
☐customer service 235
☐customer service department 77, 90
☐customize 62
☐customs broker 257
☐customs declaration form 275
☐customs inspection 275
☐cut back on 278
☐cutting-edge 159

D

☐dairy products 176
☐data-analysis 155
☐dead end 215
☐deadline 14, 30
☐deal 215
☐deal with 247
☐debate 135, 138
☐debit card 236
☐deceptive 178
☐decide 23
☐decision 135
☐declare 87
☐decline 188
☐decorate 200
☐dedicate 84
☐dedication 96
☐deduct 127
☐defect 177, 190
☐defective 185
☐defend 143
☐define 166
☐definitions 217
☐delay 289
☐delayed 277
☐delete 62
☐deliberate 162
☐deliver 38
☐delivery 255, 271
☐delivery center 255
☐delivery charge 255, 271
☐delivery station 255
☐delivery van [truck] 255
☐delivery zone 255
☐demand 248, 250
☐demonstrate 102
☐demonstration 195
☐demotion 117
☐dent 246
☐deny 288
☐depart 289, 290
☐departed 277
☐department 77, 90
☐departures 277
☐depend on 141
☐deposit 220, 276
☐depreciation of the yen 257
☐deputy branch manager 76
☐deputy manager 76
☐describe 46
☐description 197
☐deserve 106
☐design 59, 70, 194, 210
☐desirable 108
☐desire 279
☐desk 35, 50
☐detail 68
☐detailed 145
☐detain 285
☐determine 162
☐develop 168
☐devote 201
☐digit 258
☐direct 220
☐director 76
☐disagree with 165
☐discipline 114
☐discord 215
☐discover 43
☐discuss 148
☐disembarkation card 275
☐dismissal 114
☐dispatch 109
☐display 55, 201
☐disposable 181
☐dispose of 59
☐dispute 141
☐dissolve 228

INDEX

- distinctive 202
- distinguished 108
- distribute 46
- distribution industry 74
- diverse 104
- divide 83
- division 77
- dock shelter 175
- document 35, 50
- domestic 266
- dominate 78
- donate 300
- door-to-door sales 214
- dotted line 137
- doubt 189
- downsize 178
- downsizing 294
- downtown area 34, 50
- drag 286
- draw up 160
- drawer 35
- dream 24
- drive 55
- drop 307
- drop by 25
- drop off 261
- dropper 156
- dual 287
- due 208
- due date 214
- due to 186
- dummy 234
- durability 177
- durable 183
- duration 115, 130
- during 260, 271
- duty 257
- dynamic 103

E

- eager 102
- eagerly 198
- early retirement 117
- earn 121
- ease of use 196
- eco-friendly 205
- economic 304, 310
- economical 206
- economy 283
- edit 224
- editor 97, 110
- education 95, 110
- effect after termination 217
- effective 204
- effectively 202
- efficient 186
- effort 96
- elect 85
- elevator 37, 50
- eligibility 124
- eliminate 129
- e-mail address 56, 70
- e-mail newsletter 195
- embargo 257
- emergency 49
- emergency exit 37
- emit 265
- emphasize 207
- employ 21
- employee 94, 110
- employee ID card 17
- employee pass 17
- employer 94
- empty 240
- enable 108
- enact 123
- enclose 104

- enclosure 254
- encourage 129
- endorsement 115
- enforce 219
- engage 147
- engineer 97
- engineering division 77
- enhance 178
- enlarge 57
- enroll 125
- ensure 245
- entail 262
- enter 61, 276
- envelope 254
- equip 181
- equipment 156
- errand 14
- especially 205
- essential 188
- establish 48
- estimate 221
- evaluate 107
- eventually 305
- evident 162
- examine 166
- exceed 169
- except for 284
- exceptional 263
- excess 283
- excessive 243
- exchange 284
- exchange commission 276
- exchange rate 276
- excluding 264
- execute 165
- executive director 76
- exhausted 121
- exhibit 204

– 319 –

- ☑exit 45
- ☑expand 267
- ☑expect 22
- ☑expense 297
- ☑experience 95, 110
- ☑experienced 88
- ☑experiment 154
- ☑expert advisor 155
- ☑expertise 95, 110
- ☑expiration date 236
- ☑expire 248
- ☑explain 19
- ☑explanation 135
- ☑explore 166
- ☑export 257
- ☑expose 244
- ☑exposure 194
- ☑express 15, 30, 261
- ☑expression 94
- ☑expressway 34, 50
- ☑extend 218
- ☑extension 56
- ☑extensive 159
- ☑extra 48
- ☑extremely 300
- ☑eye shadow 17
- ☑eyelash curler 17

F

- ☑factory 174, 190
- ☑fade 240
- ☑failure 177
- ☑fall 309
- ☑familiar 58, 70
- ☑family allowance 116
- ☑fantastic 203
- ☑fare 236
- ☑fascinate 238
- ☑fasten 42
- ☑favorable 247
- ☑fax 57, 70
- ☑feasible 159
- ☑fee 236
- ☑feed 69
- ☑feedback 235
- ☑fellow worker 96
- ☑fiber to the home 54
- ☑field 102
- ☑file 36, 55
- ☑filing cabinet 36, 50
- ☑fill 218
- ☑fill out 164, 170
- ☑finalize 83
- ☑finance 201
- ☑financial business 74
- ☑financing 296
- ☑finger stall 35
- ☑finish up 225
- ☑fire 126
- ☑firewall 54
- ☑fit 209
- ☑fitting room 234
- ☑fix 60, 70
- ☑fixed 260
- ☑flash 197
- ☑flask 156
- ☑flatbed cart 174
- ☑flavorful 204
- ☑flight 277, 290
- ☑flight attendant 275
- ☑flight number 277, 290
- ☑floating exchange rate system 257
- ☑floor 37, 50
- ☑fluctuate 180
- ☑fluent 103
- ☑fly 289
- ☑flyer 195
- ☑focus 109
- ☑focus on 161
- ☑fold up 29
- ☑folder 36, 55
- ☑follow up 244
- ☑following 149
- ☑food industry 74
- ☑force majeure 217
- ☑forecast 306
- ☑foreign currency 276
- ☑foreign exchange market 257
- ☑forge 302
- ☑forklift 175, 190
- ☑formal 239
- ☑forming machine 174
- ☑fortunate 104
- ☑forum 134
- ☑forward 69
- ☑found 80
- ☑foundation 17
- ☑fragile 278
- ☑free newspaper 195
- ☑freelancer 114
- ☑freeze 182
- ☑freezer room 174, 190
- ☑freight 255
- ☑frequent 278
- ☑fresh 196
- ☑friendly 196
- ☑front door 37
- ☑FTTH 54
- ☑fuel 255
- ☑fulfill 24
- ☑full 204
- ☑full-time 23
- ☑function 68, 70
- ☑furnish 182
- ☑further 67

INDEX

G

- gain 305, 310
- garment bag 287
- gasoline 255
- gate 277, 290
- general 139
- general affairs department 77, 90
- general manager 76
- general partnership 75
- general provisions 217
- generate 308
- get off 286
- get on 26
- glance 28
- glasses 16
- glue 35
- go through 189
- go-between 215
- govern 268
- grab the headlines 203
- graduate 102, 110
- grant 226, 230
- graph 136, 150
- graphic 157
- graphic designer 97
- greet 49
- grip 27
- gross profit 297
- growth 294, 310
- guarantee 184
- guzzle 260

H

- hair-care products 176
- hallway 37
- hand 147
- hand out 146, 150
- handbill 195
- handle 16, 264
- handmade 196
- handout 135, 150
- handrail 15
- handset 56
- handset cord 56
- handshake 215
- hands-on 98, 110
- hangover 24
- hardly 18
- hardware 55
- hauler 254
- have a bad connection 64
- head office 76, 90
- header 56
- headline 196
- headquarters 76
- health insurance 114
- health insurance card 116
- hectic 214
- help-wanted ad 94
- hem 16
- herein 217, 230
- hesitate 63
- high quality 196, 210
- highlight 148
- high-tech 239
- highway 34
- hire 83
- hiring office 94
- hold 56
- hold on 64, 70
- home use test 155
- horizontal axis 137
- host 197
- hourly wage 115
- household appliances 176
- household products 176
- housing allowance 116
- hub 54
- huge 306, 310
- human resources 96
- HUT 155
- hypothesis 154

I

- I regret to inform you that 245
- I wonder if 65, 70
- ideal 279
- identify 164
- illustration 135, 136
- I'm afraid 67, 70
- immediate 265, 271
- impending 299
- implement 121
- import 257
- import and export merchant 257
- impose 267
- impress 147
- impressive 203, 210
- improper 48
- improve 188, 190
- in accordance with 121, 130
- in advance 247, 250
- in charge of 84
- in line 284, 290
- in need of 244, 250
- in stock 237, 250
- in use 66

☐in witness whereof 217	☐inspect 89	☐job opening 94
☐inadequate 119	☐inspection 177, 190	☐job rotation 117
☐Inc. 75	☐inspire 81	☐job seeker 94
☐incentive 107	☐install 62	☐join 106
☐include 229	☐installment payment 236	☐joint-stock company 75
☐inclusive 123	☐insure 265, 271	☐joint venture 75
☐income statement 297	☐integrate 259	☐joint venture agreement 217
☐incorporate 298	☐intend 200	☐journalist 97
☐incorporated 75	☐intensive 99	☐jump 309, 310
☐increase 119	☐internal 264	☐junk mail 195
☐incur 246, 251	☐Internet service provider 54	
☐indefinite 227	☐intersection 34	**K**
☐indicate 148	☐intervene 267	☐keyboard 55
☐individual 96	☐interview 94	☐keypad 276
☐individually 85	☐interviewer 94	☐kiosk 15
☐indoor work 214	☐intricate 149	☐kitchen products 176
☐industrial uniform 175, 190	☐introduce 124, 130	☐knowledge 95, 110
☐inevitable 119	☐invent 160	
☐inexpensive 203	☐inventory 237	**L**
☐infect 59, 70	☐invest 309	
☐inflate 308	☐investigate 165	☐label 176
☐influence 163	☐investment 296	☐labor standards law 114
☐inform 129	☐investor 296	☐labor union 114
☐informative 101	☐invoice 216	☐laboratory 37
☐in-house 45	☐involve 218	☐lack 100
☐initial 119	☐IPO 296	☐ladder 37
☐initial public offering 296	☐issue 197, 285	☐land 285
☐initiate 87	☐IT industry 74	☐laptop 54
☐initiative 215	☐item 237	☐last call 277
☐innovate 160	☐itinerary 274, 290	☐late payment 236
☐innovative 183		☐latest 161
☐input tray 57, 70	**J**	☐launch 239
☐inquire 66	☐jacket 16	☐law 229
☐inquiry 14	☐jewelry 17	☐layoff 294
☐insert 61, 195	☐job 14	☐lead 79
☐insertion 195	☐job applicant 94	☐lead to 302, 310
☐insist 224	☐job fair 94	☐leading 180

INDEX

- ☐leaflet 195
- ☐leak 180
- ☐lease 40, 50
- ☐lease contract 217
- ☐leather shoes 16
- ☐leave 64, 70, 115
- ☐legal affairs division 77
- ☐letter 254
- ☐letterhead 254
- ☐liability 297
- ☐liable for 227
- ☐license agreement 217, 230
- ☐lift 269
- ☐likely 249
- ☐limit 283
- ☐limited 75
- ☐limited express 15
- ☐limited liability partnership 75
- ☐limited partnership 75
- ☐line 234
- ☐line graph 137
- ☐line map 15
- ☐line up 240
- ☐linger 21
- ☐link 60
- ☐lipstick 17
- ☐list 169
- ☐listed company 296
- ☐litter 44
- ☐live 209
- ☐load 240, 251
- ☐lobby 37
- ☐local train 15
- ☐locate 39, 50
- ☐lock 42, 50
- ☐locker 36
- ☐locker room 175
- ☐logo 196, 210
- ☐long-term 118
- ☐look into 165
- ☐loyal 238
- ☐Ltd. 75

M

- ☐machinery 177, 190
- ☐mail 254, 259
- ☐main entrance 37
- ☐main store 76
- ☐maintain 202
- ☐maintenance 177
- ☐major 266
- ☐make a speech 89
- ☐make use of 106
- ☐makeup 17
- ☐malfunction 177
- ☐manage 80
- ☐management buyout 294
- ☐management policy 294, 310
- ☐managerial 86
- ☐mandatory retirement age 117
- ☐manufacture 184
- ☐manufacturer 176
- ☐manufacturing industry 74
- ☐market 256
- ☐market analysis 295, 310
- ☐market entry 294
- ☐market research 14
- ☐market researcher 97, 110
- ☐market share 295, 310
- ☐marketing division 77
- ☐marketing mix 295

- ☐marketing strategy 295
- ☐marvelous 207
- ☐mascara 17
- ☐mask 156
- ☐mass 301
- ☐mass media 197
- ☐material 135, 150, 174, 228
- ☐maternity leave 115
- ☐mature 82
- ☐maximize 219
- ☐maximum 120
- ☐measure 44
- ☐media 199
- ☐mediation 215
- ☐medical expenses 116
- ☐medical industry 74
- ☐meet 21
- ☐meeting time 134, 150
- ☐memo 36
- ☐memorable 196
- ☐memorandum 36
- ☐memory stick 55
- ☐merchandise 256
- ☐merchant 234
- ☐merger 294, 310
- ☐message 56, 70
- ☐messenger 254
- ☐method 157
- ☐microphone 136, 150
- ☐microscope 156
- ☐mileage 274
- ☐minimum 104
- ☐minutes 135
- ☐miss 144
- ☐missing 281, 290
- ☐mixer 174, 190
- ☐modem 54
- ☐moderate 300

– 323 –

☐moderator 135
☐modern 199
☐modest 218
☐modify 125
☐money lending business 74
☐monitor 187
☐monopolize 266
☐monthly salary 115
☐morning edition 15
☐motivate 241
☐motorbike 34
☐motorcycle 34
☐mouse 55
☐mouse pad 55
☐move out 40, 50
☐mug 35
☐multifunction printer 54
☐multinational 299
☐municipal 302
☐mutual 223, 230

N

☐name tag 17
☐nationality 275
☐nationwide 259
☐near 227
☐needs 154, 170
☐negotiation 14, 30
☐negotiator 215
☐net banking 296
☐net income / (loss) 297
☐network 54, 70
☐new item 194, 210
☐niche 305
☐non-returnable 239
☐normal 278
☐notice 36, 50
☐notify 98

☐numerous 269
☐nursing (care) leave 115

O

☐objection 135
☐objective 157
☐obligation 217, 230
☐observe 166
☐obtain 49
☐obvious 167
☐occupation 275
☐occupy 42, 50
☐offer 223
☐office 37, 50
☐office building 34, 50
☐office LAN [local area network] 54
☐office supplies 35
☐OHP 135, 150
☐on behalf of 89
☐on business 278, 290
☐on the verge of 302, 310
☐on time 277, 290
☐one-on-one 100
☐ongoing 142
☐online 225
☐online order 236
☐online payment 236
☐online research 155
☐online securities 296
☐on-the-job 100
☐open 47
☐operate 186
☐operating profit 297
☐operating system 55
☐oppose 140
☐optimistic 308, 310

☐order 41, 237, 250
☐order form 237
☐organize 145
☐out of order 189
☐out of paper 57
☐out of service 48, 50
☐out of stock 237, 250
☐out of the office 65, 70
☐out of town 280
☐output tray 57, 70
☐outside 87
☐outside work 214
☐outstanding 225
☐oven 175
☐overall 122
☐overbook 281
☐overhaul 187
☐overhead projector 135
☐overnight 24
☐overpass 15
☐overseas 84
☐overtime work 14
☐overwhelming 145
☐overwork 116
☐own 306

P

☐pack 179, 254
☐package 176, 254
☐packaging 175, 190
☐packaging machine 175
☐paid vacation 115, 130
☐panel survey 155
☐pants 16
☐panty hose 17
☐paper 57, 70
☐paper in reserve 57

INDEX

☑paper jam	57, 70
☑paper punch	35
☑paperwork	214
☑parent company	75
☑Pareto chart	137
☑park	39, 50
☑parking	34, 50
☑parking lot	34
☑participant	135, 150
☑participate	20, 30
☑participate in	145
☑partition	36
☑partner	299, 310
☑partnership	75
☑parts	177
☑part-time	118
☑part-time worker	115
☑pass	248
☑passenger	275
☑passport	275
☑passport control	275
☑patron	235
☑patronage	235, 251
☑pattern	234
☑pay	120, 130
☑pay raise	114
☑payment request	236
☑pedestrian	34
☑pedestrian overpass	15
☑penalty	236
☑penetrate	58
☑perch	45
☑perfect	81
☑perform	189
☑performance	177, 190
☑permanent	118
☑permanent job	115
☑permission	123
☑personal	264
☑personal (identification) number	276
☑personality	197
☑personnel department	77, 90
☑personnel reduction	294
☑persuade	224
☑petri dish	156
☑phone number	56, 70
☑pick up	182
☑pickup	255
☑pie chart [graph]	137, 150
☑piece	115
☑pile	43, 50
☑pilot	275
☑PIN	276
☑place	181, 295
☑plan	19, 154
☑planning department	77, 90
☑planning meeting	154
☑plant	174
☑plastic bag	234
☑plastic products	176
☑plot	301
☑plug in	69
☑point of purchase	195
☑pointer	136
☑polish	49
☑POP	195
☑portable	184
☑position	76, 90
☑positive	206
☑possess	98
☑post	47, 50, 88, 268
☑post office	254
☑postage	258
☑postal code	254
☑postcard	254
☑posting	195
☑postpone	143
☑potential	159
☑potential demand	295
☑pour	45
☑power button	55
☑power lunch	14, 30
☑PR	194
☑PR department	194
☑praise	87
☑preamble	217
☑predict	164
☑prefer	289
☑premium	116
☑preparation	154
☑prepare	168
☑prepay	263
☑present	142
☑presenter	136
☑preserve	179
☑president	76, 90
☑press conference	134
☑press corps	197
☑press release	194
☑prevent	267
☑previous	308
☑price	216
☑price competition	295
☑price slashing	295
☑price tag	234
☑print	57
☑print out	69, 70
☑printer	57, 70
☑prior	138
☑problem	154, 170
☑proceed	140
☑proceedings	135
☑process	265
☑processor	55, 256

☑produce 266	☑pumps 17	☑rate 282
☑producer 176, 256	☑punch 46	☑reach 142
☑product 256, 270	☑purchase 234, 244, 250	☑real estate business 74
☑product development 154, 170	☑purchase order 216	☑realize 43
☑product differentiation 194	☑purpose of visit 275	☑reasonable 206
☑production cut 294	☑pursue 105	☑recall 180
☑production division 77	☑put ~ into practice 161	☑receipt 236
☑professional 104	☑put out 101	☑receive 63
☑professor 97	☑put together 224	☑receiver 56
☑prohibit 209	☑put up 267	☑reception desk 37
☑projection screen 135		☑receptionist 37, 50
☑promise 206, 210	**Q**	☑recipient 255
☑promote 81		☑recognition 96
☑promotion 96	☑QC 177	☑recognize 147
☑promotional model 197	☑qualification 95, 110	☑recommend 242
☑proofread 109	☑qualify for 238	☑reconcile 222
☑proper 68, 70	☑qualitative research 155	☑reconfirm 288
☑proposal 154	☑quality assurance 177	☑recover 128
☑propose 160	☑quality control 177	☑recruit 96, 101
☑prospective 222	☑quality improvement 177	☑reduce 57, 198
☑prosperous 302	☑quantify 304	☑refer 149
☑protect 226	☑quantitative research 155	☑reference 95, 110, 157
☑protective 168	☑quantity 216	☑reflect 208, 210
☑proud 109	☑quarantine 275	☑reform 299, 310
☑prove 164	☑questionnaire 154, 170	☑refreshments 14
☑provide 125	☑quick freezer 174	☑refrigerated truck 174
☑provision 216	☑quit 118	☑refrigerator room 174
☑public 259	☑quota 214	☑refund 235, 250
☑public relations 194	☑quote 225	☑register 144
☑public relations department 77, 90, 194		☑regular employee 115
	R	☑regularly 20
☑publicity 194		☑regulate 269
☑publicity department 194	☑rack 234	☑reimburse 242, 251
☑publish 208	☑rail freight link 255	☑reject 221
☑publishing industry 74	☑railroad track 15	☑release 158
☑pull up 25	☑raise 129	☑reliability 177
		☑reliable 78
		☑reliably 207
		☑remain 280

INDEX

- remarkable 107
- remarks 277
- remote 26
- removable media [disc] 55
- remove 29
- renew 124
- renovate 48, 50
- rent 40
- rental 40
- repack 258
- repair 185, 235
- repeat customer card 195
- replace 69, 70
- replacement 235, 250
- reply 258
- report 154, 226
- reporter 97, 197
- represent 85
- representative director 76
- request form 216
- require 102
- reschedule 144
- research 154, 170
- research and development division 77
- research company 155
- researcher 154, 170
- reservation 274, 290
- reserve 146
- resolve 243, 250
- resort 116
- respectively 262, 270
- respond to 23
- respondent 167
- responsible for 86
- restore 246, 251
- restrict 58
- result 154, 170
- result in 162
- resume 179
- retail price 256
- retailer 256
- retain 120
- retire 127
- retirement age 117
- retirement benefit 117
- retrieve 65
- return 65
- revamp 61
- reveal 209
- revenue 297
- review 183
- revise 158
- reward 107
- rewrite 203
- rigid 126
- risk 128
- road network 255
- road sign 34
- roughly 307, 310
- router 54
- routine 219
- row 137, 234
- rubber band 35
- rubber gloves 156
- ruler 35
- run 38
- rundown 136
- rupture 215
- rut 117

S

- safety 177, 190
- safety device 177
- salary 114, 130
- sale 194
- sales chart 214
- sales conference 134
- sales contract 217
- sales department 77, 90
- sales meeting 14, 30
- salesperson 97
- sample 155, 195
- sampling 155
- satisfy 246
- save 68
- savings account 276
- scan 57, 266
- scandal 197
- scanner 57
- scatter graph [chart] 137
- schedule 134, 140
- scissors 35
- screen 285
- screening 94
- script 136
- search for 101
- seat 135, 150
- secretary 97, 110, 135
- section 77
- section manager [chief] 76
- secure 280
- securities company 296
- securities market 296
- security alarm 36
- see off 282, 290
- seek 99
- segmentation 295
- seize 224
- select 167, 170
- seminar 14, 30

☑ sender	255	
☑ senior	86	
☑ separate	46	
☑ serve	23	
☑ serve as	146	
☑ server	54, 70	
☑ service	114	
☑ share	19	
☑ share certificate	296	
☑ share price	296	
☑ shareholder	296, 310	
☑ shift	115	
☑ ship	263, 271	
☑ shipment	255	
☑ shipping company	255	
☑ shipping room	175	
☑ shirt	16	
☑ shoelace	16	
☑ shop	34	
☑ shopkeeper	234	
☑ shopper	235	
☑ shoulder	28	
☑ show of hands	135	
☑ show window	195	
☑ shredder	35, 50	
☑ shut down	179	
☑ side door	37	
☑ side job	114	
☑ sign	20	
☑ signboard	34	
☑ significant	306	
☑ sign-off sheet	216	
☑ single payment	236	
☑ single-lens reflex camera	197	
☑ situation analysis	295	
☑ skeptical	300, 310	
☑ skill	95, 110	
☑ skilled	103	
☑ skyscraper	34	
☑ slash	301	
☑ slight	128	
☑ slip into	27	
☑ small office/home office	114	
☑ soak	181	
☑ social insurance	114, 130	
☑ software	55	
☑ SOHO	114	
☑ solid line	137	
☑ solve	158	
☑ sort	259	
☑ sound	128	
☑ sound truck	195	
☑ spare	19	
☑ spec	177	
☑ special express	15	
☑ special offer	196	
☑ specialist	97	
☑ specialize in	103	
☑ specialty	95	
☑ specific	99	
☑ specification	177	
☑ specify	249	
☑ speed dial	56	
☑ spell	67	
☑ spend ~ on	186	
☑ spin-off	294	
☑ spokesmodel	197	
☑ sponsorship	223	
☑ spot	235	
☑ spread	201	
☑ stability	122	
☑ stack	47	
☑ staff	96, 110	
☑ staff meeting	134	
☑ stairs	37, 50	
☑ stamp	254	
☑ stand	15	
☑ stand at	182	
☑ standard	177, 265	
☑ standardize	189	
☑ staple	226	
☑ stapler	35	
☑ staples	35	
☑ state	84	
☑ state of chaos	79	
☑ statement of delivery	216	
☑ state-of-the-art	178, 190	
☑ station	208	
☑ station attendant	15	
☑ station platform	15	
☑ stationery	35	
☑ steady	301	
☑ steal	285	
☑ sterilization	175	
☑ stimulate	78	
☑ stock	249, 251	
☑ stock company	75	
☑ stock dividend	296	
☑ stock exchange	296	
☑ stock certificate	296	
☑ stock index	296	
☑ stock price	296, 310	
☑ stock price index	296	
☑ stockholder	296	
☑ stockholder's equity	297	
☑ stockholders' general meeting	296	
☑ stool	36	
☑ storage	37	
☑ storage facility	174	
☑ store	34, 242	
☑ store clerk	234	
☑ store manager	76	
☑ store sign	234	

– 328 –

INDEX

- ☑storehouse 174, 237, 251
- ☑straighten 27
- ☑strap 15
- ☑strategic 298, 310
- ☑strategy 154
- ☑strengthen 303, 310
- ☑strict 81
- ☑strive 78
- ☑struggle 79
- ☑style 234
- ☑subhead 196
- ☑subject 56, 154
- ☑submission 216
- ☑submit 21
- ☑subordinate 96
- ☑subscribe to 25
- ☑subsidiary 75
- ☑substantial 120
- ☑subtotal 216
- ☑suburb 34
- ☑succeed 218
- ☑successful 18
- ☑successive 125
- ☑such as 183
- ☑suffer 309
- ☑sufficient 146
- ☑suggest 138
- ☑suit 16
- ☑suitable 89
- ☑suitcase 275, 290
- ☑sum 41
- ☑summarize 139
- ☑summary 136
- ☑supply 221
- ☑supply room 37, 50
- ☑support 243
- ☑suppose 262
- ☑survey 154, 170
- ☑survive 298, 310
- ☑suspend 185
- ☑suspension 135
- ☑swipe 29
- ☑symposium 134
- ☑systematic 304

T

- ☑table 136
- ☑tack 36
- ☑take down 178
- ☑take effect 229
- ☑take off 284, 290
- ☑take on 219
- ☑take over 79
- ☑take place 200
- ☑takeover 294
- ☑takeover bid 294
- ☑target 154, 164, 170
- ☑target market 295
- ☑tariff 257
- ☑task 14
- ☑tax 216
- ☑tax haven 294
- ☑tear 235
- ☑telecommuting 114
- ☑telemarketing 214
- ☑telephone conference 134
- ☑telephone number 56
- ☑telescopic umbrella 16
- ☑temp agency 94
- ☑temperature 175, 190
- ☑temporarily 186
- ☑temporary 86
- ☑temporary dispatch without family 117
- ☑temporary employee 115, 130
- ☑temporary worker 115

- ☑tempt 238
- ☑tend 106
- ☑tentative 228
- ☑tentative reservation [booking] 274
- ☑terminate 228, 230
- ☑termination 217
- ☑terms 217, 230
- ☑test tube 156
- ☑test-market 161
- ☑Thank you for ~. 221
- ☑thawing room 174
- ☑therefore 229, 230
- ☑thermometer 175
- ☑thorough 143
- ☑throw away 44, 50
- ☑thumbtack 36
- ☑ticket machine 15
- ☑tie 16, 28
- ☑tie bar 16
- ☑tight 20
- ☑tights 17
- ☑time card 36
- ☑time clock 36
- ☑time limit 214
- ☑time off 115, 130
- ☑time schedule 157
- ☑timetable 15
- ☑title 157, 214
- ☑toner cartridge 57, 70
- ☑topic 135, 150
- ☑top-selling 199
- ☑total 216, 249
- ☑totaling 155
- ☑touch-type 62
- ☑tough 222
- ☑tower over 40
- ☑traceability 256
- ☑track 239
- ☑trade 307

☐ trade deficit 257
☐ trade friction 257
☐ trade surplus 257
☐ trading company 257
☐ traffic 34
☐ train station 34, 50
☐ training 94
☐ transact 303
☐ transfer 86, 117, 276
☐ transit 255
☐ transmit 263
☐ transport 262
☐ transportation allowance 116, 130
☐ transportation industry 74
☐ travel 274
☐ travel advisory 274
☐ travel agency 274
☐ travel allowance 274
☐ travel expenses 274
☐ trend research 155
☐ trial run 177
☐ trip 274, 290
☐ trophy 96
☐ turn 38
☐ turn off 60
☐ turn out 169
☐ tweezers 156
☐ 24 hours a day 244
☐ two-sided printing 57

U

☐ ultimate 169
☐ unanimous 139
☐ unbalanced 269
☐ under construction 41
☐ underestimate 81
☐ undergo 98

☐ undertake 243
☐ unemployment insurance 116
☐ uniform 17
☐ unique 109
☐ unit price 216
☐ unknown 261
☐ unleaded 260
☐ unload 261
☐ unpaid vacation 115
☐ until further notice 280
☐ unveil 198
☐ up to 260
☐ update 59
☐ upgrade 62
☐ up-to-date 60
☐ urgent 65, 70
☐ URL address 55
☐ use 279
☐ useful 18
☐ utilize 305

V

☐ vacancy 274
☐ vaccination 274
☐ valid 201
☐ vanity case [bag] 17
☐ various 47
☐ vary 282
☐ vehicle 34
☐ venue 134
☐ verbal 100
☐ verify 67
☐ vertical axis 137
☐ via 284
☐ vice president 76, 90
☐ violate 125
☐ visa 274
☐ visibility 194, 210

☐ visitor 37, 50
☐ visitor pass 37
☐ void 282
☐ voluntary retirement 117
☐ vote 135

W

☐ wage bargaining 114
☐ waive 248
☐ waiver 217
☐ wallet 16
☐ warehouse 237
☐ warm 179
☐ warning 114
☐ warp 235
☐ warrant 188
☐ warranty 235, 250
☐ waste 262
☐ waste basket 35
☐ waterproof 258, 271
☐ wear 27
☐ web 54
☐ website 54
☐ weekday 124
☐ weigh 281
☐ well-known 38
☐ whereas 217, 230
☐ white coat 156
☐ whiteboard 136, 150
☐ wholesale price 256
☐ wholesaler 256
☐ widen 269
☐ widespread 261
☐ window seat 277
☐ wireless LAN 54
☐ withdraw 287
☐ withstand 245
☐ witness 78

☑witnesseth 217
☑word of mouth 195
☑work 14
☑work gloves 175
☑work in 79
☑work on 147
☑worker 96
☑worker's accident compensation insurance 116
☑working pattern 115
☑worldwide 39
☑worth 206, 210
☑wrap 187
☑wristwatch 16
☑write down 66, 70
☑written apology 216
☑wrong 66, 70

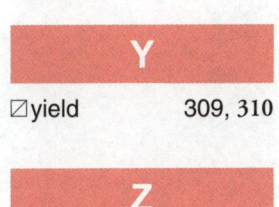

Y

☑yield 309, 310

Z

☑zip code 254

- memo -

- memo -

- memo -

【音声吹き込み】
Josh Keller（アメリカ）
Carolyn Miller（カナダ）
Nadia McKechnie（イギリス）
Brad Holmes（オーストラリア）

ビジネス現場の英単語

初版第1刷発行	2010年11月10日
編者	Z会編集部，日本アイアール
発行人	加藤文夫
発行	株式会社 Z会
	〒411-0943　静岡県駿東郡長泉町下土狩105-17
	TEL 055-976-9095
	http://www.zkai.co.jp/books/
装丁	荒井雅美（TYPEFACE）
イラスト	名渡山彩子
DTP	日本アイアール株式会社
印刷・製本	図書印刷株式会社
録音・編集	財団法人 英語教育協議会（ELEC）

© 日本アイアール株式会社　2010　★無断で複写・複製することを禁じます
定価はカバーに表示してあります
乱丁・落丁はお取り替えいたします
ISBN 978-4-86290-068-5 C0082

音声ファイルの入手方法については，切り取り線を開いて内側をご確認ください。

音声ファイルの入手方法については，切り取り線を開いて内側をご確認ください。